OXFORD MODERN LANGUAGES AND LITERATURE MONOGRAPHS

Yves Bonnefoy and Jean-Luc Nancy

Ontological Performance

EMILY McLAUGHLIN

OXFORD
UNIVERSITY PRESS

OXFORD
UNIVERSITY PRESS

Great Clarendon Street, Oxford, OX2 6DP,
United Kingdom

Oxford University Press is a department of the University of Oxford.
It furthers the University's objective of excellence in research, scholarship,
and education by publishing worldwide. Oxford is a registered trade mark of
Oxford University Press in the UK and in certain other countries

First Edition published in 2020

Published in the United States of America by Oxford University Press
198 Madison Avenue, New York, NY 10016, United States of America

British Library Cataloguing in Publication Data
Data available

Library of Congress Control Number: 2020930667

ISBN 978-0-19-884958-2

For Michael Sheringham

Contents

List of Abbreviations

Poems and Critical Texts by Yves Bonnefoy

CQ	*Ce qui fut sans lumière* (Mercure de France, 1987)
DF	*Début et fin de la neige* (Mercure de France, 1991)
DL	*Dans le leurre du seuil* (Mercure de France, 1975)
E	*Entretiens sur la poésie (1972–1990)* (Mercure de France, 1990)
HP	*L'Heure présente* (Mercure de France, 2011)
IM	*L'Improbable* (Mercure de France, 1959)
IN	*L'Inachevable. Entretiens sur la poésie, 1990–2010* (Albin Michel, 2010)
NR	*Le Nuage rouge* (Mercure de France, 1977)
PC	*Les Planches courbes* (Mercure de France, 2001)
SPV	*Le Siècle où la parole a été victime* (Mercure de France, 2010)

Texts by Jean-Luc Nancy

AE	*À l'écoute* (Galilée, 2002)
C	*Corpus* (Métailié, 1992)
CD	*La Communauté désœuvrée* (Christian Bourgois, 1986)
ESP	*Être singulier pluriel* (Galilée, 1996)
NM	*Noli me tangere* (Bayard, 2003)
PF	*Une pensée finie* (Galilée, 1990)
PP	*Le Poids d'une pensée* (Presses universitaires de Grenoble, Le Griffon d'argile, 1991)
SM	*Le Sens du monde* (Galilée, 1993)

Acknowledgements

I am hugely grateful to many people for their support whilst I was writing this book. I'd like to thank Michael Sheringham for supervising my thesis, for always making me feel excited about the project, and for being so encouraging and good-humoured at every stage. I want to thank Roger Pearson for being such an inspiring and kind tutor. His teaching made me want to study more and to become an academic myself. I am very grateful to Ian James, Ian Maclachlan, Susan Harrow, Steven Delay, Clive Scott, and the readers of my book manuscript for OUP for reading drafts and giving me such helpful feedback. Thanks to my family, Margaret, Tom, Christo, and Nick, for all their love and care. I especially want to thank my dad for talking to me, so well, about literature. Thanks to Alice for all her kindness. Special thanks to Tom, Niamh, Charne, Yasmine, and Ben for all the long chats. And every possible thanks go to Alba for inspiring and supporting me, and always making me laugh.

I was able to write this book due to the receipt of a doctoral funding award from the Arts and Humanities Research Council, a Laming Junior Research Fellowship at The Queen's College, Oxford, and a Leverhulme Early Career Fellowship at Christ's College, Cambridge. Sincere thanks to all these funding bodies and institutions for supporting my work. I'm grateful too to Wadham College, Oxford, and to all my colleagues there for their support. I would also like to thank Oxford University Press, and my editor Eleanor Collins, for helping to bring the finished book to fruition. I'm also grateful to *French Studies*, *French Forum*, and *L'Esprit créateur* for allowing me to publish in this book parts of the articles that appeared in their journals.

Introduction

Yves Bonnefoy: Ontological Performance

Yves Bonnefoy defines poetry as an act that foregrounds its own gesture of communication. In his essay '*Le Degré zéro de l'écriture* et la question de la poésie' (2000), he writes that 'la poésie est un acte'.[1] Bonnefoy suggests that the poem draws our attention to the act by which we speak and address one another, or by which we use our hands to inscribe words upon a page. In his essay 'La Parole poétique', he argues that rhythm is essential to poetry because it draws our attention to the interaction that occurs between sound and sense, matter and meaning in the scene of utterance (SPV, 201–2). What all these contentions about poetry have in common is that they stress the importance of relation. Bonnefoy presents poetry as a way of working on language so as to maximize the interactions that occur between meaningful, corporeal, and material forces in any act of thinking, speaking, or writing. For him, poetry does not emulate or represent these generative dynamics of relation but *enacts* them. The poem explores the worldly dynamics of interaction that bring its form and all other forms into being and, in doing so, it exposes existence's unpredictable creative force, its dynamic of becoming.

Throughout his career, Bonnefoy insists that finitude is the key force that inspires this conception of poetic performance. His essay 'Le Siècle où la parole a été victime' (2010) states that poetry works to 'maintenir ouverte, dans les refermements idéologiques, la voie vers la finitude' (SPV, 16). For Bonnefoy, finitude is a ceaseless expenditure that produces a continual dynamic of opening. Its endless expenditure ungrounds all presences and, in doing so, projects them outwards and into relation, bringing new constellations of being into existence.[2] Bonnefoy suggests that, when we realize the radically

[1] Yves Bonnefoy, *Le Siècle où la parole a été victime* (Paris: Mercure de France, 2010), p. 185. All subsequent references will appear within the text, using the abbreviation SPV.
[2] Yves Bonnefoy, *L'Improbable* (Paris: Mercure de France, 1959), p. 162. All subsequent references will appear within the text, using the abbreviation IM. I analyse Bonnefoy's writings on finitude in greater detail later in this introduction.

Yves Bonnefoy and Jean-Luc Nancy: Ontological Performance. Emily McLaughlin, Oxford University Press (2020).
DOI: 10.1093/oso/9780198849582.001.0001

finite or radically exposed nature of all existence, our perception of ourselves and of the world undergoes a profound change. We become aware that the precariousness and contingency that we feel is common to all existence. In this moment, we can start to feel compassionate towards and intimately connected to all other worldly beings. And Bonnefoy argues that it is this experience of connection—of 'being in relation'—that poetry articulates. The poem communicates the value and sense of our shared experiences of instability, exposure, and interaction. As Bonnefoy writes in his book on Rimbaud, the poet seeks to 'rend[re] la poésie à sa fin qui est [le] partage'.[3]

Bonnefoy never ceases to warn us, however, that this form of communication is demanding. He contends that it is deeply challenging for all human beings because linguistic consciousness inevitably tends to edit out the very dynamics of interrelation that bring it into being. In the essay 'Le Lieu d'herbes' (2010), he argues that language deforms our perception of existence. He suggests that it distances us from the physical world, placing us in a transcendental position, and encourages us to circumscribe and appropriate the presences that we perceive, reducing them to the status of objects.[4] And so, he observes in an interview in 2004, poetry is necessarily a way of resisting the normative modes of perception inscribed in us by language. It is 'ce beau combat [...] contre le langage—contre et avec le langage' (IN, 427). The poet works *on* language so as to resist the detached and appropriative modes of perception it fosters within us. Poetry offers us a means of readjusting our perception so that we can understand our contact with the world, and our position in it, in more dynamic and interactive terms.

In the essay 'Poésie et vérité' (1986), Bonnefoy laments that many twentieth-century French writers perceive the poetic act in very different terms. He suggests that they assume poetry to be 'la rupture d'une code' rather than 'la mise à distance de l'idée même de code'.[5] Bonnefoy protests that, by conceiving of poetry as a subversion of codes, these writers espouse the idea that language is a transcendental horizon. They encourage us to believe that the limits of language determine the limits of the real. Overturning this idea, Bonnefoy contends that poetry only *happens* when the poet makes the decision to resist language's hegemonic play of codes. From this moment on, Bonnefoy suggests, the poet seeks to draw linguistic

[3] Yves Bonnefoy, *Notre besoin de Rimbaud* (Paris: Seuil, 2009), p. 23.

[4] Yves Bonnefoy, *Le Lieu d'herbes* (Paris: Galilée, 2010), p. 15.

[5] Yves Bonnefoy, *Entretiens sur la poésie (1972–1990)* (Paris: Mercure de France, 1990), p. 263. All subsequent references will appear within the text, using the abbreviation E.

consciousness into exchange with the sensual, affective, and material forces that exceed its conceptual grasp. This mode of linguistic experimentation is crucial, Bonnefoy insists, because it allows us to perceive the generative dynamics of interaction that foster our own subjectivity. It shifts the emphasis from self-reflection to contact and relation and, in doing so, attunes us to the myriad ways in which human subjectivity is intimately implicated in a processual material world. What this means, Bonnefoy states in 'Poésie et vérité', is that poetry is no longer understood in epistemological terms, as an exploration of the conditions by which we know ourselves and our world *within language*. It is perceived in ontological terms as an exploration of the interaction between the diverse forces—linguistic and non-linguistic—that bring existence into being (E, 263). It is for this reason that Jean Starobinski describes Bonnefoy's *œuvre* as 'l'une des moins narcissiques qui soient'.[6] By embracing the generative nature of the act of relation, the poet seeks to foster a creative force within his poems that is general or worldly, that is instrinsically shared. As Starobinski phrases it, 'l'enjeu est un *bien* commun'.[7]

Bonnefoy uses many theatrical tropes in his poetry to alert us to the repeated and rhythmic acts of relation that bring the poem into being. His poem 'Passant, ce sont des mots', published in *Les Planches courbes* in 2001, presents itself as an inscription on a tombstone. This inscription also takes the form of a *prosopopoeia*, an address from the grave, however, as the words seek to rise up and to speak to the passer-by. The reader is addressed directly and repeatedly encouraged to listen to the sound of the voice that speaks. The poem begins: 'Passant, ce sont des mots. Mais plutôt que lire / Je veux que tu écoutes: cette frêle / Voix comme en ont les lettres que l'herbe mange'.[8] If we listen to these words, the poet suggests, we'll feel the transience of all things. We'll hear the sound of the grass slowly eating away at the text engraved on this slab of stone. As the voice urges to listen again and again, it draws us deeper and deeper in a vision of material finitude. 'Prête l'oreille', it entreats us, to hear the bee buzzing in these nearly effaced words. Hear a fainter sound still, the murmur of all our shadows, all our lives, reduced to a slight and fleeting noise as we pass through the universe. Bonnefoy writes: 'Il monte, celui-ci, de sous les pierres / Pour ne faire qu'une

[6] Jean Starobinski, 'La Poésie, entre deux mondes', in Yves Bonnefoy, *Poèmes. Du mouvement et de l'immobilité de Douve, Hier régnant désert, Pierre écrite, Dans le leurre du seuil* (Paris: Gallimard, 1982), p. 11.

[7] Ibid., p. 12.

[8] Yves Bonnefoy, *Les Planches courbes* (Paris: Mercure de France, 2001), p. 40. All subsequent references will appear within the text, using the abbreviation PC.

l'enjeu – what is at stake

chaleur avec l'aveugle / Lumière que tu es encore, ayant regard' (PC, 40). Finally, at the end of the poem, all existence is perceived in dynamic terms, as the communication of heat and light. Bonnefoy insists that our linguistic consciousness does not transcend this motion but that it emerges from the resonant or atmospheric interactions that occur between all worldly forces. As he does so, language sounds out richly, steadily reminding us that it has a sonorous and material presence as well as a meaningful one. The poem itself becomes a space of resonance, a place where linguistic, sensual, and material all reverberate together. And our linguistic consciousness is drawn into this space. We are encouraged to perceive the poem's resonant play from the inside, rather than outside. We're asked to feel the finite dynamics of worldly existence at work within us, to feel them opening us up and actively bringing us into existence.

This book investigates Bonnefoy's understanding of poetry as an ontological performance, as an exploration and an exposition of the generative dynamics of relation that bring existence into being. It explores how this conception of poetry as an ontological performance comes fully to fruition within Bonnefoy's work with the publication of *Dans le leurre du seuil* in 1975.[9] In his earlier works, the poet knows that a crucial nexus of ideas—finitude, negativity, exposure—offer him a new model for understanding human existence and poetic action. The idea of an inherently dynamic and relational poetic performance is present in the early essays, particularly 'Les Tombeaux de Ravenne' and 'L'Acte et le lieu de la poésie'. The possibility is glimpsed rather than discovered, however. In *Du mouvement et de l'immobilité de Douve* (1953),[10] *Hier régnant désert* (1958),[11] and even *Pierre écrite* (1965),[12] Bonnefoy conceives of human subjectivity and its relationship with the physical world in linguistic terms. The poetic subject is a lonely, self-conscious figure who approaches the material world from a distance. It is for this reason that the motif of the improbable quest is so central to the early collections. Bonnefoy can only *describe* or *represent* the need that he feels to deconstruct the structures of conceptual thought and to immerse himself in a world of material finitude. He does so using a series of emblematic images: Douve, ritual sacrifice, the orangery, the Phoenix, the

[9] Yves Bonnefoy, *Dans le leurre du seuil* (Paris: Mercure, 1975). All subsequent references will appear within the text, using the abbreviation DL.

[10] Yves Bonnefoy, *Du mouvement et de l'immobilité de Douve* (Paris: Mercure de France, 1953).

[11] Yves Bonnefoy, *Hier régnant désert* (Paris: Mercure de France, 1958).

[12] Yves Bonnefoy, *Pierre écrite* (Paris: Mercure de France, 1965).

stag, and the salamander. He does use performative devices such as apostrophe and dialogue to affirm his desire for a tactile and embodied poetic act, particularly in *Du mouvement et de l'immobilité de Douve*, but the performance remains purely figurative. Michèle Finck argues that Bonnefoy uses Douve's death throes and decomposition to stage a mythical theatre, one that unfolds in a separate space, and dramatizes 'le présent pur de l'événement, qui est hors du temps'.[13] The mythical images dotted throughout *Hier régnant désert* too—Perceval and the grail, the sword, 'L'Ordalie', Veneranda, the Delphes—evoke the trials that the poet endures as he endlessly attempts to cross a threshold that separates language from the physical world.[14] It is for this reason that Bonnefoy's contemporary, the poet Philippe Jaccottet, claims that his early poems unfold in 'un théâtre mental, dans le monde trompeur des essences'.[15]

It is with the publication of *Dans le leurre du seuil* in 1975 that Bonnefoy discovers the poem's own scenic potential. One of the reasons for this change is the poet's extensive experimentation with different forms of performative utterance: addresses to an unidentified other, apostrophes to inanimate things, ritualized utterances, refrains, and incantations. These structures are reminiscent of the theatrical devices used in *Du mouvement et de l'immobilité de Douve* and yet the poet now explores the theatricality of own embodied speach act, the gesture of projecting his voice outwards and addressing another person. He experiments with the meaningful, sensual, and physical qualities of his own act of communication. This process of experimentation convinces the poet that knowing the world and embracing its finitude are not incompatible acts. He is persuaded that knowing is not primarily a matter of linguistic reflection but of embodied exposure. This is what Jaccottet suggests when he writes that *Dans le leurre du seuil* is the collection of poetry in which '[Bonnefoy] a, pour la première fois, pris pied dans la réalité concrète, nommable, d'un lieu particulier, d'une saison datable'. He adds: 'le pas si longtemps souhaité "de l'amour des choses mortelles" a été fait'.[16] Jaccottet suggests that it is in *Dans le leurre du seuil* that, for the first time, Bonnefoy embraces the finitude of the gesture of speaking itself. Bonnefoy accepts that the poem is brought into being by the interaction of

[13] Finck suggests that the poems unfold in an 'espace mental mystérieusement ancré dans une terre' (Michèle Finck, *Yves Bonnefoy. Le Simple et le sens* (Paris: José Corti, 1989), p. 74, p. 55).
[14] Bonnefoy, *Hier régnant désert*, p. 122, p. 120, p. 115, p. 118, p. 149.
[15] Philippe Jaccottet, *Une transaction secrète* (Paris: Gallimard, 1987), p. 262.
[16] Ibid., p. 262.

linguistic, sensual, and material forces and that its own gesture can articulate something of the world's own dynamic of exposure.

In *Dans le leurre du seuil*, the poet reflects on his encounters with ordinary things and his romantic interactions. He explores the acts of address and interpellation in which he finds himself caught up. As he does so, he realizes that relation is not extrinsic to his being—it is not an act that a pre-existing subject performs—but that his own subjectivity emerges from dynamics of interaction. This realization makes the world feel less empty than before. It suddenly seems morely spaciously and interactively populated. And the poet has the intense sensation that he calls 'la présence'. Accepting that all forms of knowledge are contingent and co-originary, the poet feels himself to be caught up in a processual world in which all things come into being in relation. The act of knowing, conceived in these terms, becomes what Paul Claudel describes as an act of 'co-naissance',[17] and what Bonnefoy in 'L'Acte et le lieu de la poésie' describes as: '[un] savoir, tout négatif et instable qu'il soit, que je puis peut-être nommer la vérité de la parole' (IM, 178). Embracing humanity's immersion in the worldly dynamics of material finitude, Bonnefoy accepts the emergent nature of human consciousness. This is one of the key shifts that occurs in *Dans le leurre du seuil*. It is for this reason that the collection ends with the image of an unfurling and breaking wave. A series of verbs (interrupted by lengthy parentheses that have been omitted here) evoke the motion by which the wave simultaneously swells and breaks: 'S'enfle / [...], Et brûle, oui, blanchisse puis déferle / [...] La vague sans limite sans réserve' (DL, 120). Bonnefoy suggests that all existence is carried forth on this wave. Existence unfolds eternally, spends itself entirely, and holds nothing in reserve. Nothing transcends or escapes this motion. We cannot view it from above or beyond. It overtakes linguistic consciousness. We are always already immersed—before language has even attempted to circumscribe this process—in existence's dynamics of dissolution, opening, and exposure. And we can only know the world in these terms. At the end of *Dans le leurre du seuil*, Bonnefoy's use of the image of the wave signals very deliberately that the imagery of detachment and alienation that pervaded his early poetry has given way to an imagery of expenditure, exposure, and relation.

Bonnefoy does, of course, offer a very lucid account of the relationship between finitude, exposure, and relation in his early essays. From the

[17] Paul Claudel, 'Traité de la Co-naissance au monde et de soi-même', in *Œuvre poétique* (Paris: Gallimard, Bibliothèque de la Pléiade, 1967), p. 149.

beginning of his career, Bonnefoy is deeply influenced by Baudelaire's exploration of the realities of death, finitude, and embodiment in *Les Fleurs du Mal*. In 'Les Tombeaux de Ravenne' (1953), Bonnefoy critiques the way that many Western thinkers seek to master the dynamism of lived existence. He criticizes the way that Hegel privileges the synthesizing powers of human consciousness and Heidegger the disclosive powers of human consciousness (IM, 134). The young poet protests that the pre-eminence that both these thinkers grant to human capacities of perception (even if they do so in very different ways) reduces death to nothing other than an aesthetic and intellectual reality. It becomes '[u]n objet de pensée qui n'est plus l'objet réel, apaisant d'un douteux savoir l'inquiétude originelle' but also revealing the vanity of '[des] mots qui masquent la mort' (IM, 124). In the essay 'Les Fleurs du Mal' (1953), Bonnefoy argues that Baudelaire is the first poet who sets death in its proper place, unreservedly embracing the way that its negative force penetrates all physical existence and destabilizes our knowledge of it. Bonnefoy writes:

> donnant la valeur suprême à ce qui n'est que mortel, dressant les êtres dans l'horizon de la mort et par la mort, je puis bien dire, je crois, que Baudelaire invente la mort, ayant compris qu'elle n'est pas cette simple négation de l'Idée qu'aimait en secret Racine, mais un aspect profond de la présence des êtres, en un sens leur seule réalité. (IM, 162)

Death is no longer conceived as the force that negates our essentialist and idealist conception of Being. It is no longer understood to be the outer limit imposed on an individual human life, the final act of destruction that obliterates the coherence of its form. On the contrary, Bonnefoy suggests that Baudelaire conceives of death as the very limit on which being is 'dress[é]'. In other words, all beings come into existence 'dans l'horizon de la mort et par la mort'. In each instant of embodied existence, we are exposed to our end or limit. We continually confront the reality of our own dissipation and it is this very act of expenditure—and exposure—that brings us to presence. It is our 'seule réalité'. It is this reality, Bonnefoy suggests in the same essay, that makes us aware that 'le corps humain' is 'un autre théâtre, celui de l'évidence' (IM, 43). Finitude exposes what he describes as 'le *vrai discours*', 'la mort en acte' (IM, 43).

Bonnefoy argues that Baudelaire's poetry transforms our conception of death, the body, and the poetic text. In the essay 'L'Acte et le lieu de la poésie' (1959), Bonnefoy urges his reader: 'Faisons une nouvelle fois, je le propose aujourd'hui, le pas baudelairien de l'amour des choses mortelles' (IM, 172). The poet urges us to draw towards the threshold where '[l]e néant consume l'objet, nous sommes pris dans le vent de cette flamme sans ombre. Et nulle foi ne nous soutient plus, nulle formule, nul mythe, le plus intense regard s'achève désespéré' (IM, 172). Exposed to the radical finitude of embodied and material existence, he suggests that there is no formula, no structure of meaning or identity, that we can use to stabilize or instrumentalize its force. But the poet entreats us not to flee this experience of instability:

> Restons pourtant devant cet horizon sans figure, vidé de soi. Tenons, si je puis dire, le pas gagné. Car il est vrai que déjà un changement se produit. L'astre morne de ce qui est, l'élémentaire Janus, tournant avec lenteur – mais dans l'instant – sur lui-même, nous découvre son autre face. Un possible apparaît sur la ruine de tout possible. (IM, 172)

The structures of representation that we use to endow existence with order and meaning dissolve as we find ourselves on 'cet horizon sans figure'. Our sense of self is obliterated. We are 'vidé de soi'. And yet, Bonnefoy insists that this limen is 'l'élémentaire Janus'. It is a threshold between destruction and creation, ending and beginning. On this limit, our linguistic or representational understanding of the self dissolves and another experience of embodiment, subjectivity, and sense becomes possible. He affirms: 'Un possible apparaît sur la ruine de tout possible.' We start to conceive of existence as a state of exposure. The threshold becomes not merely a site of opening but a site of relation and interaction.

As Bonnefoy's understanding of the finitude evolves, he no longer perceives it simply as a force of dissolution but as an endless act of exposure. This triggers a very different understanding of contact in his work. It is no longer the act of communion that the solitary poetic consciousness yearned for in *Du mouvement et de l'immobilité de Douve* and *Hier régnant Désert*. Contact becomes a gesture that is endlessly interrupted and suspended. Interruption is not conceived in privative but in generative terms, as the force that allows contact to renew itself. This means that contact opens outwards: one force continually deflects another, projects it outwards, and exposes it anew. In poems such as 'La Terre' and 'La Voix lointaine', Bonnefoy affirms that the human subject possesses no stable or essential form that pre-exists these endlessly ungrounded acts of relation. There is no 'moi' that precedes the vocative and interactive 'je'. The 'je' comes into being as diverse forces enter into relation, continually transforming and 'singularizing' one another, and projecting the 'je' out into the world. In the essay 'La Parole poétique', Bonnefoy argues that the negativity of these processes does not inhibit our capacity to develop meaningful practices of relation. Making reference to Mallarmé's conception of 'le néant', Bonnefoy observes:

> quand on a "trouvé le néant", preuve que la personne humaine est sans fondement dans quelque absolu que ce soit, comment ne pas lever ses yeux de ce champ d'illusions pour constater, dans la société toujours active qu'une autre sorte de réalité se propose là, tout de même, avec un emploi pour les mots, une parole en évident devenir: c'est l'ensemble des êtres comme nous, et semblablement embarqués sur le même flot de matière qui se rabattra sur eux, les noiera, mais décidés à survivre, pour un instant auquel l'effort en commun confère du sens, oui, ce que l'on peut dire du sens. (SPV, 205)

Even though the human subject is 'at sea', even though there is no ground for our existence in the absolute, Bonnefoy asserts that we are not deprived of our capacity for affirmation. All subjects exist alongside other beings, 'l'ensemble des êtres comme nous'. There is nothing onto which we can grasp but, 'décidés à survivre', we reach out to one another. We communicate and cooperate. There is effort, interaction, relation, and Bonnefoy affirms that this common effort 'confère du sens'. Sense is not conceived here as something that we have but as something that is shared in the act of relation. It is a *praxis*, an activity that that does not result in any kind of exterior product or goal. Sense is articulated in the act of relation that affirms nothing other than its own gesture of sharing, 'l'effort en commun'.

This conception of sense is central to the ontological performance that Bonnefoy develops throughout his later career. The poet insists that this sense cannot be appropriated, abstracted, or put to work by any kind of formal ontology but that it is exposed in the dynamics of relation. Bonnefoy thus stresses the importance of conceiving of ontology *autrement*, of approching it as an ongoing and participative performance. Through acts of touching, speaking, listening, or writing, through the continual reverberations that occur between linguistic, embodied, and material forces, he suggests that we can explore material existence's force of exposition. We can experiment with the concrete and relational dynamics by which sense is exposed. Without mastering this process, the poetic act can participate in it. By cultivating this conception of poetic performance, Bonnefoy thus deliberately subverts the Romantic *topos* of the poetic performance that reveals or discloses Being itself. He deconstructs Romanticism's metaphysical logic of revelation because he insists that the poem does not expose anything higher or more essential than its own physical gesture. He insists that it confronts us only with its own embodied and material contingency. Nothing is revealed other than the gesture of exposure itself, this endlessly negative and generative force, this dynamic of relation in which we are all infinitely implicated and immersed.

The three chapters of this book will analyse how Bonnefoy attunes us to the generative interactions that occur between linguistic, corporeal, and material forces in the scene of poetic performance. They will use close reading to scrutinize how the poet seeks to overturn detached or circumscriptive modes of perception and to attune our linguistic consciousness to the intimate interplay with sensual and physical forces that brings it into being. The first chapter will analyse how Bonnefoy uses theatrical forms of address to explore the situated and relational nature of human consciousness in *Dans le leurre du seuil* (1975). The second will examine how the poet's experimentation with the physical distribution of words on a page allows him to explore the inherently spacious nature of material existence's dynamics of exposition in *Début et fin de la neige* (1991).[18] The third chapter will investigate how Bonnefoy plays with sound in *Les Planches courbes* (2001) and uses the reverberations of the human voice to present human subjectivity as a resonant dynamic (as opposed to a self-reflexive one).[19] This book

[18] Yves Bonnefoy, *Début et fin de la neige* (Paris: Mercure de France, 1991). All subsequent references will appear within the text, using the abbreviation DF.

[19] I only analyse Bonnefoy's 'verse' poetry in this study. I do not examine his prose poetry. We might define his verse poetry according to Agamben's definition of 'the poem': a text in which the possibility of enjambment exists (Giorgio Agamben, *The End of the Poem* (Stanford, CA: Stanford University Press, 1999), p. 111). I make this distinction between Bonnefoy's verse and prose poetry because he foregrounds tropes such as apostrophe, address, and interpellation in his verse poetry. It is in verse poetry that, as Bonnefoy argues in 'La Parole poétique', rhythm can be used most conspicuously and most dexterously to foreground the sonority and materiality of words. Our attention is also continuously drawn to the movement by which the line of poetry *turns*, foregrounding the spatial choreography of the poem's dance across the page. This book investigates how all these features of the poetic performance allow Bonnefoy to present the poem as a space of resonance between material, corporeal, and linguistic forces. I explore how he uses this space of resonance to present linguistic consciousness as an emergent force. Whilst Bonnefoy's prose poems undoubtedly relativize the structures of conceptual thought in important ways, they do so using methods that are less tactile and concrete. In his excellent study *À la souche obscure des rêves*, John E. Jackson argues that Bonnefoy deconstructs conceptual thought in his prose poems by embracing the oneiric logic of dream. Jackson writes: 'Soumis, comme Freud l'a montré, au régime des processus primaires, le rêve donne à voir un mode d'enchaînement (glissements, condensations, déplacement, inversions) propre à court-circuiter les principes de la causalité conceptuelle d'une manière comparable,

begins by examining Bonnefoy's use of theatrical tropes to foster an intimately situated or immersed practice of seeing. As the book progresses, however, it explores how Bonnefoy comes to perceive all gestures in scenic terms, insisting that all forms of action are galvanized by repeated and rhythmic interactions. In a late interview with Fabbio Scotto in 2003, Bonnefoy notes that his belief in the affinity between poetry and theatre has deepened as his career has progressed.[20] He notes:

> Le théâtre, c'est de saisir les hommes et les femmes dans leurs rapports immédiats, en des moments où l'urgence des situations, rendant évidente la finitude, prend de court la pensée, et va libérer le savoir profond. De ce fait le lieu de l'action théâtrale, sa scène, c'est celui même où la poésie se retrouve dans son travail d'écriture. (IN, 390)

Bonnefoy argues that our habitual modes of perception are challenged by the scene of theatrical performance. As bodies pass by one another by or engage with one another on the stage, we realize that we cannot abstract or comprehend these dynamics of exchange. The linguistic mechanisms that we use to distance and to appropriate worldly existence start to break down. And this failure facilitates a new way of knowing. It awakens 'le savoir profond'. We are attuned to the very dynamics of relation that bring us into being.[21] And Bonnefoy suggests that it is with this experience, this intuition, that the process of writing begins: 'la poésie se retrouve dans son travail d'écriture'.

Yves Bonnefoy and Jean-Luc Nancy

Many critics have set Bonnefoy's poetics up in opposition to the post-phenomenological deconstructionist strands of thought that emerge in France from the 1960s onwards and that flank his career. In *À la souche obscure des*

sur certains points, à la pratique poétique. Or ce court-circuitage de la logique conceptuelle représente, comme nous l'avons vu, un des plus anciens efforts de Bonnefoy' (John E. Jackson, *À la Souche obscure des rêves* (Paris: Mercure de France, 1993), p. 68).

[20] Bonnefoy observes: 'Je ressens de plus en plus la parenté de la poésie et du théâtre' (Yves Bonnefoy, *L'Inachevable. Entretiens sur la poésie, 1990–2010* (Paris: Albin Michel, 2010), p. 388). All subsequent references will appear within the text, using the abbreviation IN.

[21] Bonnefoy argues in this same interview that, by inviting us to understand signification in contingent terms, poetry also revitalizes theatre. He proposes that it effects 'cette rénovation du théâtre que seule la poésie pourrait accomplir' (IN, 390).

rêves, John E. Jackson argues that deconstruction is a '[m]ouvement qui heurte de front l'horizon de l'œuvre de Bonnefoy'.[22] Jackson argues that, dedicated to 'la présence', 'le réel', and 'l'immédiat', and privileging 'la voix' over 'la langue', Bonnefoy's poetry has little in common with a body of thought that attempts 'une "déconstruction" de la présence'.[23] In *Une pensée en mouvement* in 2008, however, Arnaud Buchs argues that there are important affinities between Bonnefoy's and Derrida's work that Jackson overlooks. He claims that the crucial preoccupation with the negativity of existence that we observe in Derrida's work is also central to Bonnefoy's œuvre:

> Habitée par plusieurs courants, traversée par des tensions qui la travaillent et repoussent toujours plus ses limites, cette œuvre semble plongée dans une mouvance qui la met constamment "à l'œuvre"; l'œuvre se fait et se défait, elle cherche toujours à dé-limiter ses propres limites.[24]

Buchs explores the common emphasis that these two writers place on the temporal and spatial dynamics of movement but concedes that they take radically different approaches when it comes to the question of ontology. Here, he puts forward an argument that bears a strong resemblance to Jackson's claims. Buchs writes that 'plus qu'à une *déconstruction* ontologique, Bonnefoy en appelle littéralement à une *reconstruction* de l'ontologie'.[25] He argues that, whilst Bonnefoy 'vise à rétablir cette métaphysique de l'être en tant que présence', Derrida 'voulait justement la dépasser en la déconstruisant'.[26]

It is difficult to see how Bonnefoy's fidelity to the negativity of existence can be compatible with 'une *reconstruction* de l'ontologie' and '[une] métaphysique de l'être en tant que présence'. The poet does affirm that his thought is ontological but he never conceives this ontology in systematic or metaphysical terms. Like Derrida, he is faithful to the operativity or dynamism that generates forms, rather than the forms in themselves. He thus does not call for a 'reconstruction' or 're-establishment' of ontology so much as a thorough reworking and reinvention of ontology that would allow us to conceive of it in dynamic and relational terms. He wants us to learn to practise ontology *autrement*, to understand it not as a system but as a performance, as an

[22] Jackson, *À la Souche obscure des rêves*, p. 60. [23] Ibid., p. 61.
[24] Arnaud Buchs, *Une pensée en mouvement. Trois essais sur Yves Bonnefoy* (Paris: Galilée, 2008), p. 9.
[25] Buchs, *Une pensée en mouvement*, p. 14. [26] Ibid.

embodied and material practice. It is the emphasis that Bonnefoy places on concrete gestures here that distinguishes his work from Derrida's aporetic textual performances. For whilst Derrida affirms the primacy of the trace and insists that its differential movement is always prior to being, Bonnefoy affirms that being is primary and that it is the temporal and spatial dynamic by which existence continually projects itself outwards in its concretude that makes the play of the trace possible. In this respect, Bonnefoy's poetics have much in common with the writings of a philosopher who was deeply influenced by Derrida and who worked with him at certain stages in his career, Jean-Luc Nancy.

Nancy's thought also begins with the movement, the dynamics of making and unmaking, that engenders all worldly productions. Like Bonnefoy, however, he does not perceive this generative motion in textual terms but in material terms. Affirming the primacy of a concrete dynamic of exposition, Nancy asserts that it is the play of material and embodied existence that permits the play of signification. The philosopher thus does not conceive the act of writing (as Derrida does) as an act that experiments with the subversive and inaugurative powers of textual aporia. He proposes that the act of writing opens up linguistic structures of signification to worldly dynamics of exposition, allowing the world's own structure of opening to act in and through the text. The act of writing is thus no longer primarily conceived as a *poesis*, he asserts, but as a *praxis*.[27] And so, like Bonnefoy, Nancy happily uses terms that Derrida places under erasure: 'la présence', 'l'être', 'l'ontologie', 'le réel', 'l'immédiat', 'la vérité', and 'l'incarnation'. Nancy proposes that the sensible and material contingency of the text's own gesture never reveals 'la présence' in a metaphysical way but that it exposes its movement 'en tant que *venue* en présence, ou encore en tant que transitivité, en tant que passage à la présence' (SM, 25). The text reveals nothing higher or more essential—nothing more appropriable—than the sensible contingency of its own textual performance. We feel the dynamics by which existence opens in and through the text (SM, 23–4).

The affinity that exists between Bonnefoy and Nancy stems from the way that they both conceive of finitude as a structure of opening. Focusing firmly on the creativity and unpredictability of material existence, their thought begins with a logic of material exposition rather than a logic of representation. This allows them to bypass the questions of splitting and

[27] Jean-Luc Nancy, *Le Sens du monde* (Paris: Galilée, 1993), p. 19. All subsequent references will appear within the text, using the abbreviation SM.

severance that is so central to the work of other twentieth-century French writers (poets such as Denis Roche, Marcelin Pleynet, or Michel Deguy, thinkers such as Michel Foucault, Jacques Derrida, Jacques Lacan, Hélène Cixous, or Luce Irigaray). This material 'turn' that occurs in Bonnefoy's understanding of finitude derives not only from his reading of Baudelaire but also from his study, under Jean Wahl's tutelage, of philosophers such as Hegel, Kierkegaard, Heidegger, Bataille, Ricœur, Granel, and Whitehead.[28] We can perceive the influence of many of the same philosophers (Hegel, Heidegger, Bataille, Ricœur, and Granel in particular) in Nancy's conception of finitude. He defines it as 'that which exists at its limits or is affected by its end, not as something external imposed on it, but as something originary', to cite Marie-Eve Morin.[29] For Nancy too, finitude is the force of ending or dissolution that leaves all things radically exposed to their outside. Being withdraws endlessly and projects itself outwards, thrusting all things into relation, and opening up new and surprising configurations of being. This dynamic of withdrawal and exposure means that no being exists in isolation but all things emerge from—come into being through—acts of relation. This dynamic of exposition is, Nancy acknowledges, at once destabilizing and invigorating, destructive and creative. But it is only by confronting this negativity, he suggests, that we can fully experience the rich possibilities of our finite existence, accepting that neither our being nor our ideas are grounded in the absolute, but that they are all to be determined through our acts and gestures, through the practice of 'being-in-relation'.

The other key term that Bonnefoy and Nancy use in a very similar way is 'le sens'. Michèle Finck writes that Bonnefoy 'détourne [...] le mot "sens" de son usage courant' in order to interiorize 'les acceptions physiologiques et spatiales du mot, au point qu'elles restructurent l'acception intellectuelle'.[30] Nancy describes sense as 'le mouvement de l'*être-à*', presenting it as an embodied and material *praxis* (SM, 25). He associates it with 'les valeurs du mouvement, du déplacement orienté, du voyage, du "tendre vers"' (SM, 25). Because of its ecstatic structure, Nancy presents sense as a force that is inherently restless. It can never be consolidated or distilled, possessed or circumscribed, precisely because it only exists in the dynamic of its exposition and circulation. This is why it is so essential to understand it in heterogeneous terms, as a force that is *at once* spatial, temporal, embodied, concrete, and

[28] See Yvon Inizan, *La Demande et le don. L'Attestation poétique chez Yves Bonnefoy et Paul Ricœur* (Rennes: Presses Universitaires de Rennes, 2013).
[29] Marie-Eve Morin, *Jean-Luc Nancy* (Cambridge: Polity Press, 2012), p. 31.
[30] Finck, *Yves Bonnefoy. Le Simple et le sens*, p. 14.

meaningful. For it is precisely the resonance that occurs between different modalities of sense that keeps sense 'inquiet' (to use Nancy's term) and perpetually on the move. In Nancy's work, as in Bonnefoy's poetry's, this dynamic understanding of sense radically overturns traditional conceptions of the human body, subjectivity, and thought. The body is no longer perceived as a compact and fleshy mass that serves as the container for thought or being; subjectivity is no longer an ethereal essence that exists prior to our embodied and worldly engagements. In *Corpus*, Nancy suggests that when we attune ourselves to the transitivity of worldly existence, we become aware that the body is not a closed structure but an open one, a site of exposition, or what he terms 'un lieu d'existence', 'un lieu à l'existence'.[31] It is in the dynamic by which bodies open outwards, entering into contact with other bodies—other openings—that 'le sens' is exposed and that existence keeps tranforming itself. Nancy argues that there is no body and no subject that precede this structure of opening. It brings human subjectivity and human corporeity into being (C, 16).

One other key point that Bonnefoy and Nancy have in common is the specifically theatrical idiom that they use to describe the exposure of the sense of material finitude. Bonnefoy suggests that theatre helps us to understand our existence according to a logic that is not representative or self-reflexive but relational. In *La Communauté désœuvrée*, Nancy calls for the same epistemological change to take place when he urges us to understand the scene of human togetherness as 'un théâtre'. He adds: 'le théâtre, ici, ne vaut plus en tant que scène de la représentation: il vaut comme le bord extrême de cette scène, comme la ligne de partage où les uns sont exposés aux autres'.[32] In *Le Sens du monde* too, Nancy writes:

> Le rideau est tombé sur la scène métaphysique, sur la métaphysique comme scène de la (re)présentation. Mais ce qui se *joue* désormais autrement, et sur un théâtre du monde [...] c'est à nouveau l'envoi d'une affirmation de l'excès absolu du sens. [...] L'affirmation nue, dénudée, d'autant plus aiguë et exigeante, du sens du monde en tant que monde. Fin de la philosophie, tâche de la pensée. Tâche de l'être-au-monde. (SM, 43)

Like Bonnefoy, Nancy proposes that theatrical performance serves as a useful model for understanding the common reality of our exposure to one

[31] Jean-Luc Nancy, *Corpus* (Paris: Métailié, 1992). All subsequent references will appear within the text, using the abbreviation C.

[32] Jean-Luc Nancy, *La Communauté désœuvrée* (Paris: Christian Bourgois, 1986), p. 164. All subsequent references will appear within the text, using the abbreviation CD.

another, 'l'être-au-monde'. The subject is thus understood as a force that emerges from a network of worldly interactions, 'un théâtre du monde', or, to return to the phrase that Bonnefoy uses in his essay on Baudelaire, 'un théâtre de l'évidence'. The world itself is understood not as a closed thing, a container for existence, but simply as the concrete dynamic by which existence opens. And the act of writing itself is not of course divorced from this conception of theatrical performance. It is perceived as another manifestation of the world's dynamics of exchange, a way of actively experimenting with the material, corporeal, and intellectual rhythms that bring all forms of worldly existence—including us—into being.

As this book explores the affinities between Bonnefoy's and Nancy's writings, it draws on Nancy's ontological texts rather than his essays on poetry. It is in these ontological texts that Nancy explores most explicitly how finitude can inspire a radically exteriorized conception of human existence in which the human subject finds itself continually overtaken by the dynamics by which existence opens outwards. Here, he develops his conceptions of contact as 'expropriation' or writing as 'excription'. Nancy thus cultivates a thought 'qui se perd tendanciellement comme "pensée" dans sa propre exposition au monde, ou qui s'y *excrit*, qui laisse le sens l'emporter, toujours d'un pas de plus, hors de la signification et de l'interprétation' (SM, 19). The philosopher insists that his writings on sense draw our attention to the *praxis* that brings any form of *poesis* into being (SM, 19). It is interesting to note, however, that Nancy's essays on poetry do not always attribute the same kind of ecstatic energy to the poetic text. It is arguable that these essays are so deeply reverential or even wary of poetry that they reify it. The poem is approached from a distance, as if it were a precious artefact. Crucially, it is not explored as it unfurls *in* the process of its making, or *in* the scene of writing or reading. In his only essay on Bonnefoy's poetry, 'Nécessité du sens', Nancy suggests that poetry harbours a metaphysical longing for closure and experiences the reality of fracture and displacement. He analyses a number of lines of verse in which he suggests that Bonnefoy uses the *coupe* to articulate this tension between container and crack, temple and fracture.[33] The account of the poems remains focused on these few

[33] Nancy sets up an opposition between poetry and metrics at the end of this essay which is revealing. He suggests that poetry expresses metaphysical longing but that the metrics of the poem are atheological. Nancy writes that, within the poem, 'le Sens, pour être le Sens, demande exemplairement le recueil, le rassemblement et la mise à l'abri. Le sens exige un temple, un horizon métaphysique, un dieu, une pose à l'antique'. He contends, however, that 'la nécessité du sens [...] exige la coupe, le transport ailleurs, la disparité des lieux et des situations,

examples and is rather static.[34] Nancy does not explore the dynamics by which Bonnefoy's poetry unfolds, exuberantly exhausting all desire for temple or icon and 'excribing' its sense. As will be demonstrated later in this book, the poet's use of the *versus* is more dynamic that Nancy allows. Bonnefoy uses its turning motion to continually interrupt sense and to reveal it anew, exposing what Nancy describes elsewhere as '[u]n sens tourné, plié et déplié vers les ouvertures des sens'.[35]

Poetry and Performance

The 'performative turn' that literary studies takes in the late twentieth and early twenty-first centuries provokes a tremendous surge of interest in the ways in which texts are operative, not merely in the scene of reading and writing, but in larger social contexts. Critics and theorists explore the peculiar agency that literary texts possess due to their semantic instability: the strange ways that meanings tend to proliferate anarchically and to contest one another within them. We might track the lineage of this idea from Mallarmé to Derrida, seeing how it is relayed from one writer to another in Derrida's reading of Mallarmé's prose poem 'Mimique'.[36] Mallarmé's text describes how Pierrot mimes the act of murder. Derrida's analysis of the text explores how its many different layers of representation intricately overlap, confusing our basic sequential conception of how action unfolds in time

l'interruption de la vérité'. He proposes that poetry exists in the tension between these two stances, between nostalgia for closure and the experience of its dissolution. He suggests that Bonnefoy's use of the *coupe* articulates this tension (Jean-Luc Nancy, 'Nécessité du sens', in *Yves Bonnefoy. Poésie, peinture, musique*, ed. Michèle Finck (Strasbourg: Presses Universitaires de Strasbourg, 1995), pp. 49–50).

[34] We see the same kind of static approach in Nancy's essay on Deguy's poetry and the distinction that he makes between 'precision' and 'exactitude'. Nancy suggests that precision seeks to approach the thing in question and believes it can accede to its presence. He then observes that 'l'exactitude est l'exigence – c'est son *etymon* – l'exigence "exagie", accomplie, à terme, sans reste: la stricte observance de la chose, de sa présence, sans le moindre écart. La chose n'est pas approchée, ni rapprochée: elle reste à son ailleurs, au lointain de son être' (Jean-Luc Nancy, 'Deguy l'an neuf!' in *Cahier Michel Deguy, Le Poète que je cherche à être*, ed. Yves Charnet (Paris: Éditions de la table ronde, 1996), p. 173). Exactitude measures the proximity and distance of the object, its accessibility and its inaccessibility. Yet it is striking to note that these terms are devoid of the emphasis on movement and excess that so characterize his philosophical texts and his writings on art.

[35] Jean-Luc Nancy and Mathilde Monnier, *Allitérations. Conversations sur la danse* (Paris: Galilée, 2005), p. 150.

[36] Jacques Derrida, *La Dissemination* (Paris: Seuil, 1972), pp. 199–317.

and space. Readers finds themselves unable to locate any kind of 'real event' that could have launched this endless series of mimings.[37] Derrida uses Mallarmé's text to suggest that, whilst humanity is always trying to locate the reality prior to the structures of representation, there is no such prior state. Reality is precisely that which is engendered by the play of mimetic structures, by its processes of repetition and differentiation. These ideas about repetition and differentiation become remarkably influential in the mid to late twentieth century. Jonathan Culler observes that theorists link the 'basic aporetic structure of texts' to their capacity for 'invention and inauguration' and so the performativity of the literary texts becomes 'a focal point for questions about agency and identity [...] in the debates about feminist theory, gay and lesbian studies, and queer theory'.[38]

This is a model of performativity that has been embraced by poets and critics alike. In French Studies, we might associate it with the semantically experimental strands of poetic exploration, 'the poets of the signifier' to use James Petterson's phrase.[39] Figures such as Denis Roche, Marcelin Pleynet, and Michel Deguy or, more recently, Christian Prigent, Dominique Fourcade, and Olivier Cadiot all explore how the play of signification within the space of the poem can disrupt preconceived structures of meaning and identity, unsettling firmly enshrined systems of power, and liberating new modes of being. As Jérôme Game writes in *Poetic Becomings*, the poem becomes 'the symbolic plane on which the production of subjectivity [...] operates'.[40] Jean-Jacques Thomas and Steven Winspur argue in *Poeticized Language* that the text's agency is 'not grounded in what words say but in the pragmatic effects that they accomplish for their audience'.[41] There is a powerful ethical impetus to this conception of performativity: the world is conceived as a 'theatre of representation' and the poetic avant-garde as the vigilant body that monitors, critiques, and adjusts the linguistic forms that we use to give meaning to our existence.

[37] Derrida writes: 'Le référent étant levé, la référence démeurant, il ne reste plus que l'écriture du rêve, la fiction sans imaginaire, la mimique sans imitation, sans vraisemblance, sans vérité ni fausseté' (ibid., p. 239).

[38] Jonathan Culler, *The Literary in Theory* (Stanford, CA, Stanford University Press, 2007), p. 140.

[39] James Petterson, *Postwar Figures of L'Éphemère: Yves Bonnefoy, Louis-René des Forêts, Jacques Dupin, André du Bouchet* (London: Associated University Presses, 2000), p. 15.

[40] Jérôme Game, *Poetic Becomings. Studies in Contemporary French Literature* (Oxford, New York: Peter Lang, 2011), p. 1.

[41] Jean-Jacques Thomas and Steven Winspur, *Poeticized Language. The Foundations of Contemporary French Poetry* (University Park, PA: Pennsylvania State University Press, 1999), p 143.

This conception of performativity has been strongly resisted by other strands of the French poetic tradition. Many critics have argued that it neglects crucial physical aspects of human experience that are not structured by linguistic consciousness. These critics have sought to develop more embodied and material conceptions of poetic agency by analysing how the poem traces the processes of exchange that occur between human consciousness and the physical world. The critic Michel Collot describes this poetic tradition—in which he includes the work of Francis Ponge, Philippe Jaccottet, Yves Bonnefoy, Jacques Dupin, and Jacques Reda—as a tradition of 'réalisme lyrique'.[42] Proposing that these poets' conception of poetic agency is profoundly influenced by phenomenology, he argues that their texts explore the dynamics by which that human consciousness finds itself profoundly implicated in its material environment.[43] He interrogates the highly formative processes of exchange that occur between the self and the physical bodies that it encounters. This is an approach embraced by many other critics, such as Jean-Claude Pinson and Susan Harrow.[44] Its crucial advantage is that it allows the critic to investigate how, as Harrow writes, 'subjectivity as a process [...] is drawn into material frames of reference' and how the human body serves as 'an exquisitely receptive interface between the self and world'.[45]

This second model of poetic performativity undoubtedly brings us closer to the materialist and realist model that we find in Bonnefoy's and Nancy's texts. Both Bonnefoy and Nancy are deeply influenced by the way that

[42] Michel Collot, *Paysage et poésie: Du romantisme à nos jours* (Paris: José Corti, 2005), p. 17.

[43] Drawing on Husserl's notion of the structure of intentionality and Merleau-Ponty's conception of corporeal sense, Collot uses 'une approche phénoménologique pour tenter de ressaisir les fondements sensibles du paysage poétique, sensoriels, et synesthétiques, kinesthésiques, et cénesthésiques, ainsi que leur retentissement affectif et leurs prolongements dans l'imaginaire' (ibid.).

[44] Jean-Claude Pinson's *Habiter en poète* argues that late twentieth-century French poetry is profoundly influenced by both the conception of *Dasein* (an ontological force that projects a pre-linguistic horizon of understanding) that is developed in Heidegger's earlier writings and the notion of dwelling that is developed in his later writings. He traces the development of a new lyric tradition that cultivates a poetics of 'l'être-au-monde' and 'la cohabitation' in a bid to foster 'une habitation lyrique du monde' (Jean-Claude Pinson, *Habiter en poète: Essai sur la poésie contemporaine* (Seyssel: Champ Vallon, 1995), p. 17). Susan Harrow's *The Material, the Real, and the Fractured Self* explores how modern poets from Rimbaud to Réda are attuned to the fragmented reality of an urban, (post-)industrial, and globalized material modernity. Her book investigates the 'self-formative activities' of a 'self-in-things' in 'the post-Baudelairean lyric' (Susan Harrow, *The Material, the Real, and the Fractured Self: Subjectivity and Representation from Rimbaud to Réda* (Toronto, Buffalo, London: University of Toronto Press, 2004), p. 4).

[45] Harrow, *The Material, the Real, and the Fractured Self*, p. 4.

phenomenology overturns 'representationalist' accounts of knowledge and affirms the primacy of humanity's experiential engagements.[46] However, it is crucial to note that Bonnefoy and Nancy do have important reservations about the way that phenomenologists portray the relationship between human consciousness and the material real. In *Le Sens du monde*, Nancy acknowledges that phenomenology (and particularly in its 'transformations heideggeriennes') opens up 'un nouvel accès au monde' by exploring how the human subject is caught up in—thrown into existence by—the dynamics of existence's own apparition (SM, 32). But Nancy argues that phenomenology continues to understand the subject's participation in the world in visual terms and conceives of the subject as the sole agent of the world's unveiling or disclosure.[47] Nancy proposes that what is needed is an immersively tactile and aural philosophy that explores the way that the human subject is endlessly overtaken and surprised by 'l'apparaître' of existence, a philosophy that 's'y laisse prendre, emporter, mettre à bout' (SM, 34). Similarly, in his ground-breaking study of Bonnefoy's poetics, *La Demande et le don*, Yvon Inizan argues that Bonnefoy departs from the phenomenological approach to material existence because he seeks to understand the concreteness of reality by conceiving of the relationships between things 'non comme surajoutées, mais comme comprises dans l'être de l'objet lui-même'.[48] In a way that brings him closer to the philosophy of Alfred North Whitehead than to phenomenology, Inizan argues, Bonnefoy presents the concrete act of relation as the active force that brings being into being. Adopting a corrective stance towards phenomenology, both Bonnefoy and Nancy affirm that sense is not the structure of relation disclosed *by* human consciousness but the structure of relation that allows *for* human consciousness to be disclosed.

The model of poetic performance that Bonnefoy and Nancy cultivate is thus more radically corporeal and materialist than those developed in accordance with phenomenological ideas. Creativity is conceived in worldly terms, as the dynamic of relation that brings all forms into being. This is not to suggest that the human subject is stripped of agency but, rather, that

[46] Dermot Moran, *Introduction to Phenomenology* (London, New York: Routledge, 2000), pp. 5–6.

[47] Nancy writes: 'pour toute phénoménologie, c'est-à-dire en définitive pour toute philosophie qui s'articule (expressément ou non) sur "un sujet" de la vision du *phainein*, il reste un point d'origine propre—immanente/transcendante—du sens, un point avec lequel, par conséquent, tout le sens se confond' (SM, 33).

[48] Inizan adds: 'il n'y a que des interdépendences. La relation n'est pas ajoutée par l'esprit, elle se donne dans des "blocs de durée", des volumes, des événements' (Inizan, *La Demande et le don*, p. 83, pp. 84–5).

agency is simply envisioned as the capacity to participate in and inflect the world's generative processes. This dynamic of inflection is steadily cultivated in Bonnefoy's poems. It becomes a rhythm in *Dans le leurre du seuil*, a hesitation or vacillation in *Début et fin de la neige*, and a resonance in *Les Planches courbes*. The poem does not mimic or represent this worldly force but exposes it. It stages an 'hésitation prolongée' between corporeal, material, and meaningful forces. It explores how these forces touch and shape one another, without penetrating or mastering one another, but always sending one another resonating outwards in new and singular ways. These repeated acts of relation give rise to apparently stable forms like the self, the human body, or the body of a text. But these stable forms are always being transformed and reoriginated. Bonnefoy thus affirms the common dynamic of exposition that allows all existence to emerge in its heterogeneity. This is what he terms 'l'un' or 'le tout'. It is for this reason that his ontology never descends into a material monism. Bonnefoy asserts that existence's dynamic of opening is primary but not that all existence is material in nature. In *Les Planches courbes*, the poet explores how the resonance of the human voice coaxes linguistic consciousness into being. Resonance becomes what we might describe as an ontological principle or disposition in this collection. The poet explores how existence reverberates outwards, spatializing and singularizing itself, allowing the different modalities of sense to emerge and to keep differentiating themselves. In *La Demande et le don*, Inizan suggests that Bonnefoy's strength as a poet is that, without eliding or dismissing our interpretative capacities, '[s]a poésie offre de penser une conception "tensionnelle de la vérité"'.[49] His poetry draws linguistic consciousness back into resonance with corporeal and material forces, attuning us to the worldly dynamics of their interaction or co-origination.

[49] Inizan, *La Demande et le don*, p. 239.

1

Performative Utterance in *Dans le leurre du seuil*

Illusion of the Threshold.

> aimer, c'est-à-dire sortir de soi
> (*Entretiens sur la poésie*, p. 59)

> Terre, ce qu'on appelle la poésie T'aura tant
> désirée en ce siècle, sans prendre Jamais sur
> toi le bien du geste d'amour
> (*Ce qui fut sans lumière*, p. 15)

'La Terre'

Bonnefoy's *Dans le leurre du seuil*, published in 1975, is generally considered to be his most ambitious volume of poetry. One long poem, divided into seven sections, it reflects on the quintessential topics that have come to define his poetic writings: the conceptual structures of language and their capacity to limit our understanding of the world; the movements and metamorphoses of physical existence; poetry's capacity to articulate what cannot be signified conceptually, the shared sense of our everyday interactions. These are questions that Bonnefoy has pursued since the beginning of his career. What distinguishes the approach that he takes in *Dans le leurre du seuil*, however, is that the poet now no longer agonizes over the distance that separates human consciousness from material reality. Embracing the embodied nature of human utterance, the poet adopts a conspicuously theatrical mode of writing and experiments with a range of different modes of address and interpellation. One poem unfolds as a series of commands; another calls out to a companion, urging her to look at a spectacle unfolding before her; another apostrophizes an inanimate material presence. Throughout the collection, Bonnefoy explores how such speech acts allow him to cultivate embodied and relational ways of thinking about finitude, subjectivity, intimacy, and community.

Yves Bonnefoy and Jean-Luc Nancy: Ontological Performance. Emily McLaughlin, Oxford University Press (2020). © Emily McLaughlin.
DOI: 10.1093/oso/9780198849582.001.0001

One of the most striking formal features of the collection is that its seven long poems are intercut with a series of dotted lines. Bonnefoy suggests that these lines represent 'des explorations que je n'ai pas faites, et dont je voulais pourtant que soit pressentie la présence obscure' (E, 66). This interruptive device means that the poems move quickly between different subject matters, styles of speech, and prosodic forms. This constant variation is what makes *Dans le leurre du seuil* such an energetic and vital text. The sinuosity of the structure is reflected in the poet's interest in highly fluid elemental forms and sections bear titles such as 'Le Fleuve', 'Deux barques', 'Les Nuées', and 'L'Épars, l'indivisible'. As we move through the collection, we gradually forge connections between a range of subtly interwoven personal narratives: the different phases in a romantic relationship, the evolution of a house and landscape, and the vicissitudes of the poet's relationship with language. It is important to note, however, that the collection still possesses a linear structure and maps a process of transformation. The first section, 'Le Fleuve', begins by evoking the poet-narrator's distress at the irreconcilable distance between the forms of artistic creation and the reality of material existence (DL, 12). It opens with an image of peaceful sleep being dashed against rocks and describes how the sleeping mind regains consciousness only to confront a raw and intractable material reality (DL, 11). Over the course of the collection, however, the poet's experimentation with diverse acts of address or relation makes him increasingly aware that the poetic act is part of this material reality. The final section, 'L'Épars, l'indivisible', ends with an image of a wave that simultaneously breaks and forms (as discussed in the introduction) (DL, 120). Bonnefoy foregrounds the finitude of the poetic gesture itself and affirms that language participates in the dynamics of contact and exposure that are common to all material existence.

This transformation of the relationship between language and the physical world in *Dans le leurre du seuil* is largely due to Bonnefoy's sustained experimentation with the performative resources of language. The poet cultivates a varied series of refrains across the collection that foreground certain grammatical components of language: imperatives, vocatives, optatives, subject pronouns, affirmations, and temporal and spatial prepositions. Bonnefoy repeats each of these formulations at the beginning of lines or stanzas, varying the contexts in which they appear, and exploring how their grammatical force differs from one phrase to the next. The action effected is sometimes deconstructive, challenging the authority of fixed linguistic structures and the patterns of thought that they produce. The section entitled 'Dans le leurre du seuil' repeats the imperative 'Heurte' and urges the reader to work within language against language, resisting its closed structures of meaning (DL, 19–21). As the collection progresses, however, Bonnefoy experiments with language's performative capabilities in more affirmative ways. The poet explores how an active and situated utterance is always already intimately implicated in the temporal and spatial dynamics of material existence. The collection ends by affirming language's capacity to celebrate fleeting instances of sensual experience, as the poet reiterates the affirmative construction 'Oui, par': 'Oui, par le soir / Quand il remue les cendres de la couleur' (DL, 106); 'Oui, par la cime éclairée / Une heure encore' (DL, 106).

This chapter examines 'La Terre', the fifth section and the most resolutely performative part of *Dans le leurre du seuil*. This section begins with a self-consciously theatrical utterance that dramatizes the poet's own speech act: 'Je crie, Regarde' (DL, 59). The poet addresses an unidentified other, perhaps a lover, perhaps the reader, urging her to look, to perceive the spectacle that is unfurling before her. The opening poems of 'La Terre' dramatize these ordinary gestures: the poet shows his companion the first flash of light on an autumn morning or the emergence of the first spring blossom. Behind these simple gestures, however, there resonates a language of myth and ritual. We perceive traces of a pre-modern form of theatre, one that dramatizes the evolution of natural and cosmic cycles.[1] In each of these poems, ritualistic utterances are pronounced in the first-person indicative and present tense, conforming to J.L. Austin's definition of a performative speech act.[2] A verbal act consecrates a crucial moment of transformation in the life of a person, a tradition, or a natural cycle. From one poem to the next, however, Bonnefoy makes the fleetingness of these gestures increasingly apparent. He undermines the authority of these ritual acts, exploring how a religious or metaphysical theatre fails to master or to transcend the finitude of worldly existence. The third poem of 'La Terre', 'Ô flamme', uses its own incantational and rhythmic structure to demonstrate that finitude cannot be vanquished by any form of ritual utterance because its performance is always already produced and consumed by it (DL, 61–3).

[1] It is worth noting that, just six years after he published *Dans le leurre du seuil*, Bonnefoy edited a dictionary of mythologies and religions (Yves Bonnefoy, *Dictionnaire des mythologies et des religions des sociétés traditionnelles et du monde antique* (Paris: Flammarion, 1981)).

[2] Austin writes of the performative utterance, 'to utter the sentence (in, of course, appropriate circumstances) is not to *describe* my doing of what I should be said in so uttering to be doing or to state that I am doing it: it is to do it'. These are often sentences, Austin notes, 'in the first person singular present indicative active' (J.L. Austin, *How to Do Things with Words* (Cambridge, MA: Harvard University Press, 1962), p. 6, p. 67).

The self-consciously theatrical poems of 'La Terre' deconstruct a mythical or metaphysical conception of poetic performance. Insisting that we can no longer conceive of the poetic act as a gesture that unfurls in space *apart* from finite material existence, Bonnefoy suggests that it is the task of the poet to develop a properly worldly practice of performance that explores how finitude brings its very gesture of presentation into being and disperses it. Bonnefoy conceives of finitude as the simultaneously destructive and creative force that steadily ungrounds existence only to project it outwards and into relation. And so, for him, a poetic performance that seeks to be faithful—or as faithful as possible—to the dynamics of finitude is a theatre of exposure. The poems of 'La Terre' use structures of address and interpellation to explore what it means to be continually exposed to other beings and presences in this way. Interrogating the sense and the ethics of existing in relation, Bonnefoy uses performative structures—vocatives, cohortatives, entreaties, appeals, commands—to develop newly embodied and relational forms of understanding. He invites us to perceive the relational dynamics that bring us into being, not from the outside, but from the inside, to develop an emergent rather than a transcendental way of knowing existence.

This intimate and relational way of knowing our world is precisely what Bonnefoy hopes to suggest when he uses the title 'La Terre'. He uses this term frequently in interviews and essays. In a 1972 interview with *Le Journal de Genève*, three years before the publication of *Dans le leurre du seuil*, Bonnefoy observes, 'ce qui vaut, ce qui est, c'est un devenir qui est assuré par l'échange, par le sacrifice réciproque des langues particulières' (E, 54). Later in the interview, he adds: 'En art comme dans la vie apprenons la parole de l'autre, et la terre adviendra, figure intense parce que lieu partagé. Tel me paraît le dessein de la poésie' (E, 59). Bonnefoy suggests that the poem surrenders the autonomy and enclosure of linguistic play, the cultivation of an idiolect, and that it privileges instead a simple gesture of opening. Fostering 'un devenir qui est assuré par l'échange', the poem makes us aware that exchange itself is generative, that the self and the world come into being through acts of relation. Its performance makes us experience the world as '[un] lieu partagé'. It restores us to our own finite material existence, to what Bonnefoy terms 'la terre'. Throughout his career, Bonnefoy defines the embodied speech act that facilitates exchange in this manner as 'la parole' and he sets this form of speech in contradistinction to 'la langue', as per Saussure's opposition. Whereas 'la langue' embroils us in a world of abstractions, Bonnefoy suggests, 'la parole' embeds us in a live situation, in a network of physical relations. When we are *engaged* in this way, we cannot so easily reduce the people or the presences around us to the status of objects. In 'La Parole poétique', Bonnefoy writes:

> Grande possible vie du langage: grâce à laquelle l'autre être humain, que tant de pensées tendent à réduire à l'état d'objet quantifiable, sera reconnu comme, oui, précisément cela, un être, dans un monde qui en devient un lieu partagé et doté de sens par ce partage. Le mot actif en sa profondeur interdit l'idéologie, se prête à l'élan de la parole. (SPV, 205)

Language is not allowed to crystallize as ideology—as a system of objectification—but remains supple and active. We perceive our interlocutor is 'un être', an undeniably vital and dynamic presence whose being is clearly in excess of signification. Bonnefoy suggests that the movement of speech between two people, two active and unpredictable beings, exposes the inherently shared nature of existence. And in doing so, it exposes its sense: 'dans un monde qui en devient un lieu partagé et doté de sens par ce partage'. 'La parole' shows us that sense is inherently shared, that it is exposed by the gesture of relation itself.

The highly theatrical exploration of finitude, exposure, and exchange that Bonnefoy delivers in 'La Terre' has much in common with Nancy's writings on these subjects in *La Communauté désœuvrée*, published in 1986, eleven years after *Dans le leurre du seuil*. This important work on community presents finitude as a dynamic of exposure and interaction. Nancy writes: 'la finitude elle-même n'*est* rien, qu'elle n'est pas un fond, ni une essence, ni une substance. Mais elle paraît, elle se présente, elle s'expose, et ainsi elle *existe* en tant que communication' (CD, 72). Nancy suggests that finitude's ecstatic motion outwards gives rise to all phenomena, provoking what he describes not as their 'apparition' but their 'comparution'. He writes: 'la finitude *com-paraît* et ne peut que *com-paraître*' (CD, 72). Everything that comes into being does so through a dynamic process of exposure and interaction: 'l'être fini se présente toujours ensemble, [...] toujours dans l'être-en-commun et comme cet être lui-même (CD, 72). Nancy suggests that it is difficult to use language to talk about the finite dynamics that shape all our interactions in this way. He observes: 'Peut-être ne faut-il chercher ni mot ni concept, et reconnaître dans la pensée de la communauté un excès théorique (plus exactement: un excès sur le théorique) qui nous obligerait à une autre *praxis* du discours et de la communauté' (CD, 66). One might suggest that Bonnefoy's use of theatrical structures in 'La Terre' elaborates 'une autre *praxis* du discours et de la communauté'. He uses the theatrical structures of address and interpellation to dramatize the gestures of exposure that precede and exceed the representations of language. He demonstrates how utterance presents itself 'dans l'être-en-commun et comme cet être lui-même'.

If we compare 'La Terre' to the poetry produced by Bonnefoy's peers at this time, poets such as Dupin and du Bouchet, we get a clearer idea of just how innovative its performative practice is. Dupin and du Bouchet both pursue a resolutely negative approach in this period, insisting that it is only through a deconstructive approach to the conceptual structures of language that the poet can gain access to the physical world. Both use constant images of cutting, breaking, violence, violation, destruction, and death. Inflicting violence upon words, they hope to reveal something of its vital material plasticity. Dupin describes his poetry as a 'chant qui est à lui-même sa faux'.[3] Michel Collot suggests that Dupin's work deconstructs stable linguistic oppositions in order to reveal the fertile power of chaos.[4] At the end of *Dans le leurre du seuil*, Bonnefoy insists that he has pursued a very different aim in this collection. He writes: 'Non, ne démembre pas / Mais délivre, et rassure. "Écrire", une violence / Mais pour la paix qui a saveur d'eau pure' (DL, 116). He insists that violence must always be a means and not an end. He contends that any process of deconstruction must ultimately serve to renew our capacities for affirmation.

The Advent and Sacrifice of the Poem

The first three poems of 'La Terre' reflect on experiences of birth and death. They all echo certain pre-modern rituals that were used to celebrate the passage of things into or out of being. They can be read respectively as an Ur-myth, a fertility ritual, and a sacrificial ceremony. The first poem opens with the highly performative utterance, 'Je crie, Regarde'. The poet dramatizes his own speech, presenting it as a spontaneous cry, and points towards a presence that is unfurling before him (DL, 59). Bonnefoy uses these exclamations and gesticulations—which will be repeated in the opening lines of the next poem in the sequence—to introduce the theme of advent. Etymologically, 'advent' comes from the Latin 'adventus', meaning 'arrival'.[5]

[3] Jacques Dupin, *Gravir* (Paris: Gallimard, 1963), p. 16.
[4] Michel Collot, *La Matière-émotion* (Paris: Presses Universitaires de France, 1997), p. 195.
[5] 'Advent', in *Oxford English Dictionary*, http://www.oed.com, accessed 9 August 2017.

The presence that gradually comes into sight in this first poem is the light. The poem bears witness to the arrival of the dawn sun and pursues the traces of its beams of light. The second poem dramatizes the poet's reaction to the arrival of the first almond blossom after winter. There is a thematic shift in the third poem, 'Ô flamme', as renewal gives way to loss, and advent to sacrifice. The poem's structure of address changes too as the poet turns away from his audience in order to apostrophize a flame and to reflect on the nature of destruction. It is in this poem that the poet realizes that birth and death are not distinct events, and that one event is not to celebrated and the other lamented. 'Ô flamme' suggests that birth and death are coterminous in every gesture. With this realization, the promise of redemption and transcendence that underpinned the first two ritualistic performances seems increasingly hollow to the poet. And so, in 'Ô flamme', he develops a properly finite model of poetic performance: one that celebrates its own advent and sacrifice, its expenditure without reserve.

The first poem of 'La Terre' is remarkably energetic. In the moments following the apparition of a dawn light, the poet points towards its remaining traces: 'Je crie, Regarde, / La lumière / Vivait là, près de nous!' (DL, 59). The imperatives and deictics all perform the act of pointing. The noun 'Lumière' is isolated, as if by appearing alone in this way it could become a substitute for the presence of the light itself. The use of the verb '[v]ivait' presents the light as a vital or even animate force. The poet scours its traces, longing to retain them, but the reiteration of the shifting deictic 'ici' suggests their inherent fleetingness: 'Ici, sa provision / D'eau, encore transfigurée. Ici le bois / Dans la remise. Ici, les quelques fruits / A sécher dans les vibrations du ciel de l'aube' (DL, 59). Enjambments run excitedly from one line to the next. Each time the poet fixes the light for an instant, it slips away, and the poet must point again. And yet, as this light moves, shifting from one form to another, a series of phenomena are steadily revealed: the water, the hangar, and the fruit. A landscape gradually appears before us, illuminated, 'dans les vibrations du ciel de l'aube'. The poet at first stresses the ordinary nature of scene. Even as he points in amazement towards this light, he insists that the world is the same as it has always been and that poetry too performs almost the same task as always, producing 'Presque les mêmes mots' (DL, 59). Yet, as the poem progresses, a force rises up between the poet and his companion, or, perhaps, between the poet and the reader: 'Mais, vois, en toi, en moi / L'indivis, l'invisible se rassemblent' (DL, 59). The internal rhyme in 'vois, en toi, en moi' mimics the rising of this presence. It is as if, in response to 'vois', the sound [wa] becomes apparent 'en toi' and 'en moi'. The repetition and inversion of sounds in 'L'indivis, l'invisible' too suggest the complicit but contradictory workings of this force. It is invisible but undivided, imperceptible but omnipresent.

The poet's excitement culminates in the final stanza as the light itself seems to arrive. Fronting the subject pronoun, Bonnefoy stages a dramatic arrival: 'Et elle! n'est-ce pas / Elle qui sourit là' (DL, 59). The inversion signals the poet's uncertainty as to the nature of this presence. The reader is at first not sure whether 'elle' marks cultural or grammatical gender. And yet, as this figure smiles, it becomes clear that a female figure has appeared.[6] She then speaks: '("Moi la lumière, / Oui, je consens")' (DL, 59–60). Her speech is strangely ritualized, as if she were responding to some form of ceremonial request. She issues an affirmative, identifies herself, and gives her consent. Delivered in the first-person present indicative, this utterance is a perfect Austinian performative speech act.[7] It falls across the line end, as if to suggest its transgressive or extravagant nature. It appears between parentheses and *guillemets* too, setting itself apart as doubly 'other'. The poem ends with one final enjambment as the light crosses the horizon, 'Penchée, guidant les pas / D'on dirait un soleil enfant sur une eau obscure' (DL, 60).

The first poem of 'La Terre' dramatizes a constant succession of arrivals. Very little is explained—the poet only observes that nothing has changed—and almost everything is performed. The light appears, a feeling arises between the poet and his companion, a female figure arrives, and then a 'sun-child'. Puncturing the poetic utterance and performing the act of consent, even the light's speech makes a direct incursion into the poem. With each of these arrivals, the poet can only gesture towards each new presence, summoning our attention and pointing. As he does so, a conspicuous religious imagery intercedes, suggesting that we interpret the advent of this light in a divine sense. Touched by the first rays of light, the water is 'encore transfigurée'. The force that unites the couple is '[l]'indivis, l'invisible'.

[6] 'La lumière' becomes an active and animate female presence within the poem. It is precisely the way that the subject pronoun is transformed from 'it' to 'her' in the metaphysical scene of advent that interests the poet.

[7] Austin of course dismisses the use of a performative utterance within a poem or on the stage as being 'non-serious', 'a mockery, like a marriage with a monkey' (J.L. Austin, *How to Do Things with Words*, p. 24). Derrida's reading of Austin's text insists, on the contrary, that the serious act is indistinguishable from the non-serious act. This is the very distinction that Derrida notoriously challenges in 'Signature événement contexte' by insisting that all speech acts are defined by 'une citationalité générale' (*Marges de la philosophie* (Paris: Les Éditions de Minuit, 1972), p. 387). Bonnefoy too seems to be reflecting on the purportedly authentic nature of ritualistic utterances.

The female figure appears 'dans la certitude du seuil'. In anthropology, the threshold, 'the transitional or liminal phase-place', is often conceived as a 'gateway to the divine'.[8] In an image which has endless mythical, anthropological, and poetic resonances, the light finally leads 'un soleil enfant' over the horizon.

Bonnefoy's opening poem emulates the Mallarmean model for poetic performance, 'le drame solaire'. Mallarmé considered the setting and the rising of the sun to be the archetype for all death and resurrection myths. Heavily influenced by George Cox's *Manual of Mythology*, which he adapted in French as *Les Dieux antiques*, Mallarmé suggested that the sacrificial hero of all world myths and religions is precisely the same figure: the sun god. Structures of myth and ritual can thus be seen to emulate the pattern of the sun's death and resurrection. Gardner Davies, citing Mallarmé, suggests that: '[l]e "grand et perpétuel sujet de la Mythologie" est l'évolution quotidienne et annuelle du soleil, son voyage à travers le ciel vers l'horizon occidental, et la succession des saisons'.[9] Mallarmé himself writes: 'Persée, Bellérophon, Héraclès, Thésée, Achille, Apollon, Odyssée, Sigurd, Rustem, et une légion d'autres, ne sont que des formes différentes d'une seule et même personne; et l'idée de cette personne est issue de phrases qui décrivaient originairement la marche du soleil dans son orbe annuel et quotidien'.[10] Mallarmé suggests that the steady re-enactment of this scene allows humanity to explore the cyclical nature of life and death and to construct a pattern that is 'ontologically consoling', to use Roger Pearson's phrase.[11] The first poem of 'La Terre' very deliberately opens with this seminal theatrical trope that Mallarmé uses to construct his theory of poetic performance. Bonnefoy's sequence initiates a new cycle in the never-ending performance, the resurrection of 'un soleil enfant'.[12]

The second poem of 'La Terre' depicts another manifestation of *le drame solaire*: the blossoming and the pollination of an almond tree. The almond tree is the first tree to flower after winter in Western Europe and is therefore

[8] Alexander Moore, *Cultural Anthropology, The Field Study of Human Beings* (San Diego: Collegiate Press, 1998), p. 145.

[9] Gardner Davies, *Mallarmé et le drame solaire* (Paris: José Corti, 1959), p. 33.

[10] Stéphane Mallarmé, *Œuvres complètes*, 2 vols, ed. Bertrand Marchal (Paris: Gallimard, Bibliothèque de la Pléiade, 1998–2003), II, p. 1518.

[11] Roger Pearson, *Stéphane Mallarmé* (London: Reaktion, 2011), p. 67.

[12] In Rimbaud's poetry, the same connection is forged between the breaking of dawn and the arrival of a child. In *Illuminations*, 'Aube' ends with the same archetypal image of advent: 'L'aube et l'enfant tombèrent au bas du bois' (Rimbaud, *Œuvres complètes*, ed. André Guyaux (Paris: Gallimard, Bibliothèque de la Pléiade, 2009), p. 306).

an ancient symbol of rebirth.[13] The first poem showed us the emergence of the first rays of dawn sun in Autumn but this poem takes place on a Spring night. The poet cries out as he did in the first poem, urging us to bear witness to the apparition of flowers upon the gnarled old branches of the almond tree:

> Je crie, Regarde,
> L'amandier
> Se couvre brusquement de milliers de fleurs.
> Ici
> Le noueux, l'à jamais terrestre, le déchiré
> Entre au port. Moi la nuit
> Je consens. Moi l'amandier
> J'entre paré dans la chambre nuptiale.
>
> (DL, 60)

The poem alternates long and short lines, an abundant eleven syllables evoking the tree's efflorescence, and then our attention is focused on the short two-syllable line, 'Ici'. The 'here' and 'now' is presented as a space of arrival. The knotty and ragged form of rough-barked almond suddenly flourishes. It stages a triumphant entry as if it were a boat, bedecked with white sails, entering port. In this exultant moment, another voice cuts through the poet's speech, mid verse and mid stanza. It is the night that now speaks and performs the act of consent: 'Moi la nuit / Je consens'. This voice is not marked by parentheses or *guillemets* as the voice of the light was. It blends with the poet's speech. And in the next breath, the voice of the almond tree breaks through. Bearing its rich blossoms into the bridal chamber, it performs a kind of fertility ritual. It's as if the botanical process of pollination consecrates the sexual act of procreation. As these two voices make a direct incursion into the poem, the poet witnesses the intervention of a transcendental presence. Two hands descend from the sky and a divine being pollinates the seed. These hands 'Prennent / Comme passe une ondée,

[13] In many world religions, the almond seed is the symbol of virgin birth. The Greek God Attis was conceived when Nana, the virgin nymph, placed a ripe almond on her breast (Christine Schnusenberg, *The Mythological Traditions of Liturgical Drama: The Eucharist as Theatre* (Mahwah, NJ: Paulist Press, 2010), p. 193). In Christian art, the virgin Mary and Jesus are symbolized by the almond or the almond branch. The 'mandorla', meaning almond nut in Italian, is the almond-shaped contour that surrounds the figures of Mary and Jesus in traditional Christian art (Elizabeth E. Goldsmith, *Sacred Symbols in Art* (Whitefish, MT: Kessinger Publishing, 2003) p. 67).

dans chaque fleur, / La part impérissable de la vie' (DL, 60). As the seed is formed, the renewal of these ephemeral material forms is envisaged as a form of eternity: 'l'à jamais de la fleur éphémère' (DL, 61).

Bonnefoy begins the first poems of 'La Terre' with an exploration of the advent of two natural cycles: sunrise and pollination. Like Mallarmé, he investigates how the spectacles that we witness in the natural world, 'l'évolution quotidienne et annuelle du soleil, son voyage à travers le ciel vers l'horizon occidental, et la succession des saisons', mould the poetic, theatrical, mythical, and religious imagination. He explores how one spectacle gives rise to another and how humanity gives communal form to these temporal rhythms. As the poet explores the dynamics by which existence is miraculously renewed, the poetic language hovers between the quotidian and the marvellous in a way that is reminiscient of Rimbaud's poetry. The third poem, however, shifts the focus away from renewal and considers questions of consumption and loss instead. Although Bonnefoy continues to experiment with the theatrical structures of religious ritual by staging an apostrophe to a flame, he now presents a very different enactment of *le drame solaire* and develops a different model of poetic performance. Etymologically, 'apostrophe' comes from the Greek for 'to turn away'. As the priest turns his back on the congregation to face the altar, the poet turns away from his companion to address the flame directly, speaking to it 'as if it were alive, present, and capable of understanding'.[14] As the poet's attention turns away from the rising sun and the fertilized seed to the sacrificial fire, he questions the disappearance of life. He apostrophizes the flame repeatedly, endowing it with a new set of epithets each time. Its ephemeral presence becomes a model for various kinds of human action. Love, sex, procreation, and poetry are all envisaged as a kind of sacrificial burning.

The poem begins by extolling the paradoxical nature of this force that simultaneously flourishes and consumes itself: 'Ô flamme / Qui consumant célèbres, / Cendre / Qui dispersant recueilles' (DL, 61). The address to the flame quickly becomes an address to the ash, to this fine powder that at once disperses and deposits that which is burned. The 'flamme' is used as an image for the finite, and thus sacrificial, nature of all existence. Images of sacrificial fire merge with images of 'la fièvre' or sexual 'burning' to suggest the finite nature of physical passion: 'Flamme, oui, qui effaces / De la table sacrificielle de l'été / La fièvre, les sursauts / De la main crispée' (DL, 61). As

[14] *The Princeton Encyclopedia of Poetry and Poetics*, ed. Alex Preminger (2nd edn, Princeton: Princeton University Press, 1974), p. 42.

the sacrificial table becomes the lovers' bed, sex is presented as a feverish excess that burns intensely and consumes itself. The conjunction that follows suggests that this burning has a purpose. The convulsive pleasure of sex fades 'pour que la pierre du ciel clair / Soit lavée de notre ombre, et que ce soit / Un dieu enfant qui joue / Dans l'âcreté de la sève' (DL, 61). In an image that is clearly redolent of the solar drama, the sacrificial table becomes a sky and the passing of each of our shadows is conceived as a sacrificial cleansing, a dissolution that permits renewal. And in spite of its tireless consumption, the feverish burning of sex leaves a deposit, 'la sève', from which another 'dieu enfant' emerges.

The poet leans over the flame and laments his sacrifice. He perceives only 'L'impatience, l'ardeur, le deuil, la solitude / Dans ta fumée' (DL, 62). Passion exhausts itself and the poet perceives only loss and desolation. His own finitude is perceived as an absolute sacrifice, as the loss of something essential. And yet, as the poet leans again—and this motion will become an almost tropistic gesture across the poems of 'La Terre'—he reaches towards the child: 'Je me penche sur toi, aube, je prends / Dans mes mains ton visage' (DL, 62). Perceiving the child as a dawn, the poet suggests that the passing of one era gives rise to another. Bonnefoy suggests that the individual experiences this simultaneous ending and beginning only through its exposure to the other. By reaching towards the child, by taking its face in his hands, he shares in its 'aube'. With the exhaustion of a sexual passion comes another form of relation. The poet exclaims: 'Qu'il fait beau / Sur notre lit désert! Je sacrifie et tu es la résurrection de ce que je brûle' (DL, 62). As the poet addresses this newborn child, he feels, not so much the redemption or recuperation of past losses, but the necessary conjunction of loss and renewal.

With this realization, the structure of the apostrophe changes. The poet no longer dedicates his utterance to a solitary flame but, rather, apostrophizes a series of divergent objects, greeting them all as 'Flamme'. As he leaned towards the child, so he reaches out towards a diverse series of physical things. The poem's closed ritual theatre is suddenly opened up to the varied presences of the material world. The poet hails last year's bedroom, this apparently solid structure, as a passing boat: 'Flamme, notre chambre de l'autre année, mystérieuse / Comme la proue d'une barque qui passe' (DL, 62). He lauds the changing shapes of the light on the wall, which pass with no concern for our finite existence. Greeting each object in turn, Bonnefoy creates the sensation that they are all slipping past. He evokes a world of material things that, in their finitude, are a series of passing and thus vital forces. Mixing modern and historical, religious and secular references, he finally declares: 'Flamme l'ampoule / Où manquait Dieu / Au-dessus de la porte de l'étable' (DL, 62). This is a modern technological manifestation of the light imagery that has run throughout all these poems. Yet the 'ampoule' is also a container that holds the Eucharist during Communion. Here is a light and a stable that contain no divine presence, no 'soleil enfant'. And yet, the poet greets the 'ampoule / Où manquait Dieu' as a 'flamme'. He suggests that every material thing is an ephemeral flame. Everything is consumed and, yet, for a moment, everything stands revealed in its numinosity.

In the final lines of the poem, the ritual of sacrifice itself is greeted as a passing flame: 'Flamme la pierre / Où le couteau du rêve a tant œuvré' (DL, 63). The metaphysical ambitions that are expressed by the gesture of sacrifice are overturned here. The poet no longer seeks to exchange destruction for resurrection, the ephemeral for the essential. He presents the sacrificial ceremony itself as a flame, insisting that its gesture does not transcend the ephemeral 'burning' of existence. The dream of transcendence is swallowed up by finitude itself. Sacrifice is no longer conceived as a human process with human ends; all existence is perceived a 'Flamme qui va [...]'. Nancy reflects on the relationship between finitude and sacrifice in a very similar way in *Une pensée finie* when he writes:

> Dire que l'existence est offerte, c'est employer un mot du vocabulaire sacrificiel, sans doute (et si nous étions dans la langue allemande, ce serait le mot même: *Opfer, Aufopferung*). Mais c'est pour essayer de marquer que l'existence, s'il fallait la dire sacrifiée, n'est en tout cas sacrifiée par personne, et n'est sacrifiée à rien. "L'existence est offerte" veut dire la finitude de l'existence.[15]

Nancy suggests that everything is always already sacrificed and that it is sacrificed by no one and for no one. Existence is a constant expenditure that will not be instrumentalized in any form of ritual or performance. It is 'l'insacrifiable' precisely because it is always already 'offered up' (PF, 104). Nancy writes: 'L'existant arrive, il a lieu, et cela n'est qu'un être-jeté au monde. Dans cet être-jeté, il est offert' (PF, 102). In a similar manner, Bonnefoy presents existence as a flame that flashes into being and expires. He suggests that this 'burning' can neither be appropriated nor transcended. 'Ô flamme' thus ends with the words 'Flamme, / Dans la paix de la flamme, / L'agneau

[15] Jean-Luc Nancy, *Une pensée finie* (Paris: Galilée, 1990), p. 101. All subsequent references will appear within the text, using the abbreviation PF.

du sacrifice gardé sauf' (DL, 63). The ephemera of the world are embraced as ephemera. The lamb is not sacrificed but kept safe, entrusted to finitude: 'Flamme, / Dans la paix de la flamme'. In Bonnefoy's poem, as in Nancy's text, each and every being becomes the 'dieu enfant': a Christ that is always already offered up.

The first three poems of 'La Terre' bear witness to or address the spectacle of fire: the dawn sun, the arrrival of blossom with the arrival of the Spring sun, and the expenditure of a flame. Bonnefoy uses these three motifs to reflect on the cyclical nature of existence, the steady disappearance and renewal of light, blossom, and life. He reflects on models of poetic performance that have sought to redeem these events in metaphysical terms. Using the religious motifs of advent and sacrifice, Bonnefoy reflects on ritual or ceremonial acts that seek to transcend the finitude of existence, to master its limits by commanding its origin or its end. 'Ô flamme' critiques this model of poetic performance, insisting that nothing in existence can be offered up, that everything is always already coming into and passing out of being. The poet protests that finite existence is pure expenditure and that nothing transcends this 'general economy'. If Bonnefoy's understanding of finitude overlaps with Nancy's here, it is surely because both are reflecting on the motif of sacrifice and are influenced by Bataille's writings on it and 'l'économie générale'.[16] Stuart Kendall writes that Bataille reflects on how:

> organising our lives and the lives of our communities around large-scale expenditures – as in sacrificial acts and festivals that traditionally accompanied transitional moments in individual life, births, adolescence, marriage and death, as well as transitional passages in natural life, the passages of the earth through the solar year – links human life to larger patterns of expenditure.[17]

Bataille's analyses of 'these patterns of expenditure' present sacrifice as a moment of pure disappropriation that abolishes the mastery of the Hegelian subject. Sacrifice is an experience that cannot be 'put to work'. As James phrases it, it cannot be 'incorporated into the dialectical activity of negation and determination which make up the life of the subject'.[18] There is no

[16] See Georges Bataille, *La Part maudite, précedé de La Notion de dépense* (Paris: Éditions de Minuit, 1967).

[17] Stuart Kendall, 'Expenditure', in *Georges Bataille. Key Concepts*, ed. Mark Hewson and Marcus Coelen (Abingdon, New York: Routledge, 2016), pp. 84–5.

[18] Ian James, *The Fragmentary Demand, An Introduction to the philosophy of Jean-Luc Nancy* (Stanford, CA: Stanford University Press, 2006), p. 181.

gesture that the subject can use to recuperate or redeem this negativity, to master its expenditure without reserve. Bataille relishes the motif of sacrifice precisely because it negates, as Elisabeth Arnould-Bloomfield writes, 'utilitarian relationships with the world' and exposes a 'desire to join, in consumption, the ever-changing fluidity of being—whose preferred trope is indeed, the sun'.[19] The radiance of the sun's light exposes the endless processes of consumption and renewal to which all existence is subject. By surrendering to its boundless expenditure, Bataille seeks to participate fully in an endlessly mobile and mutable physical world.

Similarly, Bonnefoy suggests that, as much as humanity may strive to transcend finitude, it is the general economy within which all human action unfurls. A poetic gesture cannot be raised up or held apart from the dynamics of finite existence. There is no ritual that can consecrate a discrete beginning or ending, or redeem some kind of transcendental form. In 'Ô flamme', we witness the sacrifice of this aspiration towards transcendence. Of course, this is not to suggest that the poem renounces its aspirations to communicate or to touch upon the sanctity of existence. Certainly, Bataille perceives sacrifice's excessive gesture as that which brings about communication with—rather than a communion with—the sacred. In a very similar manner, Bonnefoy suggests that finitude exposes the sanctity of material existence. The final sequences of 'Ô flamme' celebrate the passing or the consumption of the poem itself. As soon as each utterance or image is pronounced, it is swallowed up by the rhythmic structures of the poem. 'Ô flamme' affirms that the poetic act is as ephemeral as any other gesture. Bonnefoy suggests that the only gesture that is capable of articulating the sanctity of finite existence is one that allows itself to be consumed and that, in doing so, exposes the vitality and the urgency of existence.

We might suggest that Bonnefoy embraces a Bataillean model of performance as opposed to a Mallarmean one in these poems. Bonnefoy emulates Mallarmé's enactments of *le drame solaire* but, as the poems progress, we become increasingly aware that they also critique the way that he puts its pattern or rhythm to work in his poetry. Although Mallarmé does view the ritual performances of *le drame solaire* from an anthropological perspective that relativizes their metaphysical ambitions, he still affirms that its cosmic rhythm, its cycles of death and resurrection, offer a glimpse of a pattern that transcends the amorphous flux of finite material existence.

[19] Elisabeth Arnould-Bloumfield, 'Sacrifice', in *Georges Bataille, Key Concepts*, ed. Hewson and Coelen, p. 105.

Bonnefoy is uneasy with the way that Mallarmé presents his own enactment of the *drame solaire* as a systematic and articulative totality, perpetuating the metaphysical logic of the myth itself. For Bonnefoy, the spectacle of light or fire is the essentially finite performance that consumes such totalizing desires. He allows a Mallarmean language of myth and ritual to echo throughout the opening poems of 'La Terre', citations drifting from one poem to another, so that its closed and authoritative forms can be swallowed up by the repetitive performance of the poem itself: 'Flamme, de salle en salle, / Le plâtre, / Toute une indifférence, illuminée. // Flamme l'ampoule [...]' (DL, 62). Taking the advent and sacrifice of fire as its model, the poetic performance asserts its ephemeral and thus irreducible existence. The poetic performance becomes the flame: an ephemeral speaking that burns up the poet's aspirations to transcendence or eternity. The poem accepts that it is continually coming into and passing out of being, that advent and sacrifice are coterminous in each and every gesture.

Breaking the Fourth Wall

In 'Ô flamme', Bonnefoy develops a model of poetic performance that celebrates the sanctity of all transient gestures. The poet had struggled in his earlier collections to reconcile the stasis of the act of inscription with the shifting reality of finite existence. In *Yves Bonnefoy, Le Simple et le Sens*, Finck observes that Bonnefoy only managed to confront death in *Du mouvement et de l'immobilité de Douve* by staging a gesture that 'pulvérise le temps pour le réduire à un instant spasmodique'.[20] Caws too suggests that the poems of *Pierre écrite* celebrate transient moments of sensual experience by constructing minimalist tableaux, in which '[t]ime loses its force, as all movement turns into mere painting, frozen for our unhurried and motionless aesthetic enjoyment'.[21] 'Ô flamme' therefore represents an important performative breakthrough for Bonnefoy. And yet, in the same gesture, it provokes a certain anxiety. The fourth poem reflects on the devastating effect that such a thinking of finitude can have on the theoretical architecture of the Western tradition and on the conceptual structures that shape our lives. Structured around the same performative refrain as

[20] Finck, *Yves Bonnefoy. Le Simple et le sens*, p. 74.

[21] Mary Ann Caws, *The Inner Theatre of Recent French Poetry* (Princeton: Princeton University Press, 1972), p. 168.

opening poems, 'Et, tard, je crie', the poem repeatedly calls for our attention and urges us to look or to listen. It has the same kind of enumerative or list-like structure as the final stanzas of 'Ô flamme'. Yet, whereas 'Ô flamme' hailed a procession of numinous phenomena, this poem greets a series of fractured or failed things: a lost music, an unravelling wind, a torn fishing net, illegible signs, a tumbled-down house. We are told in the opening lines that it presents '[d]es mots que le feu accepte' (DL, 63). This is a fire or a 'burning', however, that does not reveal the sanctity of things. It shows us only dissolution and degradation. Sifting through the debris of a tradition, the poet exclaims at the lateness of the hour. He explores how a belief in the unmasterable nature of finitude can result in a sense of ontological disintegration.

Many critics have explored the self-critical nature of Bonnefoy's poetry, scrutinizing how it sets up transcendental images as foils, dramatizing the flights and evasions to which language lends itself, and deconstructing these linguistic transports in order to accede to the finite and contingent nature of 'le réel'.[22] In *Une Pensée en mouvement*, Buchs writes: 'Aux yeux du poète, l'image incarne la lutte que se livrent le langage et la réalité, et la critique de l'image est au fondement de son esthétique'. He continues: 'l'image est un mal nécessaire, [...] elle peut et [...] elle doit être dépassée dialectiquement'.[23] The performative formulations that Bonnefoy repeats throughout the poems of 'La Terre', 'Je crie, Regarde' or 'Je crie, Écoute', dramatize this self-critical treatment of the image. The poet points at a series of images in this poem, assuming a certain critical distance from them and presenting them as cultural artefacts. Here, however, he is not critiquing images of the ideal or the divine, as he did in the opening poems of the sequence, but images of dysfunction. He is critiquing a culture of disintegration and deconstruction that has pervaded the Western psyche. He warns us that the failure of systems of conceptual thought should not convince us of the failure of the world. He issues a similar warning in an essay on Garache's paintings in *Le Nuage rouge*: 'prenons garde à ne pas faire *être*, en les infusant à nos signes par une déviation de l'intelligence première, les forces d'un mal—d'une catastrophe—qui n'est pas le fait de la terre' (NR, 260).

[22] See, for example, John T. Naughton, *The Poetics of Yves Bonnefoy* (Chicago: University of Chicago Press, 1984); Ronald Gérard Giguère, *Le Concept de la réalité dans la poésie d'Yves Bonnefoy* (Paris: A.-G. Nizet, 1985); or Patrick Née, *Yves Bonnefoy: Penseur de l'image. Ou les Travaux de Zeuxis* (Paris: Gallimard, 2006).

[23] Buchs, *Une pensée en mouvement*, pp. 94–5.

The poet addresses his companion or reader once again in the fourth poem. Now, however, he signals with alarm that that her very presence seems to be diminished. One negative follows another, as the poet describes the etiolation or the evacuation of her being: 'Je crie, Regarde, / Ta conscience n'est pas en toi' (DL, 63). Continually negating the preposition 'en', the poet describes the erosion of the self's interiority, the dispersal of perception and feeling: 'L'amont de ton regard / N'est pas en toi, / Ta souffrance n'est pas en toi, ta joie moins encore' (DL, 63–4). With this loss of subjective autonomy comes a general sense of disorder. The poet cries out, urges us to listen, and then observes: 'Une musique a cessé. / Partout dans ce qui est, / Le vent se lève et dénoue' (DL, 64). We listen only to find that the music that we seek has vanished. We pursue some kind of lost harmony. The wind rises, only to unravel insidiously, '[p]artout dans ce qui est'. The first and last words of this sentence, 'Partout' and 'dénoue', enclose in a chiastic internal rhyme, reinforcing a sense of the all-encompassing nature of the degeneration. The *vers impair* too enacts this unravelling motion. After the six-syllable line, the seven-syllable line creates an effect of slackness and surplus. In the final stanza of 'Le Cimetière marin', Valéry pits the human intellect against the chaos of the physical world with the words 'Le vent se lève! ... il faut tenter de vivre!'[24] In Bonnefoy's poem, the wind rises and simply unravels. Bonnefoy suggests that an opposition between the ordering force of the human *cogito* and the disorder of the physical world is no longer sustainable. Making reference to Valéry, perhaps the last great poet of this humanist tradition, Bonnefoy suggests that this music has ceased.[25]

In the next sequence, human consciousness is presented as a torn net. The weave of this net has fallen slack, so now we perceive nothing but the gaping holes between the threads: 'Aujourd'hui la distance entre les mailles / Existe plus que les mailles, / Nous jetons un filet qui ne retient pas' (DL, 64). The final line here is what Jérôme Thélot calls an 'alexandrin boiteux'.[26] The first six syllables cast out hopefully and the final five fall short, suggesting

[24] Paul Valéry, *Œuvres*, 2 vols, ed. Jean Hytier (Paris: Gallimard, Bibliothèque de la Pléiade, 1969), I, pp. 1503–4.

[25] John E. Jackson writes: 'ce qui est mis en cause dans ces vers, comme a été ébranlée la préséance de la conscience sur l'être, n'est rien d'autre, justement, que le pouvoir ordonnateur de l'esprit dans sa prétention de s'asservir le réel en lui donnant forme d'œuvre. Tel est le sens de cette "musique" qui a cessé—musique close de l'œuvre, sans doute, au sens où le voulait, par exemple, la poésie symboliste—et qui remplace le bruit du vent, qui est celui de l'*ouvert* du monde' (Jackson, *La Question du moi. Un aspect de la modernité poétique européenne. T.S. Eliot, Paul Celan, Yves Bonnefoy* (Neuchâtel: A la Baconnière, 1978), p. 314).

[26] Jérome Thélôt, *Poétique d'Yves Bonnefoy* (Geneva: Droz, 1983), p. 33.

their own failure to enclose upon the world. The alexandrine itself, whose twelve syllables once articulated a perfectly coherent thought, is now 'un filet qui ne retient pas'. The poem evokes a world of increasing complexity in which our projects can no longer be fulfilled or completed: 'Achever, ordonner, / Nous ne le savons plus' (DL, 64). The poet apostrophizes scored out words and rust-marks: 'Ô ratures, ô rouilles / Où la trace de l'eau, celle du sens / Se résorbant s'illimitent' (DL, 64). He uses the apostrophe, this archetype of poetic pretension, to suggest the extent to which poetry's aspirations have declined. As sense has dispersed, becoming evanescent and ungraspable, there is nothing to distinguish words and scorings, intentional inscriptions and accidental markings. These 'ratures' perhaps even suggest that lines of erasure that deconstructionist thinkers such as Heidegger and Derrida use to suggest that the meaning of a word is inappropriable or endlessly deferred. The poetic address strays haphazardly from one term to the next, from 'ratures' to 'rouilles' to 'Dieu', suggesting the interchangeability of all these terms. They have all been scored out in precisely the same way. God, this ultimate signifier of worth, is now the 'paroi nue / Où l'érosion, l'entaille / Ont même aspect désert au flanc du monde' (DL, 64). The assonantal play on 'l'érosion, l'entaille' echoes the alliteration of 'Ô ratures, ô rouilles'. It suggests that everything now rhymes, arbitrarily, vacantly. Nothing has any special ontological status and everything resonates with the same emptiness.

The poet exclaims at the extreme lateness of the era: 'Comme il est tard!' Like the Decadents at the end of the nineteenth century, he feels that he is observing the death throes of a civilization. Unable to fix or impose any kind of vision of his own, the poet simply bears witness to a chaotic stream of fractured images. One hopeful vision looms briefly but it quickly slips away again: 'On voit un dieu pousser quelque chose comme / Une barque vers un rivage mais tout change' (DL, 64). But a vision of salvation no longer delivers us. It merely illuminates our thoughts for a second and passes by. In the final lines of the stanza, the language of crisis gives way to the language of catastrophe and apocalypse: 'Effondrements sur la route des hommes, / Piétinements, clameurs au bas du ciel' (DL, 64). The ravaged landscape that the poet describes here, this 'lande du sens', recalls T.S. Eliot's *The Waste Land*. Bonnefoy writes: 'C'est comme si le feu avait pris feu, / Et ce second brasier, dépossession, / Comme s'il prenait feu encore, dans les hauts / De l'étoffe de ce qui est' (DL, 65). The fire or the light that revealed the sanctity of existence at the beginning of 'La Terre' now consumes itself endlessly, fuelled by nothing other than its own negativity. Bonnefoy suggests that what might have been a home has been turned into a wasteland. Humanity seeks illumination in nothing other than the conditions of its own disinheritance, 'ce second brasier, dépossession'.

The procession of images of fractured things culminates in one key image. Urging his reader to look once again, the poet points to a tumbled-down building:

> Regarde,
> Le quatrième mur s'est descellé,
> Entre lui et la pile du côté nord
> Il y a place pour la ronce
> Et les bêtes furtives de chaque nuit.
>
> (DL, 65)

The poet urges us to observe the break in the fourth wall: 'Regarde, / Le quatrième mur s'est descellé'. 'Se desceller' means 'ouvrir ce qui est fermé hermétiquement ou semble l'être' or 'défaire ce qui est fermé d'un sceau'.[27] There is a fissure in that which appeared to be perfectly sealed. Through the breach, wild plants and animals enter the house. The bramble and the wild nocturnal creatures are images of the improper and the outcast. The undomesticated finds a place within the domicile. The breaking of this wall is again evoked as the breaking of a seal: 'Le sceau de la présence a éclaté / Sous la poussée rocheuse' (DL, 65). The phrase 'le sceau de la présence' awakens ideas of the sovereignty, authenticity, and the enclosure of presence.[28] Like 'le sens' that evaporated in the earlier stanza, this ideal of a perfectly self-contained presence now disperses. It gives way 'Sous la poussée rocheuse'. It succumbs to the finitude and movement of material existence.

Bonnefoy uses the image of the delapidated house to represent the fallen ideals and the fractured architecture of our era. He also uses it, however, to make a reference to Brecht's notion of breaking the fourth wall: 'Le quatrième mur s'est descellé'. Criticizing traditional practices of theatrical representation that present the stage as a perfectly enclosed and separate

[27] 'Desceller', in *Centre national de ressources textuelles et lexicales*, http://www.cnrtl.fr, accessed 17 May 2018.

[28] A 'sceau' is a 'Cachet où sont gravés en creux des signes propres à une autorité souveraine [...] et qu'on applique sur une matière molle, cire ou plomb, afin que l'empreinte en relief ainsi réalisée atteste l'authenticité, l'autorité, la validité des documents sur lesquels il est apposé, ou les close afin d'en tenir caché le contenu' ('Sceau', in *Centre national de ressources textuelles et lexicales*, http://www.cnrtl.fr, accessed 17 May 2018). It is precisely the notion of the perfect authenticity and authority of the seal that Derrida deconstructs in *Limited Inc.*, using the concept of iterability (Jacques Derrida, *Limited Inc.* (Paris: Galilée, 1990), p. 66).

space, Brecht 'broke' the line that separates the 'imaginary' world of the play from the 'real' world of the audience.[29] He opened up this closed performative space up to the contingent interactions of everyday life.

In Bonnefoy's poem, as this seal is broken, plants and wild animals move in through the breach. Bonnefoy insists that, just as there can be no self-contained and transcendental philosophical ideal, there can be no enclosed performative space. The theatricality and the reality of existence coexist. In each and every act, they are inextricably intertwined. The sealed and sovereign space—language, presence, the stage, the poem—is fractured. The poet embraces this rupture and steps into the breach: 'J'entre donc par la brèche au cri rapide' (DL, 65). As he does so, there is an overturning of the despair with which the poet greeted 'l'aspect désert' of the 'rouilles' and the 'ratures'. Language no longer seems like a failed purveyor of presence. The failure of closure is suddenly perceived not as a catastrophe but as source of possibility.[30] The breach is associated with an articulative release, an uninhibited form of verbal expression. What represented the external limit of an enclosed space—the clearly defined outer limit of a self-enclosed presence, a property, or a proper form—now becomes a space of opening and interaction. As he breaks the fourth wall, the poet realizes that this site of exposure is the space of poetic performance. It is the place in which all things find themselves opened up to and set in contact with other entities.

This new performative freedom is symbolized by the play of the light: 'la lumière joue avec la lumière / Et le signe est la vie / Dans l'arbre de la transparence de ce qui est' (DL, 65). As the poet insists that there is no possible separation between the ideal and the real, between the poem and everyday reality, he evokes a state of play between forces. He insists that language participates in the physical world just as much as any other phenomenon: 'le signe est la vie / Dans l'arbre de la transparence de ce qui est' (DL, 65). Language is conceived as play and performance, as part of the movements and metamorphoses of existence. And so, the poet calls out once again, 'Je crie, Regarde, / Le signe est devenu le lieu' (DL, 66). This revelation comes

[29] Brecht initiated theatrical techniques that acknowledged the artificiality of the divide between stage and audience, such as having an actor play the role of spectator. He sought to expose, as Meg Mumford writes, 'the efforts of traditional theatre to hide and hypnotize' (Meg Mumford, *Bertolt Brecht* (Abingdon: Routledge, 2009), p. 66).

[30] Bataille used the image of 'la brèche' throughout his career to suggest the capacity that all forms have to rupture, open, and to overflow. In *L'Expérience intérieure*, he describes a rapturous experience, and observes: 'dans la brèche, le sujet, l'objet sont dessous, il y a passage, communication, mais non de l'un à l'autre: l'un et l'autre ont perdu l'existence distincte' (Georges Bataille, *L'Expérience intérieure* (Paris: Gallimard, 1978), p. 67).

with a vision of forked lightning: 'Sous le porche de foudre / Fendu / Nous sommes et ne sommes pas' (DL, 66). Merging luminous and architectural images, Bonnefoy suggests that this performative use of language sets us in a new theatre or church. The streak of lightning that darts across the sky for a second becomes our new 'edifice'. Accepting that being cannot be contained or fixed by our conceptual structures, the poet suggests that we can only affirm our actions tremulously from one moment to the next, as our existence continually dissolves and emerges: 'Nous sommes et ne sommes pas'.[31] Issuing two further imperatives in the final lines of the stanza, the poet urges us to break through the fourth wall, to abandon conceptual ideals of closure and fixity, and, in doing so, to step outside the context of our dispossession: 'Entre avec moi, obscure, / Accepte par la brèche au cri de faim' (DL, 66). We're asked to accept the liminal nature of our existence and the unstable reality to which it gives rise. The cry that unfolds on the threshold *between*, at the intersection of diverse forces, is not one of fullness or satisfaction but one of hunger. As we go forward in relation, Bonnefoy suggests, no gesture is ever full and complete. It is inherently contingent, which is to say, open-ended and unsated. It is always left wanting. We find ourselves trembling always somewhere between desire and lack: 'Nous sommes et ne sommes pas'.

In the final line of the poem, the imperative 'Regarde' is replaced with the cohortative 'Soyons'. The poet no longer points towards the image from a critical distance but he now assumes its full performative force: 'Et soyons l'un pour l'autre comme la flamme / Quand elle se détache du flambeau, / La phrase de fumée un instant lisible / Avant de s'effacer dans l'air souverain' (DL, 66). Addressing his companion once again, he urges contact and sharing. He proposes that the couple give themselves over to one another, experiencing their togetherness as a flame, a momentary life spurt. Their actions will be like a trail of smoke or a written phrase, a brief trace that lingers a while and disperses. It is the air that swallows these traces that is presented as the sovereign force here, not the two subjects of the action. As the poet and his lover embrace one another ecstatically, they accept the radically exteriorized nature of their existence. They accept that they come into being on the *limen* or threshold between self and other. Like the flame that sparks outwards as it reacts with the oxygen in the air, their interaction is the very performance that brings them into being.

[31] The third chapter of this book explores this syncopation of existence and non-existence, the constant grounding and ungrounding of being.

The fourth poem of 'La Terre' dramatizes a crisis of form. It reflects on the way that the finitude of existence erodes the ideal of the autonomous and sovereign form, whether it is conceived as the self, presence, the poem, or the stage. As the poet sifts through images of failed or broken things, the voices of different literary and philosophical figures resonate behind his words. We can hear Valéry's ailing dream of intellectual order. But we also intuit Bataille's conception of 'la brèche' not just as a place of disintegration but as a place of opening. We hear echoes of Brecht's resistance to closed practices of representation and his experimentation with theatrical gestures that come into contact with or unfold in ordinary, everyday spaces. Bonnefoy aligns Bataille's and Brecht's reflections on the limit here, 'la brèche' and 'le quatrième mur', in ways that are highly suggestive. He teases out the preoccupation with exposure that manifests itself in both the philosopher's and the dramatist's work: their fascination with the way that the self opens at its limits onto the other. Returning to the image of the flame at the end of the poem, Bonnefoy suggests that this is precisely the same thinking of finitude that emerged from 'Ô flamme'. He presents finite existence as the continuous process of ending and opening, dissolution and exposition that means that each entity is always intimately exposed at its own limits. He suggests that all existence unfurls upon a tremulous threshold. The self's continual exposure to the other is thus an inherently performative dynamic that elicits Brechtian practices of interaction and improvisation. In the final lines of this poem, Bonnefoy embraces this newly liminal performative space. No longer crying out and dramatizing a spectacle that is happening 'over there', in a separate or other space, he addresses his companion directly, dramatizing nothing more than his own act of address. He celebrates a relational gesture, a brief moment of play or sharing, urging 'Soyons l'un pour l'autre comme la flamme'.

Bonnefoy's thinking of finitude is shaped by Bataillean notions of liminality and exposure in 'Et tard, je crie'. Similar Bataillean motifs play an important role in Nancy's thought. In *After Bataille*, Patrick ffrench writes: 'With Bataille, we are brought to the threshold of the question of the subject, a threshold from which other possibilities may be glimpsed, even if not by Bataille himself.' He then adds: 'This threshold is the starting point, it seems to me, of the work of Jean-Luc Nancy.'[32] The fourth poem of 'La Terre'

[32] Patrick ffrench, *After Bataille. Sacrifice, Exposure, Community* (Leeds: Legenda, 2007), pp. 80–1. Whilst Bataille is a key influence in shaping both Nancy's and Bonnefoy's conception of the limit, it's also important not to ignore Maurice Blanchot's writings on this question. In

dramatizes this threshold and reflects on the possibilities to which it might give rise. Bonnefoy suggests that finitude must be conceived not simply as a form of dissolution that fractures stable forms but as an opening, a dynamic of exposure that fosters interaction and communication. In *Une pensée finie*, Nancy defines finitude as '[n]on une pensée de la limitation, laquelle implique l'illimité d'un au-delà, mais une pensée de la limite comme cela sur quoi, infiniment finie, l'existence s'enlève, et *à* quoi elle s'expose' (PF, 48). He argues that such a thinking of finitude marks the end of an era of closed representations of the world and the beginning of an era of newly performative action that unfolds in the world or even as world, what he describes as 'un théâtre du monde', '[une] tâche de l'être-au-monde' (SM, 43). As noted in the introduction to this book, he makes the same point in *La Communauté désœuvrée*, observing: 'le théâtre, ici, ne vaut plus en tant que scène de représentation: il vaut comme le bord extrême de cette scène, comme ligne de partage où les uns sont exposés aux autres' (CD, 194). Much like Bonnefoy's 'Et, tard, je crie', Nancy's conception of finitude causes him to reimagine theatre as an exploration that occurs at the outer limit of the stage. He urges writers to embrace this new performative space, to explore the thresholds that run between us and all through us, revealing us to be exposed and relational beings.

Bataille, Klossowski, Blanchot: Writing the Limit, Leslie Hill writes that Blanchot perceives death as that which 'determines human life without remainder' but 'death is also that which escapes negation, from which no separation is possible, and which human labour cannot overcome; it is an obscure constraint that can never be experienced for itself by any living human self'. Because death is 'constitutive of what is human but it necessarily exceeds all that is human', Hill writes, human beings are exposed to death, not as a 'familiar possibility', but as a 'strange impossibility' (Leslie Hill, *Bataille, Klossowski, Blanchot: Writing the Limit* (Oxford: Oxford University Press, 2001), p. 182). For Blanchot, therefore, our exposure to death is always double. Human beings experience death, on the one hand, as freedom and activity and, on the other hand, as negation and separation. The gap between these two versions of death remains irreconcilable. Blanchot suggests that language can alert us to this state of possibility/impossibility. It exposes an endless process of inscription and effacement that allows the subject to come into being and that simultaneously dissolves it. Writing thus alerts us to the strange temporality of our existence: 'the fate of writing is irreducibly liminal. It cannot ever begin or end except by interrupting itself, by way of a break or rupture that, like death, is an event that has always already happened but is nevertheless always still to come. Writing belongs to no present, then, save an empty one' (Ibid., p. 194). The *limen* is thus a site of perpetual rupture and interruption. What results is a conception of exposure that is far more intractable, antagonistic, and violent than that which we encounter in Nancy's and Bonnefoy's writings. The liminality of writing shows us that human beings 'are in reality never alone. They are subject to the irremediable effects of death's possibility; they share in a language, partake of a family, belong to a community, participate in a history. But the result is neither peace nor harmony, but confrontation, struggle, violence' (Ibid., p. 183).

'Retrouvons-nous': Contact, Togetherness, Exposure

The call for a fiery embrace at the end of 'Et, tard, je crie' inspires a series of love poems in the central sections of 'La Terre'. The first begins with the performative refrain 'Retrouvons-nous' as the poet calls for intimacy and contact with his lover. Echoing the final lines of the previous poem, the poet envisions this embrace as a luminous outpouring. As the poet steadily renews his appeals for contact across this sequence, the poem unfolds in a series of highly reiterative and rhythmic structures that gain an almost incantational force. A series of short poems then follow that repeat the image of the cry but reimagine it in a range of different ways, drawing on a range of different scenes from the poet's life.[33] From one poem to the next, he reflects on the excessive nature of the lovers' sexual relationship but he insists that this ecstatic experience of sharing is not unique. He insists that the 'outpouring' that occurs in sex is a fundamental or ontological dynamic. Sexual contact is merely a heightened experience of ecstasy that alerts us to radically exteriorized and radically shared nature of all human existence and all material presence.

'Retrouvons-nous' is at first glance a very traditional love poem. The poet addresses his loved one and calls for renewed contact, for a sexual union. The opening lines of the poem envisage this union as a high and luminous embrace, an outpouring of light and feeling:

Retrouvons-nous
Si haut que la lumière comme déborde
De la coupe de l'heure et du cri mêlés,
Un ruissellement clair, où rien ne reste
Que l'abondance comme telle, désignée.

(DL, 67)

A clear stream of light 'déborde / De la coupe de l'heure et du cri mêlés'. As the poet describes this outpouring, the verb 'déborde' spills over the line end in an enjambment. The zeugma also blends two distinct formulations, aligning the ecstatic nature of both the flow of time and the lovers' cry. Both

[33] Bataille also uses the motif of the cry to reflect on the ecstatic nature of human subjectivity. What Bataille terms 'inner experience' is, Gerhard Poppenberg writes, 'being-outside-the-self, rapture'. Poppenberg observes: 'Erotic ecstasy is an access to inner experience for Bataille, one with a privilege equal to that of mystical experience' (Gerhard Poppenberg, 'Inner Experience', in *George Bataille. Key Concepts*, ed. Hewson and Coelen, p. 112).

forces are seen to disperse outwards simultaneously, 'mêlés', like the two lovers' bodies. As the poem moves into another enjambment, Bonnefoy suggests that this motion holds nothing in reserve: 'rien ne reste / Que l'abondance comme telle, désignée'. As the lovers cry out, existence is revealed in its profusion. Nothing is kept and existence is exposed in its excess, its ceaseless expenditure.

The next stanza reiterates the same plea: 'Retrouvons-nous, prenons / À poignées notre pure présence nue' (DL, 67). The poet yearns to take possession of the 'nous', of their shared physical presence, as if it were one entity or essence. Repeated plosive alliterations suggest the virulence of this desire. The cohortative 'prenons' reaches wistfully across the enjambment. And the poet pursues the object of his desire: 'Sur le lit du matin et le lit du soir, / Partout où le temps creuse son ornière, / Partout où l'eau précieuse s'évapore' (DL, 67). He seeks to grasp it everywhere and, yet, everywhere, time hollows its rut and disperses presence. Presence is an endless passage and so all things have to keep reaching out towards one another. The poem's reiterative syntax evokes this endless reaching and this endless dispersal. The poet can only keep renewing his entreaties: 'Portons-nous l'un vers l'autre comme enfin / Chacun toutes les bêtes et les choses, / Tous les chemins déserts, toutes les pierres' (DL, 68). There is a subtle interplay between the fricative alliteration of 'chacun', taken up in 'chemin' and 'choses', and the dental alliteration repeated in 'tous' and 'toutes'. Bonnefoy counterpoints the singularity of the individual act by which 'chacun' reaches out and the endless proliferation of these singularities, repeated by 'tous' and by 'toutes'. The poet's longing to take possession of 'notre pure présence nue' finds itself endlessly dispersed by these reiterative formulations. The discrete instance of desire reveals itself to be part of an infinitely larger and endlessly dispersive rhythm.

Halfway through the poem, these rhythmic structures are interrupted by the isolated imperative, 'Regarde'. It functions as a kind of *volta*, halting the steady passage of subclauses. Bonnefoy uses it to make an important equation: 'Regarde, / Ici fleurit le rien' (DL, 68). It seemed for a moment that this poet might define this force but he describes it only in negative terms. It is 'le rien' but it is a nothing that flourishes, that takes endlessly different forms from one clause to the next. It blossoms forth in insistent sibilant and velar alliterations: 'Ici fleurit le rien; et *s*es *c*orolles, / *S*es *c*ouleurs d'aube et de *c*répuscule' (DL, 68). Its endless different gradations of colour play across the dawn and the dusk sky. The poet witnesses 'ses apports / De beauté mystérieuse au lieu terrestre' (DL, 68). He suggests that its ceaseless metamorphoses give it its mysterious beauty. And in the final lines of this sequence, the poet observes: 'C'est l'or qui est en nous: or sans matière, / Or de ne pas durer, de ne pas avoir' (DL, 68). Bonnefoy insists that its metamorphoses *are* the value of finite worldly existence. He suggests that its shifting forms are 'l'or'. And yet, as soon as he does so, the appositional syntax that runs throughout the whole poem starts up again and empties this symbol—'l'or'—of any kind of substantial, appropriable, or preservable value. What the poet values is a gold that we cannot have or keep, whose value is coterminous with our very existence and exposed 'en nous'.

Across this first long stanza, Bonnefoy equates 'notre présence nue' to 'le rien', to 'la beauté', and to 'l'or'. Each time he seems to be on the point of defining one of these terms, he equates it to a steady stream of others. He sets it in apposition with a series of clauses that strip it of any definition. And so, all the words that he uses—'la présence', 'le rien', 'la beauté', 'l'or'—are stripped of their traditional significance. They are all presented as dynamics of exposition that are endlessly productive and endlessly ungraspable. The poet's reflections on this force of exposition culminate in the final two stanzas of the poem in which he presents this force as divinity itself. The two final stanzas constitute two halves of one logically argued sentence. The main clause appears in the first line of the second stanza, the subclause in the first line of the third and final stanza: 'Et tant vaut la journée qui va finir / [...] Que tu peux nommer Dieu ce vase vide' (DL, 68–9). Bonnefoy suggests that finitude gives ephemeral experience such vitality that we might call finitude God. As he makes this statement, the poet breaks into the appositional syntax that dominates the poem. Both clauses are steadily paraphrased across the final two stanzas: 'Et tant vaut la journée qui va finir, / Si précieuse la qualité de cette lumière, / Si simple le cristal un peu jauni [...]' (DL, 68). Each apposition stresses the singularity of a particular moment of experience, the specific gradation of the light, or the tint of the coloured glass. Each image rises and falls, showing us how each particular detail passes in a way that is at once poignant and pleasurable. And the contact that occurs between the two lovers is presented as another such fleeting interaction. They are presented as two voices that journey side by side, that are frequently parted. When they find each other, they delight in one another: 'Et si satisfaisantes, l'une pour l'autre, / nos voix, qui eurent soif de se retrouver' (DL, 68).

The final stanzas suggest that the dynamic that produces and disperses all things, that brings the lovers together and causes them to part, can be considered divine. Yet, like the gold that was neither appropriable nor preservable, this is a divinity who does not exist: 'Dieu qui n'est pas, mais qui sauve le don, / Dieu sans regard mais dont les mains renouent, / Dieu nuée, Dieu enfant et à naître encore' (DL, 69). It is not that finitude reveals existence's true or transcendental value. On the contrary, he suggests that finitude exposes the value of existence precisely because it holds nothing in reserve. It voids the notion of transcendental value and, in doing so, restores value to the dynamics of worldly exposition: the formation of a cloud, the birth of a child. This voiding of the transcendental is suggested by the recurrent images of empty forms in the final stanza, 'vase vide', 'vaisseau', 'voûte'. These words all begin with the letter 'v', itself another empty container. The same form appears, inverted, above the word 'voûte', the circumflex rising above the word in an arch: 'Dieu voûte pour l'étoile incertaine du sel / Dans l'évaporation qui est la seule / Intelligence ici qui sache et prouve' (DL, 69). This final image once again suggests that value is not an essence or extract. It is not the deposit of salt that is valuable but the motion of evaporation. It is 'la seule / Intelligence ici qui sache et prouve'. In this remarkable final statement, Bonnefoy affirms that intelligence can no longer be conceived as a human faculty. It is no longer the process by which human consciousness authenticates and proves a reality and thus confers value upon it. Insisting that intelligence cannot be located above or outside existence, Bonnefoy proposes that only the dynamics of existence can affirm the reality and the worth of existence. Existence can only be authenticated by its own dynamics.

Across the stanzas of 'Retrouvons-nous', Bonnefoy foregrounds the reaching motion by which one lover goes towards the other. He uses the poem's highly reiterative structures to affirm the value of intermittent experiences of contact and sharing. He suggests that the value of contact cannot be understood without embracing the temporal and spatial dynamics that part the lovers and make them reach continually out towards each other again. As he does so, the poetic syntax deconstructs traditional conceptions of affirmation. What is affirmed across the stanzas of the poem is never delimited or defined. On the contrary, one term is endlessly equated with another, 'la présence', 'le rien', 'la beauté', 'l'or', or 'Dieu'. An appositional syntax subjects all these terms to endless processes of redefinition. And due to these reiterative and appositional structures, the noun is stripped of any form of transcendental value. Just as in the final stanzas, the withdrawal of God restores value to the contingent dynamics of earthly existence, so the dispersal of the value of the noun restores value to the movement of the lines of verse. Value is allowed to circulate *between words*. It becomes a force shared and spent in the act of relation. And affirmation too becomes a necessarily reiterative process, a gesture that reaches endlessly outwards without grasping, without affirming anything other than its own open-ended gesture of relation.

'Une ontologie à venir'

'Retrouvons-nous' is followed by a cluster of very short poems that all repeat the central motif of the cry. The cry becomes emblematic of the kind of performative gesture that the poet is striving towards. Having delivered a paean to the negativity of finite existence in 'Retrouvons-nous', Bonnefoy experiments in this series of diminutive poems with ways in which the experience of human togetherness can nonetheless still be affirmed in language. The poet cultivates another kind of practice of affirmation here, one that is less rhythmic and more punctual, one that affirms what 'nos mains' and what 'notre terre' might be in brief formulations in the subjunctive mood. Insisting once again that the negativity of existence does not mean that we have to abandon our affirmative impulse, Bonnefoy develops a mode of affirmation that seeks to remain faithful to the contingency and ephemerality of the experience of togetherness. The first of these poems begins with the words, 'Et nos mains se cherchant / Soient' and the second, 'Et notre terre soit'. We can read these subjunctives as expressions of desire (the optative that appears in liturgical formulations such as 'Dieu soit loué') or as hypotheses (contingent and unverifiable statements of what might be). Finck writes, '[l]e subjonctif est le signe linguistique de la simultanéité du désir et du manque'.[34] However we choose to read them, it is clear that a statement in the indicative would not suffice. The poet seeks to affirm an uncertain process of negotiation that is in search of some form of identity but that never fully arrives at it or achieves it.

[34] Michèle Finck's analysis of how Bonnefoy uses the subjunctive to move towards 'le simple' is revealing. She writes, 'Le poète ne peut parler du "simple" que sur le ton de la prière: "Tout nous soit simple". Le subjonctif est le signe linguistique de la simultanéité du désir et du manque. La poésie moderne ne peut accomplir l'avènement du "simple", vers lequel cependant est tendue sa prière. Le poème à la fois promet le "simple" et le dérobe à l'instant même où il semble sur le point de l'offrir ("de loin"). La poésie de Bonnefoy est fondée sur la coexistence de la promesse et du retrait' (Finck, *Yves Bonnefoy. Le Simple et le sens*, pp. 170–1). Finck, however, has a tendency to present the poet's progression towards 'le sens' or 'le simple' as a teleological movement, as if 'le simple' and 'le sens' were something that could be grasped. This chapter suggests that the movement itself—the movement forwards or towards—*is* the very sense and the very simplicity of existence. The desirous and uncertain reaching of the subjunctive mood *is* the shared sense of our coexistence.

The first of these formulations in the subjunctive mood envisages that the couple's fleeting encounters might take the form of a more permanent or substantial union: 'Et nos mains se cherchant / Soient la pierre nue / Et la joie partagée / Une brassée d'herbes' (DL, 69). The poet wishes that the endless searching of one hand for another, one body for another, might be fixed in naked stone; that 'la joie partagée' might simply materialize as '[u]ne brassée d'herbes'. The plural noun governed by a present participle, 'nos mains se cherchant', gives way to a noun in the singular, 'la pierre'. The restlessness of the lovers' desire translates into a stable and self-contained substance. Yet, as soon as the poet tests out this hypothesis, he starts to reflect on the dynamism of sex and of the sharing that it permits: 'Car bien que toi, que moi / Criant ne sommes / Qu'un anneau de feu clair / Qu'un vent disperse' (DL, 69). What seems to be an unending and unbreaking 'anneau' is simply an 'anneau de feu', quickly dispersed by the wind. Such is its transience that, after the event, one will not even know if it happened: 'on ne saura / Tôt dans le ciel / Si même eut lieu ce cri' (DL, 69–70). The future tense is followed by a preterite, 'annulant l'acte jusque dans l'apparence de son non-accomplissement', to use Blanchot's formulation.[35] Blanchot writes these words about Mallarmé's famous formulation 'RIEN [...] N'AURA EU LIEU [...] QUE LE LIEU'.[36] Even as the poet looks forward desirously, he is aware that he will look back at loss and dispersal. By the final stanza, however, in spite of loss and uncertainty, one hand is already finding the other again: 'Toutefois, se trouvant, / Nos mains consentent / D'autres éternités / Au désir encore' (DL, 70). And so, after the dream of a permanent or palpable union, the hands turn from '[d]'autres éternités' to consent '[a]u désir encore'. They consent to the repetition of desire.[37] Playing on the double meaning of 'encore', Bonnefoy suggests that desire is 'still' to be realized and always to be realized 'again'. The hand consents to this restlessness, going 'still', 'again' towards the other: 'se cherchant', 'Criant', 'se trouvant'.

Bonnefoy's use of the subjunctive mood here suggests the contingency of the dynamics of relation. In the present moment, we move towards one another in anticipation and uncertainty. The next poem begins: 'Et notre terre soit / L'inachevable / Lumière de la faux / Qui prend l'écume' (DL, 70). The poet speaks—perhaps wistfully, perhaps speculatively—of 'notre terre', of the 'lieu partagé' that he described in the 1972 interview cited at the start

[35] Maurice Blanchot, *Le Livre à venir* (Paris: Gallimard, 1959), p. 294.
[36] Mallarmé, *Œuvres complètes*, I, p. 400.
[37] I will return to this crucial image of consent in the final section of this chapter.

of this chapter. Bonnefoy depicts a sharing that is consummately finite in this poem. He compares it to the light that glints off the scythe as life disappears with the greatest ease, like a blade skimming froth. Yet it is not, he insists, that death is the singular and unfailing truth of human existence: 'Et non parce qu'est vraie / Sa seule foudre' (DL, 70). The poet does not embrace a nihilistic vision of existence—'Bien que le vide, clair, / Soit notre couche' (DL, 70)—even if he understands its logic. Even though the world may be foundationless, even though two lovers are only smoke beaten back off the sacrificial fire, the repeated falling of the scythe draws us on towards desire: 'Pour sa retombée / Qui nous unit, / Blé de la transparence, / Au désir encore' (DL, 71). The scythe suggests the steady sweep of the blade at harvest time and the steady recurrence of death as *La Faucheuse* claims each and every human life. It beats a steady rhythm, as its cycles of life and death move steadily onwards. Bonnefoy suggests that the negativity of existence, the notion that 'le vide, clair, / Soit notre couche' (DL, 70), does not preclude the resurgence of life. Rather, it is the rhythm of death, there always in the background, that quickens and intensifies the rhythms of desire.

The sense of 'notre terre' does not take the form of a stable image, as in the image of 'nos mains' becoming 'la pierre nue'. It emerges as a rhythm: as the repetition of cycles of life and death and as the ebb and flow of human desire.[38] The 'nous' is never united with itself. As the scythe 'nous unit / Au désir encore', we are simply reconciled to the rhythm of existence. Human existence perpetuates itself and repeats itself without ever completing itself. The first line of this poem reads, 'Et notre terre soit / L'inachevable', and the poems of 'La Terre' emulate this unending force. They do not foreclose possibility or crystallize as fact. They venture a desire or a hypothesis, move towards a sense of our shared being, and then they repeat this performance. In the opening of *Être singulier pluriel*, Nancy writes:

> la répétition est condition de l'affirmation. Je dis: "cela est, que cela soit". Ce n'est pas un "fait", et cela n'a rien à voir avec une évaluation d'aucune espèce, c'est le retranchement d'une singularité dans son affirmation de l'être: une touche de sens'.[39]

[38] We see a similar use of repetition all through 'La Terre' and *Dans le leurre du seuil* as a whole. Large sections of 'Dans le leurre du seuil' and 'Deux Couleurs' are structured around the refrain 'Plus avant que' (DL, 23–43). The entirety of 'L'Épars, l'indivisible' is structured around the refrain 'Oui, par...' (DL, 103–21).

[39] Jean-Luc Nancy, *Être singulier pluriel* (Paris: Galilée, 1996), p. 24. All subsequent references to the latter book will appear within the text, using the abbreviation ESP.

Like Bonnefoy's poetic performances in the subjunctive mood, Nancy suggests that we venture an affirmation and we affirm it only by repeating this venture, over and over again. We venture the sense of the 'nous' together, and we affirm it together, over and over again. We go forward saying: 'cela est, que cela soit'.

For Bonnefoy, the 'nous' is something that is ventured in the subjunctive mood. It is an inherently contingent and futural reality, always to be enacted and re-enacted, to be gone towards and to be imagined anew. The poet's successive performative refrains ('Retrouvons-nous', 'Portons-nous l'un vers l'autre', 'Et nos mains cherchant / Soient', 'Et notre terre soit') are part of this never-ending performance. In *Être singulier pluriel*, Jean-Luc Nancy writes:

> la "pensée" de "nous", antérieure à toute pensée – et, en vérité, sa condition même –, n'est pas une pensée représentative (pas une idée, une notion, un concept), mais une *praxis* et un *ethos*: la mise en scène que la comparution est. Nous y sommes déjà, toujours déjà, à chaque instant. Ce n'est pas une nouveauté – mais il faut, il *nous* faut, chaque fois la réinventer, chaque fois entrer en scène à nouveau. (ESP, 94)

There is a marked similarity between Bonnefoy's performative poetics that explore the contingent dynamics of our exposure to one another and Nancy's thinking of 'la mise en scène que la comparution est' which is not 'une pensée représentative'. Refusing to ground thought in a static figure or concept, both the poet and the philosopher insist upon the present moment of performance. They suggest that, spatially, ethically, we always already appear alongside one another. We are committed to a 'nous' that is always to be performed and always to be reinvented. Like Nancy, Bonnefoy perceives the inherent theatricality of the impermanence of the words and the gestures that we share, and of our constant need to approach one another, to reinvent our relationships, over and over again. All these notions are present in the wistful refrain with which the sixth poem of 'La Terre' began: 'Retrouvons-nous'.

The poetic act becomes analogous to the sexual act: the ephemeral cry of sexual pleasure and the ephemeral sharing between two bodies. The poetic performances all seek to 'rend[re] la poésie à sa fin qui est [le] partage', to return to the formulation cited earlier. The next poem of this short central cluster, however, evokes the cry of the newborn child. It is not the transience of the cry that is now foregrounded but its singularity. The exploratory performances in the subjunctive mood are suddenly punctured by a dramatic address and an assured present tense: 'Éternité du cri / De l'enfant qui semble / Naître de la douleur / Qui se fait lumière' (DL, 71). This first stanza addresses or invokes the 'Éternité du cri'. The eternity it describes seems to stem from the cry's infinite capacity for renewal. As it is released, suffering gives way to light and brings new life. After this invocation, the second stanza presents a simple constative statement: 'L'éternité descend / Dans la terre nue / Et soulève le sens / Comme une bêche' (DL, 71). This 'éternité' descends upon the earth and turns the soil upwards. At once a downwards and upwards motion, it is a kind of *bouleversement*. It collides with the earth and 'le sens' rises up, as if thrust up by a shovel. Bonnefoy thus presents the arrival of the child as 'le sens'. It is as if, upon hearing the cry of the newborn, the poet's conceptual reckoning of the world is dismantled and he too is thrown back upon the naked earth. The pre-existing structures of human thought offer no template that can comprehend or translate this singular 'naissance de sens'. Nancy presents birth itself as a similar kind of 'surgissement' that overturns our conceptual structures and exposes 'le sens'. In *Le Poids d'une pensée*, he writes:

> Dès l'aube de la pensée contemporaine, dès Hegel (il suffit de relire l'introduction de la *Phénoménologie*), "naissance" est un mot pour dire un excès absolu sur la représentation. Déjà, Hegel saisit le savoir essentiel – celui qui *enfantera* le savoir absolu – comme ce mouvement de surgir *et de nier toute représentation donnée avec ce surgissement*, aussi bien que toute représentation *de* ce surgissement.[40]

Like Nancy, Bonnefoy presents birth as a *surgissement* that undermines representation. The poet's attempts to affirm the nature of the cries of sexual pleasure and 'la joie partagée' are punctuated by this short poem. It is only half the length of the previous two poems and it is perhaps the most powerful poem of all of those in 'La Terre'. It presents a cry that *undoes* any generalization, a cry that we can only respond to by allowing the conceptual systems with which we map the world to fall away. This singularity, Bonnefoy suggests, is 'le sens'.

The last of these short poems evoking the cry reverberates with all the different manifestations of the cry that we have seen so far: the cries of

[40] Jean Luc-Nancy, *Le Poids d'une pensée* (Grenoble, Québec: Presses universitaires de Grenoble, Le Griffon d'argile, 1991), p. 131. All subsequent references will appear within the text, using the abbreviation PP.

sexual pleasure, of suffering and death, and of birth. It returns to the first-person present indicative and to the utterance with which 'La Terre' began: 'Je crie'. Now, the poet himself simply performs the cry. It is as if, having heard the newborn child, the poet opens his lungs and cries too. Breaking the run of quatrains, Bonnefoy presents a single sentence that stretches over a tercet and a couplet:

> N'étant que la puissance du rien,
> La bouche, la salive du rien,
> Je crie,
>
> Et au-dessus de la vallée de toi, de moi
> Demeure le cri de joie dans sa forme pure.
>
> (DL, 73–4)

Using the present participle in the negative, 'N'étant que', the poet depicts himself as nothing more than a negative force, a groundless vigour. He depicts only the ouverture of his mouth and the saliva within it, figuring himself as nothing but a spacious or fluid opening. He cries out 'Je crie' and these two small words linger in the empty space between stanzas. And as we move into the second stanza, this cry resonates in the space between two bodies, 'au-dessus de la vallée de toi, de moi'. There is no union between one person and another. The valley or the gulf between them remains. And yet, there is a sharing and a communication across a divide. This sharing, Bonnefoy suggests, is the joy of human existence: 'le cri de joie dans sa forme pure'.

The motif of the cry is steadily repeated until the poet finally enacts this gesture himself. The last of this central cluster of very short poems foregrounds this embodied and relational gesture of communication. It privileges the act of communication itself and not the communication of a particular message. The poem becomes a cry that is simply released, let go. And with this gesture, the vision of poetry as a form of appropriation or preservation is also let go. The power of these two small words, 'Je crie', lies in the fact that they do not seek to preserve or protect anything. In the interaction that occurs between two bodies, the cry is offered up. In *La Communauté désœuvrée*, Nancy writes, 'la communication n'est pas celle d'un message—mais elle a lieu' (CD, 181). He adds, 'Que l'œuvre soit offerte à la communication, cela veut dire qu'elle soit effectivement *offerte*, c'est-à-dire présentée, proposée et abandonnée sur la limite commune où se partagent les êtres singuliers' (CD, 182). For both Bonnefoy and Nancy, the cry is offered up between two bodies. It expends itself ecstatically 'sur la limite commune'. In doing so, this gesture of communication attunes us to the fact that these two bodies are always already exposed to one another. It affirms the generative and the indeed joyful nature of their common exposure. Bonnefoy suggests that this dynamic of relation in all its singularity exposes 'le sens'. It brings sense to light or gives birth to it. Nancy, similarly, argues that sense is not said but that it is exposed in the act of speaking: 'Le sens d'être n'est sans doute jamais dans ce qui est dit – dans les significations –, mais il est à coup sûr dans ceci, qu'"il est parlé", au sens absolu de l'expression' (ESP, 46–7). Acts of speaking, crying out, or addressing the other articulate a sense that cannot be signified. Nancy writes: '*l'être lui-même nous est donné comme le sens*. L'être n'*a* pas de sens, mais l'être lui-même, le phénomène de l'être, c'est le sens' (ESP, 20).

When the poet urges 'Retrouvons-nous' in the central sections of 'La Terre', he's calling to his lover and seeking intimacy. And yet, in the same gesture, the poet is also speaking to his reader and to a wider community. He urges us, 'nous'—the couple, the group, the collective—to rediscover what it means to be together, to exist alongside one another. This is not to suggest that Bonnefoy's love poem becomes a mere vehicle for ontological enquiry. On the contrary, love inspires this philosophical intuition. The experience of being intimately exposed to and transported by another person is so profound for the poet that it infects his entire view of existence. He becomes convinced that, in spite our inclinations towards sollipsism and self-reflexivity, experiences of contact and exposure are primary. When the poet urges 'Retrouvons-nous' in 'La Terre', he is appealing to us to rediscover this primary state of being-in-relation. Bonnefoy seeks linguistic formulations that could affirm the nature of sharing whilst still allowing it to remain contingent and unpredictable. From one poem to the next, he affirms the nature of 'Nos mains' and 'Notre terre' in the subjunctive mood. Each short little poem reaches towards and seeks to communicate something of the 'nous'. Each attempt emulates the endless reaching motion by which the lovers hands seek one another. Eventually, it is the poetic performance itself and its gesture of address that articulates this motion. The poem enacts the cry that occurs between the two lovers. Its address communicates the reality of their exposure to one another, what Nancy describes as 'l'être-avec de tout ce qui est, lui-même nu et inévaluable' (ESP, 22).

For Bonnefoy, all these poetic performances together articulate the beginnings of an ontology, one that is yet to realize itself and indeed cannot realize itself. He presents this ontology as 'l'inachevable'. Similarly, in *Être singulier pluriel*, Nancy writes:

> Ce *nous* du sens, qui est le sens, ce sens qui est l'être du "nous" avant toute anthropologie, avant tout humanisme et tout antihumanisme, exige une ontologie qui est encore à venir, ce qui ne veut pas dire qu'elle viendra, mais peut-être qu'elle est en elle-même, comme pensée, ordonnée à la dimension d'un "venir" ou d'un "survenir": celui de notre comparution, qui est notre présentation dans l'élément du sens. Cette présentation n'a pas elle-même de signification, elle a seulement lieu, sans cesse, à travers d'innombrables significations. Elle ne procède pas comme la reconnaissance ni comme l'identification de ceux – *nous* – qui sont présentés. Elle procède comme une exposition: nous *sommes* exposés, c'est là notre être – ou c'est le sens de l'être. (ESP, 95)

Nancy suggests that sense is communicated by our very togetherness. This is not a sense that can ever be encapsulated or signified. On the contrary, it simply arrives in the very dynamics of our exposure and its ontology thus always remains 'à venir'. As we appear alongside one another and interact, we are always unsettled or changed by these interactions. We are always exposed to the 'venir' or 'survenir' of 'notre comparution'. For Bonnefoy, this is 'le sens' that is communicated by the cry of sexual pleasure or suffering, the cry of the mother in childbirth or of the newborn child. In sex, death, or childbirth, Bonnefoy suggests that we surrender to the ecstatic nature of existence, to the dynamism that ungrounds and renews existence and exposes one person to another. In the central poems of 'La Terre', each new gesture of contact, each repeated poetic performance, perpetuates this shared experience of 'le sens'. In this respect, Bonnefoy's 'ontologie à venir' is perhaps nothing other than a thinking of our existence as rhythm: rhythms of life and death, sowing and harvesting, touching and parting, affirmation and negation. Each of these rhythms takes us onwards and no closer to resolution.

Consent

The motif of consent recurs in the early poems of 'La Terre'. In the first poem, the poetic discourse is interrupted by the voice of the light which pronounces: '("Moi la lumière, / Oui, je consens")' (DL, 59–60). In the second, this same formulation appears again but, this time, it is absorbed into the poet's speech: 'Moi la nuit / Je consens. Moi l'amandier / J'entre paré dans la chambre nuptiale' (DL, 60). This gesture initially appears to be some form of metaphysical act. The light, the night, or the almond tree seem to consent to the poet's will and enter into a state of communion with him. Across the poems of 'La Terre', this metaphysical conception of the poetic act is deconstructed as Bonnefoy insists that no human gesture can transcend or master the finitude of worldly existence. And so, in the central poems of 'La Terre', consent takes on a new meaning. The gesture is re-envisaged in finite and relational terms as the lovers' hands: 'consentent / D'autres éternités / Au désir encore' (DL, 70). The lovers consent to the tropistic way in which they have to keep reaching out towards one another, according to the rhythm of desire. They embrace the ecstatic force by which finitude projects all being outwards and thus leaves all things exposed. Etymologically, 'consentir' comes from Latin; 'consentire' means 'to feel with or together'.[41] The lovers thus affirm the inherently relational nature of their existence and the fact that feeling is always a matter of 'feeling-with'.

The theme of consent dominates the final sections of 'La Terre'. The final poem re-enacts the performative utterance with which the sequence began, 'Moi la lumière, / Oui, je consens'. It is the poet, however, who now performs this gesture at the end of 'La Terre'. No other voice cuts across the poetic discourse to perform this act. The poet repeats this formulation until it resembles an incantation. Each time he utters this phrase, he reformulates it. Between the disjunctive pronoun 'moi' and the conjunctive pronoun 'je', the poet inserts a different noun phrase each time. The poem thus opens with the words 'Oui, moi les pierres du soir, illuminées, / Je consens. // Oui, moi la flaque' (DL, 74). The poet thus speaks with or alongside the stones or the puddle. As the poet sees the stones illuminated by the evening sun, he seems to recognize that he comes into being with or alongside them and that they too emerge in relation to him. The formalization and enactment of this grammatical impossibility is crucial to the poet's act of consent. By sharing the space of enunciation, by setting 'moi' and 'les pierres' in apposition, Bonnefoy challenges the autonomy and pre-eminence of the 'je'. He refuses not just the oppositional logic of the Latinate sentence but, also, the Hegelian concepts of subject and object, and even the Levinasian concepts of self and other. Opposition gives way to apposition, to what Nancy

[41] 'Consent', in *Online Etymological Dictionary*, http://www.etymonline.com, accessed 1 September 2018.

describes as 'la comparution'. The poet affirms the essentially relational nature of all existence, including human subjectivity. In *Être singulier pluriel*, Nancy writes,

> La comparution doit donc signifier – tel est désormais l'enjeu – que le "paraître", c'est-à-dire la venue au monde et l'être au monde, l'existence comme telle, est strictement inséparable, indiscernable du *cum*, de l'*avec* où il a non seulement son lieu et son avoir-lieu, mais aussi – et c'est la même chose – sa structure ontologique fondamentale. (ESP, 83)

Bonnefoy's appositional structure affirms an ontological principle similar to that to which Nancy refers: a thinking of existence as coexistence, an ontology of 'being-with'. It is no accident of course that the noun 'sens' appears homophonically within the verb, 'je consens'. Bonnefoy suggests that the act of relation exposes the 'sens' (or the 'con-sens') of finite material existence.

As the poet repeats the act of consent, the subject pronoun 'moi' is set in apposition with very different noun phrases: 'Oui, moi la flaque / Plus vaste que le ciel, l'enfant / Qui en remue la boue, l'iris / Aux reflets sans repos, sans souvenirs, / De l'eau, moi, je consens' (DL, 74). The puddle is a small form that has immense capacities for reflection. The child stirs up the mud at the bottom and different images dart across its surface, 'sans repos, sans souvenirs'. The many meanings of the word 'l'iris' resemble these shifting reflections. 'L'iris' is the iris of an eye, perhaps the child's eye, one pool of liquid reflected in another. Yet, 'l'iris' also suggests Iris, the messenger of the gods who displayed her sign as a rainbow. 'L'iris' is of course also the flower that grows near water. As transient reflections of the 'iris' flicker across the surface of a puddle, various permutations of the word's meaning flicker in the reader's mind. The word itself has 'reflets sans repos, sans souvenirs'.

Bonnefoy suggests that the subject position 'je' is just as capacious as this puddle. His reiterative construction 'Oui, moi [...] moi, je consens' frames an incredibly diverse range of noun clauses. It allows the poet to delay the arrival of the verb, leaving the subject position open, and permitting the accumulation of an endless number of appositional clauses. Between 'moi' and 'je', the subject position can encompass the poet narrator, the puddle, the child, the 'iris', the shifting forms in the mud, the shifting reflections in the water, and even the shifting nature of the language used. The subject becomes an infinitely receptive category. It is open to and constituted by the happenings of the physical world and the happenings of language. Like the puddle, it is receptive, permeable, and shifting. The poet thus consents to forms that are ephemeral and long-lasting: 'Moi la nuée / Je consens. Moi l'étoile du soir / Je consens' (DL, 75). He embraces the banal and the epic:

> Moi le départ
> Des maçons attardés vers les villages,
> Moi le bruit de la fourgonnette qui se perd,
> Je consens. Moi le berger,
> Je pousse entre la fatigue et l'espérance
> Sous l'arche de l'étoile vers l'étable.
>
> (DL, 75)

The biblical image of the shepherd following the star echoes the image of the birth of the 'soleil-enfant' with which 'La Terre' began. The poetic voice becomes the voice of the shepherd. He represents a weary but hopeful mankind, waiting for a miraculous birth. In the next line, however, the image of the shepherd and its freight of Christian history, shifts out of focus. An August night beds down the animals in the stable. As in so many of the poems of 'La Terre', an image rises for a moment and then metamorphoses into something else. The stanza ends with an image of sleep, as if to suggest that all these visions are mere dreams, fitful projections of the human mind, each one as contingent and fleeting as the next.

In this final poem, the ceremonial language with which 'La Terre' opened finds itself transformed. Whereas the act of consent initially suggested that authority was passed from one figure to another, from a metaphysical presence to the poet, here it becomes a simple act of relation. Bonnefoy insists that he has no special dominion over existence, no means of mastering its boundaries, and he consents to finitude, to the force that exposes us endlessly at our limits. The prefix 'con-' in the verb 'consentir' suggests precisely that. It suggests that, before there is any feeling, there is exposure and relation. Throughout 'La Terre', Bonnefoy has steadily been exploring how different subject pronouns—'je', 'tu', and 'nous'—allow us to inhabit the world in different ways. He has experimented with structures of address and interpellation in particular. In the final poem of 'La Terre', he finds a way to speak appositionally. In this respect, the poem's long incantional structure thus has a therapeutic function. It sets us, as we speak, in a relationship of parity with the beings and presences of the physical world. It teaches us to feel outside of the subject positions allotted to us by language. It trains us to speak, not from a transcendental position, but from an emergent one. It is no accident either that the poem's incantational structure gives it a choral resonance. A refrain is a formulation that is taken up and repeated by a large number of voices. It draws the detached and passive listener into a ceremony and makes her an active participant.[42] The more the refrain is reiterated, the more we feel its sonority, the more we pour ourselves into its rhythms and its resonances. We can imagine it passing from one voice to another, being taken up by a group. With this gesture, poetic language becomes, not a means of signification, but a place of cohabitation. It becomes, to return to the earlier quotation, 'un lieu partagé et doté de sens par ce partage'.

An Ontological Performance

In the poems of 'La Terre', Bonnefoy seeks to develop a form of poetic performance that is faithful to the dynamics of finite existence. He begins by commemorating the rituals and festivals of the pre-modern world that, in Stuart Kendall's words, 'gave communal, material form to expenditures, linking them to the passage of time, to cycles of life at cosmic, seasonal, and human scales'.[43] Adopting this anthropological perspective, he emulates a Mallarmean conception of poetic performance as a therapeutic ritual that celebrates the temporal rhythms of human, social, natural, and cosmological existence. And yet, as he does so, he critiques the notion that such a practice assuages human anxiety because it offers us a transcendental glimpse of pattern. He insists that, if *le drame solaire* is a meaningful model for poetic performance, it is because the sun's orbit of the earth and the changing of the seasons are performances from which nothing can be extracted or retained. A light radiates outwards, exposing a motion that no human gesture, no form or rhythm, can master. A Bataillean thinking of finitude as pure expenditure is used to correct the residual transcendental impulses that persist within Mallarmé's conception of poetic performance.

[42] The ceremonial nature of this final poem is suggestive of Mallarmé's writings on performance, ritual, and the ceremony of the Book. In his 'Notes en vue du Livre', Mallarmé envisages a performance, based on the Christian Eucharist, in which the audience would 'consecrate' the poet's 'Lecture'. Between the poet and the audience, the text would at once be administered and embodied (Mallarmé, *Œuvres complètes*, I, pp. 617–22). Bonnefoy's fidelity to the finitude of existence produces a very different conception of the poetic performance in 'La Terre'. Whereas Mallarmé envisages the ceremony in transcendental terms as the consecration of the poet's exchange with his audience, Bonnefoy envisages a litany that is nothing other than a series of existential acts: the self reaches out to the other, still, again, consecrating nothing other than the ecstatic and desirous rhythm by which existence projects us outwards and into relation.

[43] Kendall, 'Expenditure', in *Georges Bataille, Key Concepts*, ed. Hewson and Coelen, p. 78.

Bataillean motifs—sacrifice, the limit, exposure, excess, ecstasy, the cry—are dotted throughout 'La Terre'. Bonnefoy cultivates each one of these images according to the logic of finitude's boundless expenditure. At times, this allows him to perceive possibilities that Bataille does not and to develop these motifs in novel ways. The notion of ecstasy becomes crucial, as does Bataille's attendant idea of the community of lovers. Yet Bonnefoy resists Bataille's idea that communication between the lovers is inevitably caught between fusion and *déchirement*. He presents sexual climax as an experience of exposure that reveals the radically exteriorized nature of all existence. Crucially, Bonnefoy suggests that the sexual act is not in any way exceptional. It simply attunes us to the ecstatic nature of all material existence, to its originary dynamic of opening. We see Nancy rework Bataille's conception of the community of lovers in a very similar way in *La Communauté désœuvrée*. Nancy writes: 'Les amants exposent, sur la limite, l'exposition des êtres singuliers les uns aux autres, et le battement de cette exposition: la comparution, le passage et le partage' (CD, 95). The lovers show us that all existence unfolds at the limit. This exposure is rhythmic and generative. The 'battement de cette exposition' steadily opens each of us up, exposing one singular entity to another. Nancy suggests that this is the very rhythm of our 'com-pearance'. Nancy writes: 'Passant à sa limite, la finitude passe "de" l'un "à" l'autre: ce passage fait le partage' (CD, 87). He suggests that this gesture of exposure distributes existence. It shares it out and divides it up, giving things form. This is what Nancy describes as 'l'extase du partage' (CD, 64).

Both Bonnefoy and Nancy perceive the subject's actions as participating in and perpetuating this infinitely larger rhythm, a continuum, as Kendall writes in reference to Bataille, 'wherein entities circulate as energies through couplings and conjunctions [...] in constant convulsive transformation'.[44] This is why the notion of performance is central to both their works. They both refuse to conceive of writing according to a logic of representation, as a gesture that inscribes its meaning in a space apart from worldly existence. They insist that the poetic or philosophical act must surrender to existence's rhythm of expenditure and exposure, allowing itself too to unfold ecstatically. The text must explore the *praxis* and the *ethos* of its own gesture of presentation. And so Bonnefoy foregrounds the poem's own structures of relation. He had of course already experimented with such theatrical structures in collections such as *Du mouvement et de l'immobilité de Douve*. It is in 'La

[44] Kendall, 'Expenditure', in *Georges Bataille, Key Concepts*, ed. Hewson and Coelen, p. 82.

Terre', however, that Bonnefoy affirms for the first time that the poem's own performance can expose ontological dynamics of exchange. He presents the poem's own act of address or relation as an ontological disposition. The text opens onto the world and affirms this aperture. And Bonnefoy insists that affirmation itself is nothing more than this gesture. It is what Nancy describes in *Être singulier pluriel* as 'l'acte d'être-au-monde *et d'être-monde*' (ESP, 7).

Hence the vital importance that the act of stepping into 'la brèche' holds for Bonnefoy at the end of 'Et tard, je crie'. One might suggest that this gesture deliberately seeks to counter critical and negative forms of textual exploration, particularly Derridean deconstruction, that were becoming ever more prominent throughout the 1960s and 1970s. Bonnefoy insists that it is not enough to lament the failure of closure or to trace the limitations of the structures of 'logocentric' thought. He presents the breach as a place of action, 'la brèche au cri rapide'. He protests that the limit of the text must be the place where we engage with the very forces that exceed language. To accept the limit as a place of endless distancing, to accept the absolute alterity of the exterior world is, Bonnefoy argues, to repress language's capacity for engagement with material, affective, and corporeal forces. It is to repress its crucial ethical function. It is for this reason that, when Bonnefoy makes his inaugural address to the Collège de France and takes up the chair formerly held by Barthes, he states:

> nous avons perçu un clivage de l'être-au-monde, mais nous risquons d'en subir, *par oubli de l'action qu'on lui opposait*, les conséquences catastrophiques. [my emphasis] (E, 186)

Bonnefoy insists that a salutary process of deconstruction should be undertaken *in order to affirm* a newly mobile and dynamic thinking of human relation. He suggests, in other words, a deconstructive approach dominated by a Levinasian thinking of the selfsame and the other should give way to one that is guided by a Bataillean thinking of exposure.

This experience of exposure allows the poet to affirm a newly performative conception of ontology. Bonnefoy's poetry celebrates its ability to affirm the sense of existence and all that is common to existence. Poetry can do so, Bonnefoy hastens to add, because it no longer conceives of sense in essentialist or substantialist terms, according to a model of appropriation. Bonnefoy understands sense as a birth or an arrival, as the exposure of existence's own 'structure d'exposition'. The poet uses gestures of address, interpellation, or consent to articulate this experience of sense. He explores its originary force, the way that it emerges, new and singular, each time, in each act of relation. Bonnefoy uses the poem's own *praxis* to affirm that, whilst we don't *have* anything in common, we *are* in common. We are all part of what Nancy terms: '[la] communauté *de* la finitude'. Nancy writes: 'la finitude "est" communautaire, et [...] rien d'autre qu'elle n'est communautaire' (CD, 68). We all share the same experience of contingency. It is this fragile and unpredictable sharing that produces 'le cri de joie dans sa forme pure' in 'La Terre'. As Nancy writes:

> Il n'y a pas de sens si le sens n'est pas partagé, et cela, non pas parce qu'il y aurait une signification, ultime ou première, que tous les étants auraient en commun, mais parce que *le sens est lui-même le partage de l'être.*
>
> (ESP, 20)

For both Bonnefoy and Nancy, sense is the very dynamic by which existence is shared out and divided up. Its mode of articulation restores us to 'la terre', to the world's own ontological performance, for it reveals the exposed nature of all existence. It reminds us that the space that we're in is 'un lieu partagé et doté de sens par ce partage'.

2
In a World of Material Presence, *Début et fin de la neige*

> c'est la profondeur comme telle qui du coup
> se signifie à l'encontre, s'indique non abolie
> 'Quelques notes sur Mondrian' (NR, 136)

> Pour dire la présence, la poésie doit élaborer
> un lieu qui vaudra pour tous.
> 'Poésie et vérité' (E, 267)

Début et fin de la neige

In *Dans le leurre du seuil*, physical intimacy and sexual contact serve as models for understanding what Bonnefoy describes as 'une économie de l'être-au-monde' (E, 21). The poet suggests that the ecstasy experienced in sex is not unique in relation to all other human acts but that, on the contrary, it exposes a dynamism and a sharing that is common to all existence. Dramatizing the acts of address by which one lover reaches out to another, Bonnefoy not only explores the rhythmic forms of interaction that expose human subjects to one another but he affirms that these very forms of interaction bring us human subjects into being. As the poet embraces the endlessly unstable but endlessly generative nature of 'being-in-relation' at the end of 'La Terre', it is important to note that he 'consents' not merely to a lover, friends, or community but to a wide array of different material phenomena. Bonnefoy suggests that the human subject is intimately exposed to stones, puddles, clouds, and even the sound of a van's engine. The incantational sequence with which 'La Terre' ends signals that the poet is already reflecting in 1975 on the impact that his relational ontology will have on the human subject's understanding of its relationship to its material environment.

Yves Bonnefoy and Jean-Luc Nancy: Ontological Performance. Emily McLaughlin, Oxford University Press (2020). © Emily McLaughlin.
DOI: 10.1093/oso/9780198849582.001.0001

This area of reflection becomes increasingly prominent in Bonnefoy's work in the late 1980s and early 1990s with the publication of *Ce qui fut sans lumière* (1987)[1] and *Début et fin de la neige* (1991). The poet dramatizes certain moments in which, as he engages with material things, touching them or attempting to grasp them, the distance that separates him from them dissolves and he feels himself being absorbed into an endlessly spacious and productive material universe. In this instant, he explores how contact is no longer understood in appropriative terms, as a way of approaching and encircling things from the outside, but as a spacious activity that allows material bodies to continually open outwards, to emerge from and withdraw back into the nothingness at the heart of existence. The poet investigates how this spacious mode of sensing allows him to embrace the immersed nature of its own subjectivity: the way that his own consciousness emerges out of the spacious interaction that occurs between embodied, material, and cerebral forces. As Bonnefoy writes of the poetic act in 'Poésie et vérité': 'voilà la réalité qui se diversifie dans son dire, sans désormais se fragmenter, s'extérioriser' (E, 267).

As its title suggests, *Ce qui fut sans lumière* (1987) is a collection of poetry that questions the relationship between illumination and darkness, discovery and loss. After the remarkably affirmative performance of *Dans le leurre du seuil*, this next collection of verse poetry reflects on the way that the instrumentalist structures of conceptual thought can be held at bay momentarily but inevitably come to dominate our perception once again, causing us to objectify material reality and to set ourselves apart from it. In 'La Voix encore', Bonnefoy writes: 'La nuit est prompte et lourde à retomber / Sur le bleu du dehors du monde, dont la voix / Va te sembler trompeuse, te faire mal' (CQ, 28–9). The subject loses its sense of intimate connection with the presences that surround it. Linguistic consciousness circumscribes and immobilizes them once again. And when finitude inevitably erodes the stable conceptual structures that we erect all around us, we cast the blame for this disorder and negativity on the physical world itself. Its 'workings' or 'mechanics' seem flawed or even deceitful. Bonnefoy writes in 'La Voix encore': 'Et le cri de la nuit est âcre dans l'huile / Des gonds de toute chose' (CQ, 29). The human subject's capacity to transcend existence and to give it form proves to be illusory. We find ourselves immersed in an amorphous

[1] Yves Bonnefoy, *Ce qui fut sans lumière* (Paris: Gallimard, 1987). All subsequent references will appear within the text, using the abbreviation CQ.

and endlessly chaotic material world. We intuit what Mallarmé describes as 'le néant' during *la crise de Tournon*. And yet, in this moment, Bonnefoy once again urges us to 'tenir le pas gagné'. He suggests that, if we are prepared to relinquish the expectations that the structures of conceptual thought foster within us, we can perceive our participation in this material flux in a very different manner. The final lines of this stanza in 'La Voix encore' thus read: 'Le poids même du fer sur la pierre témoigne / De corps suants, courbés / Sur le bâtir mystérieux et le sens' (CQ, 29). The hinge embedded in the stone bears witness to the human body's action on the stone and the stone's action on the human body. These two forces are engaged in a process of making that remains mysterious, that is not controlled or mastered by either party. Acting upon one another, these two forces are transformed in unpredictable ways. Bonnefoy suggests that this process exposes 'le sens'. Sense is articulated through the open-endedly and indeterminately creative dynamics of this 'bâtir mystérieux'. The poet does not control it or direct this process from the outside but participates in it from the inside.

In *Début et fin de la neige*, published in 1991, just four years after *Ce qui fût sans lumière*, Bonnefoy's offers his most in-depth account—and surely his most coherent vision—of the human subject's participation in the material world. It is a short collection of poetry, written after the period that Bonnefoy spent living and working in Massachusetts, and it is devoted to a single subject matter: snow. It is as if the poet's discovery of an American Winter with its 'fifth element', snow, spurs a fresh set of reflections about the material world and the human subject's place in it. Bonnefoy makes references to Lucretius' treatise on Epicurean atomism in the collection, giving one short poem the title 'De rerum natura' (DF, 122). In many of the poems, as the poet watches snowflakes swirl through the air, we are reminded of Lucretius' accounts of watching dust motes dance in a beam of sunlight. In Lucretius' text, the act of watching these dancing particles changes the viewer's understanding of both matter and the space that surrounds it. Similarly, Bonnefoy's 'De rerum natura' opens with the words 'Lucrèce le savait: / Ouvre le coffre, / Tu verras, il est plein de neige / Qui tourbillonne' (DF, 122). The snow's atmospheric presence makes the poet aware that space itself is not an empty and exterior medium, an inert gap between one material body and another. Gaseous, alive with dancing particles, the air is actively and generatively material. Matter too is not as solid as we normally assume. As Lucretius writes, '[v]oid is enmeshed in things and is where movement gets it start'.[2] The spacing of existence is what makes the material world so mobile and mutable. We need only to assume a much larger perspective—or a much smaller one—to see that matter continually dissipates and emerges, withdraws and presents itself. Throughout *Début et fin de la neige*, Bonnefoy uses the snow to cultivate an atomistic or atmospheric vision of the productively spacious nature of material existence. Experimenting with the spatial dynamics of the poem's own performance, he seeks to resituate linguistic consciousness and the human gaze back *within* the spatial dynamics of worldly existence. Without relinquishing notions of transcendence, illumination, agency, and creativity, he seeks to conceive of these experiences in spacious, dynamic, and material terms.

In the essay 'Le Lieu d'herbes' (2010), Bonnefoy describes how the structures of linguistic consciousness can distort the subject's vision of the world. He suggests that 'notre conscience du monde [...] subit le langage comme une sorte de prisme au travers duquel la perception de ce qui est connaît une diffraction et se déforme et à des moments se dédouble, s'irisant de couleurs d'apparence alors surnaturelle'.[3] He continues: 'notre pratique de la réalité est troublée autant que construite par le langage'.[4] The poet suggests that language causes us to perceive the world in Platonic terms. To use Timothy Clark's phrase, linguistic consciousness seems to show us 'the underlying essence, the non-changing template or masterplan, so to speak, of which phenomena are merely a copy, the sensible manifestation'.[5] In many of the poems of *Début et fin de la neige*, Bonnefoy explores how the hand that reaches out to touch a snowflake does so in the hope of capturing a more essential reality. And yet, the snowflake evaporates in the poet's hand or dissipates as it falls through the air. The poetic subject seeks an underlying essence or form but encounters nothing other than the negativity of existence itself, the endlessly spatializing motion by which existence presents itself and withdraws. On many different occasions, Bonnefoy compares this experience to *Noli me tangere*, the biblical scene in which the risen body of Christ evades the touch of Mary Magdalene. Bonnefoy uses this biblical scene to reflect on the way he finds himself intimately exposed to the negativity of existence. He senses that he—like the snowflake—has no origin or ground that is not exposed to this negative force. Permeating all existence, this negativity is at work in his own body and even in his thoughts. And it

[2] Lucretius, *De Rerum Natura*, trans. Alicia Elsbeth Stallings (London: Penguin, 2007), p. 47.
[3] Bonnefoy, *Le Lieu d'herbes*, p. 15. [4] Ibid.
[5] Timothy Clark, *Martin Heidegger* (Abingdon: Routledge, 2002), p. 31.

actively deconstructs the appropriative modes of thought that purport to master it. The poet thus becomes increasingly aware his subjectivity does not transcend this negativity, that his mind is not an autonomous container that safely stores away his representations and impressions. He no longer perceives himself as a subject of reflection but as a subject of action: caught between creation and destruction, presence and absence, his being is continually propelled outwards into an endlessly changing material world.

In his critical writings, Bonnefoy refers to the experience of finding himself immersed in a productively spacious material world as 'la présence'. In the essay 'Poésie et liberté', published in 1989, just two years before *Début et fin de la neige*, Bonnefoy describes 'la présence' as '[c]ette impression de participer à une réalité soudain plus immédiate et pourtant aussi plus une et plus intérieure à notre être' (E, 310). In this essay, and in others, particularly the more recent essay '*Le Degré zéro de l'écriture* et la question de la poésie' Bonnefoy explains the perceptual shift that occurs in the experience of 'la présence' by using an anecdote about watching a leaf fall hesitantly from a tree. Bonnefoy describes how he becomes aware, as he watches the leaf fall, that his mind is anticipating the trajectory of the leaf's descent, mapping it in linear terms before the leaf has even fallen.[6] But the leaf hesitates as it falls—Bonnefoy repeats the verb 'hésiter' many times—oscillating in mid-air. As it does so, the poet forgets 'la ligne et ses points' (SP, 177). He no longer perceives the leaf as a discrete and solid body that moves through an empty space. Nor does he perceive himself as a distant observer, detached from the scene before him. The leaf as it falls is perceived in Bergsonian terms as 'un fragment de la durée', as one instant in existence's concretely creative force of becoming (SP, 177). It is 'moins une partie que le tout, ce tout étant le monde qui nous entoure, et dont rien nous montre qu'il est plus ou moins, ou autre, que la feuille qui se dissipe dans son sein qui n'est pas l'espace' (SP, 177). The notion of vacant and static 'outside' space that surrounds stable objects and the poet's own body reveals itself to be an illusion. The poet perceives the concrete temporal and spatial force by which the whole world evolves and feels his own body moving, evolving, and falling with it. Bonnefoy writes: 'nous n'avons plus de réalité séparée en cet Un que notre propre durée de

[6] This anecdote appears in the essay 'Poésie et liberté' in 1989, just three years before *Début et fin de la neige* (Bonnefoy, *Entretiens sur la poésie*, pp. 308–31 (p. 311)). It also appears in the essay 'Le Degré zéro de l'écriture' (Bonnefoy, *Le Siècle où la parole a été victime*, pp. 167–91 (p. 177)).

feuille qui tombe de l'arbre nous réinscrit. D'où un allègement de tout l'être. On pressent ce qui pourrait être une divine gaiété' (E, 311).

Critics have rightly stressed the importance of place in Bonnefoy's accounts of 'la présence'. Patrick Née suggests that presence is the experience of 'un lieu de l'être, ou un être-au-lieu'.[7] Describing it is as 'une abdication heureuse de la souveraineté du sujet', Michèle Finck asserts that '[i]l ne s'agit plus de régner sur le lieu mais de laisser le lieu régner en soi. "L'ordonnance" est une expérience de la dépossession, de la déposition du moi'.[8] Strikingly, however, even as critics describe 'la présence' as an experience of 'la déposition du moi', they still tend to describe it using a language of communion. Finck describes 'la présence' as 'la fusion du moi et du réel';[9] Giguère presents it as 'l'expérience d'unité de la conscience et des choses'.[10] Pamela A. Genova, in her article 'White on Black on White: Yves Bonnefoy's *Début et fin de la neige*', suggests that the poem becomes a space 'in which the self can render the exterior internal, in which the *Tout* is joined with the *Moi*, in which finally contradiction is overcome and a kind of ultimate salvation is offered up'.[11] It is important to stress, however, that Bonnefoy very deliberately deconstructs a Christian and metaphysical logic of communion by foregrounding the simultaneously creative and destructive force of the spatial dynamics by which material existence unfurls. 'La présence' is not the fusion of the self and the world, as if these were two separate entities that would be reunited. It is the realization that the human subject is not separate from material existence because it is always already ungrounded by its dynamics of exposition and thrust out into the world. As in the poems of 'La Terre', Bonnefoy develops a post-metaphysical and post-Christian understanding of what the diverse beings and presences of material existence have *in common*. They are all exposed in the same way to the radical exteriority of existence. This is the experience of 'l'un' or 'le tout' that the poet affirms.

Bonnefoy's understanding 'la présence' therefore has much in common with Nancy's conception of sense as a state of 'être-à' or 'être-avec'. What is most striking, however, is that the poet and the philosopher use—and steadily return to—the same key images when they seek to explain the inherently spacious nature of this experience of 'being-towards'. Nancy also

[7] Patrick Née, *La Poétique du lieu dans l'œuvre d'Yves Bonnefoy ou Moïse sauvé* (Paris: Presses Universitaires de France, 1999), p. 289.

[8] Finck, *Yves Bonnefoy. Le Simple et le sens*, p. 224.

[9] Ibid., p. 242.

[10] Giguère, *Le Concept de la réalité dans la poésie d'Yves Bonnefoy*, p. 65.

[11] Pamela A. Genova, 'White on Black on White: Yves Bonnefoy's *Début et fin de la neige*', *Romance Studies*, 23.2 (2005), 143–58 (p. 144).

draws upon ancient atomistic philosophy, citing Democritus. In *Le Sens du monde* (1993), he suggests that Democritus affirms 'l'espacement originaire en tant que matérialité' (SM, 95). Nancy suggests that the image of the *clinamen* allows us to reflect on the unpredictably productive nature of the spacious dynamics of material existence and to explore 'l'écart et le contact, l'assemblage, la séparation, la tangence, l'entre-deux et l'entrechoc de l'*il y a* diffracté singulier' (SM, 97). Nancy also reflects at length on the biblical story of *Noli me tangere* and the iconic paintings of it, devoting a whole book to them: *Noli me tangere. Essai sur la levée du corps*.[12] Nancy published this book in response to Derrida's accusation in *Le Toucher, Jean-Luc Nancy* that Nancy's tactile conception of sense perpetuates a long metaphysical tradition that privileges the act of touching.[13] Nancy responds to this critique by asserting that he has always understood contact as a dynamic that is endlessly spaced, dissolved, and deferred. For him, it is precisely the constant dissipation of touch that makes it so endlessly productive or disseminative. As Geoffrey Bennington writes: '[c]ontact is never established or given as presence, it is (only) the rhythm and vibration of its own touching and separating. [...] The subject is subject to the outside, as you say, always already. [...] touch is already withdrawing *in* its touch, vibrating away and becoming, intrinsically, a trace of itself, a trace of touch.'[14] In other words, touch is envisaged, not as the act that the human subject performs, but as the act that exposes the human subject. Its constant dissipation means that the subject of touch is always dispersed by its ebb and flow, carried out into the physical world by it, onto the next instance of contact, and the next.

The other key overlap between Bonnefoy's and Nancy's respective engagements with the material world is the active way in which they distinguish their approach from a phenomenological one. Both are aware that they are indebted to Heidegger's conception of *Dasein*, of 'being-there' or being 'thrown into existence'. Like Heidegger, Bonnefoy and Nancy affirm that the human subject is 'always already' projected into a pre-linguistic horizon of shared worldly sense.[15] However, as I suggested in the introduction

[12] Jean-Luc Nancy, *Noli me tangere. Essai sur la levée du corps* (Paris: Bayard, 2003). All subsequent references to the latter book will appear within the text, using the abbreviation NM.

[13] Jacques Derrida, *Le Toucher, Jean-Luc Nancy* (Paris: Galilée, 2000).

[14] Geoffrey Bennington, 'In Rhythm: A Response to Jean-Luc Nancy', *SubStance*, 40.3 (2011), 18–19 (p. 18).

[15] Clark points out that Heidegger develops a holistic conception of sense. He writes: 'a sense of the whole [...] precedes the parts of which it might seem constructed. Heidegger's view is a *holism*, i.e. the sense of things overall precedes and makes possible a grasp of the relevance and implication of the specific parts' (Clark, *Heidegger*, p. 19).

to this book, they are both critical of the anthropocentric way that Heidegger conceives of *Dasein* as the force that actively spatializes and temporalizes being and so entrances the sense of existence. Bonnefoy and Nancy present the sensible contingency of material existence as an inherently spatializing and temporalizing force that precedes and exceeds human consciousness, that continually overtakes human consciousness and thrusts it outwards. It is for this reason that the motif of falling is so prominent in Bonnefoy's work. His subject falls hesitantly forwards—it 'ex-ists'—just like the leaf or the snowflake. Bonnefoy suggests that not only is human subjectivity not the sole locus of creativity or agency in the world but that human subjectivity only comes into being through its participation in larger creative processes, in worldly dynamics of spatial exposition. Agency is thus presented as a distributed force, as a dynamic that is not realized by human consciousness but by thoroughly consensual or cooperative forms of worldly activity. Human agency in particular is envisaged as a form of inflection or involvement. As Philippe Jaccottet writes in *La Semaison*: 'On peut encore à tout moment modifier la vie / Avec beaucoup d'attention et de douceur / (Infléchissement perpétuel du cours des choses [...])'.[16]

A great deal of the criticism on late twentieth-century French poetry and the subject's relationship to the material world is deeply influenced by phenomenological ideas. This chapter stresses the importance of conceiving of Bonnefoy's relationship to the material real in post-phenomenological terms.[17] Rather than investigating how Bonnefoy's writing *mediates* between human subjectivity and material reality, this chapter investigates how his work displaces the opposition between these two forces, making us aware of their common dynamic of exposition. In this respect, we might suggest that Bonnefoy's writings anticipate the new generation of materially-oriented poets that has emerged in recent decades. We might point to Marie-Claire Bancquart's meditations on geological and evolutionary time, her reflections on humanity's embeddedness in immensely long and slow material processes. We might also compare Bonnefoy's atomistic or atmospheric texts on snow to Christopher Tarkos's notion of 'le patmo' ('le pâte-mot'), his conception of language as a kind of paste, compote, or purée that immerses

[16] Philippe Jaccottet, *Oeuvres* (Paris: Gallimard, La Bibliothèque de la Pléiade, 2014), pp. 335–418 (p. 396).

[17] Critics often read the work of poets such as Ponge, Réda, Dupin, du Bouchet, and Bonnefoy using a phenomenological paradigm to understand the relationship between the poetic subject and the material world. As discussed in the introduction to this book, the use of phenomenological models is very explicit in works such as Pinson's *Habiter en poète* or Collot's *Paysage et poésie*. Collot and Pinson both have chapters on Bonnefoy's poetry that offer phenomenological readings of his work.

human consciousness.[18] What is perhaps most innovative about Bonnefoy's exploration of the agency of material presence, however, and what distinguishes his work from Bancquart's and Tarkos's writings, is the emphasis that he places on the spacing of existence. By stressing the actively spatializing nature of mattter, Bonnefoy prevents his thought from congealing into a monistic materialism. He focuses on the inherently spacious way that diverse forces—material, corporeal, cerebral, linguistic—continually coexist and interact.

'Noli me tangere'

St. John's Gospel is the only gospel that describes Mary Magdalene's encounter with the resurrected Christ and Christ's warning to her not to touch him, saying: 'Noli me tangere'. This episode has inspired a long tradition of iconographic paintings, some of the most famous of which are by Rembrandt, Dürer, Correggio, and Titian. The paintings all centre around what Nancy describes as 'un jeu de mains remarquable' (NM, 55): one hand reaches out in desire or humility; the other hand is raised in warning or withdrawal. There is often a near or slight touching at the moment of the refusal of contact. The scene of *Noli me tangere* is explicitly alluded to twice in *Début et fin de la neige*, in the short poem 'Noli me tangere', early in the collection, and in the long poem 'Hopkins Forest', late in the collection. The scene is also subtly reconfigured in many other poems which feature images of hands pushing away hands, suspended or missed instances of contact. The poet often describes how he reaches out to touch or take possession of the snow and how it retreats from his grasp, saying 'Non, ne me touche pas' (DF, 26).

Début et fin de la neige opens with a series of short poems that resemble light sketches, as if each of them is trying to approach the snow with as much lightness and delicacy as possible. We are perhaps reminded of Bancquart's advocation—possibly informed by Bonnefoy's approach—of '[les] minces traces'. She writes: 'Plus que belle éloquence, ces langages diffus / pénètrent profond.'[19] In many of the short poems at the start of *Début et fin de la neige*, Bonnefoy reflects on the metaphysical aspirations that the act of touch inspires. In 'Le Peu d'eau', the poet holds a snowflake for a moment and expresses his desire to assure it an eternal life: 'À ce flocon / Qui sur ma main

[18] See, for example, Marie-Claire Bancquart, *Dans le feuilletage de la terre* (Paris: Belfond, 1994) and Christophe Tarkos, *Écrits poétiques* (Paris: P.O.L., 2008).

[19] Bancquart, *Dans le feuilletage de la terre*, p. 44.

se pose, j'ai désir / D'assurer l'éternel' (DF, 16). The snowflake melts upon contact, however: 'Mais déjà il n'est plus / Qu'un peu d'eau, qui se perd / Dans la brume des corps qui vont dans la neige' (DF, 16). The desire for eternity is met with evaporation and dispersal. The next poem in the series, 'Neige', explores the figure of touch in similar terms. It describes the fleeting way that the snow lingers on the poet's scarf and gloves and compares its presence to the most fragile of flowers, the poppy. The poet recalls that, as he held the poppy last summer, his hand 'rêva [...] Que l'absolu est à portée du monde' (DF, 17). The poppy's very fragility seems to offer contact with some otherworldy force. And now, as the poet sees the snowflakes melt on his clothes, he has the same intuition: 'Pourtant, quelle promesse / Dans cette eau, de contact léger, puisqu'elle fut, / Un instant, la lumière!' (DF, 17). As the material slips towards the immaterial, the poet feels as if he is brushing lightly up against the absolute. The poem ends, however, on a cautionary note: 'Circé / Sous sa pergola d'ombres, l'illuminée, / N'eut pas de fruits plus rouges' (DF, 17). In Homer's *Odyssey*, Circé is the goddess who laces food and wine with a magical potion in order to enchant Odysseus' crew.[20] Bonnefoy suggests that the reddest and most alluring of summer fruits—much like 'cette illusion, le coquelicot'—tempt us to betray the very ephemerality that they embody. Paradoxically, the transience of existence quickens our desire for the absolute. Bonnefoy suggests that this temptation is a cruel lure.

A similar lightness of touch characterizes 'Noli me tangere', the ten-line poem that evokes a single snowflake's solitary descent across an empty blue sky. The poem echoes the story about watching a leaf hesitate for a moment as it falls into the long grass that Bonnefoy recounts in his talks and essays. Here too, Bonnefoy describes how the snowflake hesitates as it falls. The opening line inverts the subject and the verb in order to foreground this motion:

> Hésite le flocon dans le ciel bleu
> À nouveau, le dernier flocon de la grande neige.
>
> Et c'est comme entrerait au jardin celle qui
> Avait bien dû rêver ce qui pourrait être,
> Ce regard, ce dieu simple, sans souvenir
> Du tombeau, sans pensée que le bonheur,
> Sans avenir
> Que sa dissipation dans le bleu du monde.

20 Homer, *The Odyssey*, trans. E.V. Rieu (Harmondsworth: Penguin, 1945), p. 165.

"Non, ne me touche pas", lui dirait-il,
Mais même dire non serait de lumière.

(DF, 26)

The last snowflake of the season perhaps hesitates because it is too small or light to fall. It seems to tremble on the brink of expiration. The poet compares himself as he watches it to the figure of Mary Magdalene: the one who dreams of what could be—contact, presence, possession, love—and who reaches out to touch. A series of negatives are used to describe the figure upon whom Mary looks, reducing him to nothing but a gaze. He looks impassively at the world, without remembering, thinking, or desiring. He exists only in the present moment, a present that is already slipping away, bringing him closer to his 'dissipation dans le bleu du monde'. He says 'Non, ne me touche pas' and, as he does so, his words dissolve into the light, 'Mais même dire non serait de lumière'. Even his words of refusal slip away, becoming only incandescence, and refusing to be touched.

The poem compares this tremulous snowflake to the risen and departing Christ. It does not function as religious analogies generally function, 'resurrecting' an apparently insignificant material presence by revealing its essential form or true meaning. We are not granted access to the absolute that lies beyond the material. Bonnefoy's snowflake simply dissipates 'dans le bleu du monde'. It does not withdraw towards an 'elsewhere'. No interior or secret essence is redeemed. All that the snowflake shows us is the voiding motion at the very heart of material existence. And it is this voiding motion that awakens thoughts of the biblical scene of *Noli me tangere*, the image of the body whose sanctity resides in the fact that it is withdrawing and disappearing. Bonnefoy thus offers a vision of transcendence that is neither divine or Platonic but, rather, finite and material. He associates the sacred, this force which touches us intimately but which cannot be possessed, with the negativity at the heart of physical existence. Nancy, in his reading of the biblical story and the paintings of it, suggests that Jesus's gesture of refusal is nothing other than the dynamic of departure or withdrawal that animates all material presence. Nancy writes:

> Ce n'est pas que Jésus se refuse à Marie-Madeleine: c'est que le vrai mouvement de se donner n'est pas de livrer une chose à empoigner, mais de permettre le toucher d'une présence, et par conséquent l'éclipse, l'absence et le départ selon lesquels, toujours, une présence doit se donner pour se présenter. (N, 82)

As Bonnefoy's snowflake evaporates, becoming only light, so the risen body of Christ withdraws. Nancy suggests that this withdrawal exposes 'l'éclipse, l'absence et le départ' at the heart of existence. We are touched by this force of withdrawal, even though it is a force that we cannot grasp. We are intimately exposed to the motion by which material existence continually voids itself or empties itself out, exposing itself even as it disappears 'dans le bleu du monde'.

The opening poems of *Début et fin de la neige* probe the sense of wonder that the transience of material existence can inspire in us. They interrogate the way that, as a fragile flower fades or a snowflakes melts, the poet feels the material substance of things hovering uncertainly between the material and the immaterial, the tangible and the intangible. Bonnefoy describes the sensation of broaching a limit within material existence, one of those thresholds that Jaccottet likens to 'une porte qui serait à la fois, inexpliquablement, entrouverte et verrouillée'.[21] The poet feels himself to be drawing close to the immaterial, the absolute, or the divine. Knowing that the hand that seeks to appropriate in the act of touching seeks more than the transience of this world, the poet feels the allure of the absolute, even if he knows it to be a lure. This brings us to an interesting point of 'contact in separation' between Bonnefoy's poetics and deconstructionist philosophy. Bonnefoy's poetry is far more willing to explore the moments in which we succumb to such metaphysical desires than philosophers like Derrida or even Nancy. Indeed, Bonnefoy offers an in-depth study of the allure of the metaphysical in *L'Arrière-pays*. He dramatizes intense cycles of aspiration and disappointment, hope and loss, presenting what he describes as 'une radioscopie des vouloirs en jeu'.[22] And yet, once he has done so, he deconstructs these desires. Exploring the connections between touch and metaphysical ambition, he offers a cautionary exposition of a haptocentric metaphysics. He suggests that, at the root of the metaphysical impulse, there is nothing but the experience of transience itself. The threshold that inspires a longing to accede to a divine essence is the eternally dissolving threshold of transient physical existence. Bonnefoy's brief but highly suggestive poems about snow all suggest that our desire for sanctity does not disappear with our loss of faith in the existence of God. They suggest that this very impulse towards the transcendent is awakened in us originally by the dynamics of finite material existence. We reach upwards and outwards, almost tropistically, he suggests, but we need not reach towards another world. We can reach towards and

21 Jaccottet, *Œuvres*, p. 820.
22 Yves Bonnefoy, *L'Arrière-pays* (Geneva: A. Skira, 1972), p. 100.

become intimate with the alterity within this world, the voiding motion that mobilizes our terrestrial existence and brings it into being.

The scene of *Noli me tangere* is also used to alert the reader to the energizing and animating nature of the negativity of material existence in the long poem 'Hopkins Forest'. The first three stanzas explore the poet's desire to grasp the essential sense behind the world's shifting physical appearances. They present three visual images, each of which is suggestive of a different practice of representation: painting, drawing, and photography. Each of these images presents a vision of a chaotic and destructive material reality that will not reveal its essential meaning or pattern. 'Hopkins Forest' as a whole explores this experience of refusal. It investigates how exposure to the unrelenting negativity of material existence can throw us into a profound state of ontological crisis. In the final stanzas of the poem, it is once again the scene of *Noli me tangere* that allows the poet to challenge and reimagine these feelings of loss and devastation. Reflecting on this scene of refusal and withdrawal, the poet becomes aware that negativity does not obliterate existence but only the essentialist vision that he has projected onto it. The negativity of finite material existence is thus no longer perceived as the force that refuses the poet's desires and blocks his intimacy with the physical world. On the contrary, Bonnefoy suggests that it attunes us to the common dynamism and spaciousness of all existence. It makes us realize that we too are produced by these worldly dynamics of presentation and withdrawal.

'Hopkins Forest' opens with a heavily painted image. The poet describes a dream in which he goes out to fetch water and finds himself 'en présence d'un autre ciel' as the sky empties and an unadulterated blackness reigns (DF, 35). On this black background, in the left-hand corner, just above the horizon, one burning cluster of red stars appears: 'Il y avait un amas d'étoiles rougeoyantes / Comme un brasier, d'où montait même une fumée' (DF, 35). This apparition resembles some form of sign or portent. We are reminded of Mondrian's *The Red Cloud*, the painting that Bonnefoy uses for the title of his 1976 collection of essays on poetry and art, *Le Nuage rouge*. In his essay on this painting, Bonnefoy describes this cloud as 'une lettre d'un alphabet inconnu, [...] comme un *signe*, au sens où un vol brusque d'oiseau ou un rocher d'aspect insolite le furent si constamment pour la conscience archaïque'.[23] The sign that appears in the poet's dream seems ominous. The sky empties of all recognizable forms and the poet confronts a pure

[23] Yves Bonnefoy, *Le Nuage rouge* (Paris: Mercure de France, 1977), p. 116. All subsequent references will appear within the text, using the abbreviation NR.

blackness, an unbroken expanse of emptiness. The enigmatic cluster of red stars smokes forebodingly. If Bonnefoy is reflecting on Mondrian's red cloud here, he perhaps also has Garache's red figures in mind. In *Le Nuage rouge*, he suggests that these red figures are portents that herald the arrival of a cruelly materialist epoch, one in which humanity sees itself 'cruellement par le dehors, [...] dans la brutale raréfaction de nos raisons d'exister' (NR, 312). He likens Garache's red forms to '[des] appels d'étoiles lointaines, fatalités comme en percevaient dans le ciel les astrologues pessimistes de l'antique Babylonie' (NR, 312).

The second stanza of 'Hopkins Forest' offers a mirror vision of the first. Having walked out and looked up towards the sky, the poet now returns home and looks down at an open book. The blackness of the sky gives way to whiteness of the page, and all that was richly painted before is now sparely drawn. The poet looks at the text on the page and it suddenly refuses to yield any meaning: 'Page après page, / Ce n'étaient que des signes indéchiffrables' (DF, 35). Words are perceived from the outside, as mere graphics. They are 'Des agrégats de formes d'aucun sens / Bien que vaguement récurrentes' (DF, 35). The poet traces these recurrent patterns but finds himself unable to unlock their meanings. If the red stars were a portent of destruction, this seems to be the catastrophe that they foretold. The poet confronts a world of sterile surfaces in which language no longer grants any purchase on its material forms. The page looms below the text, 'une blancheur d'abîme' (DF, 35). In a telling simile, Bonnefoy suggests that it is as if 'l'esprit', the human mind or spirit, is falling there: 'Comme si ce qu'on nomme l'esprit tombait là, sans bruit, / Comme une neige' (DF, 35). Without noise or resistance, the human mind falls through the white space of the page. Bonnefoy presents a vision of a material universe where everything is subject to the same processes of material entropy. We are all falling, like snowflakes or atoms. The poem ends with an image of perseverance but it is hard to say whether the gesture is heroic or bathetic. The stanza simply concludes with the words 'Je tournai cependant les pages' (DF, 35).

Bonnefoy's description of meaning draining away from language and the human spirit swirling off into the abyss here bears a striking resemblance to Mallarmé's descriptions of his *crise de Tournon*. In an interview, Bonnefoy describes this crisis as Mallarmé's intuition of 'le caractère à jamais subjectif et incohérent de la signification, "vaine forme" produite par le hasard', as the realization that 'nous ne sommes donc qu'une "présence" – à nous-mêmes ou à autrui et dans l'univers – de simple apparence, sans substance, absence en fait, le néant'.[24] The poet becomes aware of the essential negativity of existence, the way that it continually voids or empties itself, depriving us of any form of absolute or foundation. A similar revelation occurs in the third stanza of 'Hopkins Forest'. This time, however, it is triggered by a photograph. The poet describes being on a train in America, travelling between two utterly random locations, when he sees 'Dans un journal ouvert à deux pas de moi, / Une grande photographie de Baudelaire, / Toute une page' (DF, 36). The isolated four-syllable line, 'Toute une page', suggests the poet's disbelief. This large photographic image of Baudelaire circulates amongst the commuters. Its mass-produced image flashes up from the pages of a random newspaper. And the poet suggests that it appears 'Comme le ciel se vide à la fin du monde / Pour consentir au désordre des mots' (DF, 36). Baudelaire is of course not only Bonnefoy's most cherished poet but the poet who devoted himself to 'le culte des images'[25] and who warned of the dangers of photography, accusing it of producing '[des] progrès purement matériels'.[26] Bonnefoy's essay '*Igitur* et le photographe' reflects on the effect of the creation of the first photographic image on the nineteenth-century imagination. He argues that its creation triggered 'une sorte d'épiphanie de l'absence, où paraît le non-être de tout ce qu'on ressentait comme être: en somme, un enseignement de ce que Mallarmé va appeler le Néant'.[27] In the third stanza of 'Hopkins Forest', it is as if Baudelaire's worst fears have been realized. Bonnefoy sees contingency itself, 'le non-être', laying seige to Baudelaire's face. And the world is perceived cruelly, from the outside, in its raw material negativity. Nothing has any kind of fixed or essential value. Nothing can be redeemed by the human gaze and its vision of existence.

The final stanzas of the poem describe how the poet reflects on this dream and this memory as he walks in Hopkins Forest one Autumn. Watching the forest fill up with snow, the poet starts to perceive the negativity that confronted him in these two scenes in a new light. He asks whether it is the expectation generated by language, the desire to read the world as if it were a set of signs and to grasp its meaning, that cause him to perceive its material

[24] Yves Bonnefoy, *Lieux et destins de l'image* (Paris: Le Seuil, 1998), p. 243.

[25] Charles Baudelaire, *Œuvres complètes*, 2 vols, ed. Claude Pichois (Paris: Gallimard, Bibliothèque de la Pléiade, 1975–6), I, p. 701.

[26] Baudelaire, *Œuvres complètes*, II, p. 618.

[27] Yves Bonnefoy, '*Igitur* et le photographe', in *Mallarmé 1842–1898, Un Destin d'écriture*, ed. Yves Peyré (Paris: Gallimard, Réunion des musées nationaux, 1998), p. 64.

processes as disordered and sterile. By perceiving the snowflakes as 'signes', contradictorily, do we produce a vision of '[un] monde dévasté' (DF, 36)? As the poet considers this possibility, he is startled by the apparition of a punctual spot of colour on the horizon. Snow levels the entire landscape, obliterating all colour, 'mais un toit au loin, une planche / Peinte, restée debout contre une grille, / C'était encore la couleur' (DF, 36–7). This board is a simple but curious presence. It remains stubbornly upright, refusing to be flattened, continuing to reveal its colour as everything else is painted white. The board rises up, mysteriously, impossibly, as if offering some form of epiphany. It is 'mysterieuse / Comme un qui sortirait du sépulcre et, riant: / "Non, ne me touche pas", dirait-il au monde' (CQ, 37). This painted board is like the young god that steps out of the tomb, laughing, in the scene of *Noli me tangere*. It seems to appear on the threshold between presence and absence, the tangible and the intangible. It insists that there is no explanation for what is happening here. Or rather, there are many explanations and this painted board, this material presence, rebuffs each one, lightly, laughingly, saying 'Non, ne me touche pas'. It tells us that the world's material presences are not our object. They are not within our grasp. Similarly, reflecting on the scene of *Noli me tangere*, Nancy writes:

> Non, rien n'est disponible ici: ne cherche pas à t'emparer d'un sens de cette vie finie, ne cherche pas à toucher ni à retenir ce qui essentiellement s'éloigne et en s'éloignant te touche de sa distance même [...] comme de ce qui, en décevant définitivement ton attente, fait surgir devant toi, pour toi, cela même qui ne surgit pas, cela dont la surrection ou l'insurrection est une gloire qui s'emploie à décevoir et à écarter ta main tendue vers elle. Car son éclat n'est pas autre chose que le vide du tombeau. (NM, 30)

Nancy suggests that presence touches us 'de sa distance même'. It touches us *from* a distance and *with* its distance, exposing us to the very emptying or dissolving motion that Bonnefoy perceives within the snow, the sky, and language. This is the only epiphany that presence stages, the philosopher insists. It shows us its own ungrounding and emptying out and, yet, there is nothing to be uncovered or grasped here.[28] There is only the force by which presence emerges in its singularity, its excess, refusing to be grasped or enclosed. As Nancy eloquently phrases it, 'son éclat n'est pas autre chose que le vide du tombeau'.

[28] As Nancy writes in *Le Sens du monde*, 'l'essence y est privée de son essentialité, mais cette privation n'est privation de rien' (SM, 54).

In the final stanza of the poem, Bonnefoy confesses frankly, 'Je dois vraiment beaucoup à Hopkins Forest' (DF, 37). He suggests that the forest stays with him: 'Je la garde à mon horizon, dans sa partie / Qui quitte le visible pour l'invisible / Par le tressaillement du bleu des lointains' (DF, 37). Hopkins Forest stays on the periphery of the poet's vision, 'à mon horizon'. It slips off into the distance, in a quivering line of blue. Bonnefoy suggests that it was in 'Hopkins Forest' that he discovered the liminal nature of his own worldly existence, the way that the sensing subject is simultaneously exposed to visible and invisible, material and immaterial forces. And now, the poet keeps returning to this *limen*. He probes colour and even sound, strains to hear 'à travers les bruits' (DF, 135). He peels back layers of dead leaves on the forest floor, 'poussant du pied les feuilles mortes / D'autres années' (DF, 37). This pursuit no longer triggers a sense of crisis or loss as it did in the opening of the poem. On the contrary, the poet eagerly awaits the moment in which the ground seems to give way beneath his feet: 'ce sol 's'ouvre / À l'infini'. One line of poetry falls through into the next in an enjambment as the ground—this apparently solid substance, this foundation or base—opens onto infinity (DF, 135). In the empty space, the poet sees leaves falling there: 'ces feuilles y tombent / Sans hâte, ou bien remontent, le haut, le bas / N'étant plus, ni le bruit' (DF, 37). It is as if they are decomposing, falling through the earth. As one short clause follows another, as monosyllables and negative constructions proliferate, conceptual oppositions dissolve. There is no longer any up or down. There is no longer even any sound, 'sauf le léger / Chuchotement des flocons' (DF, 37). Whispering lightly, its mobile forms seem to speak some infinitely delicate and inaudible language. This whispering or rustling mass surges at the end of the poem as these particles '[s]e multiplient, se rapprochent, se nouent' (DF, 37). In this instance, the poet sees the world differently. He feels himself immersed in a swirl of particles: '– Et je revois alors tout l'autre ciel, / J'entre pour un instant dans la grande neige' (DF, °37).

The poem ends with a traditional image of transcendental or metaphysical revelation, a vision of 'l'autre ciel'. Yet this vision does not lead upwards or outwards, towards some exterior reality, but back towards the earth. The *other sky* becomes the interior infinite that the poet glimpses in the trembling line of the horizon or in the decomposing humus, the illimitable motion by which the material slips towards the immaterial, being towards nothingness. As Celan or Heidegger conceive of divinity as the withdrawal or 'passing' of the gods, Bonnefoy re-envisages the transcendental in dynamic and materialist terms, as the very void or the depths out of which existence is continually emerging.[29] It becomes what Nancy describes as the 'trans-immanence' of existence. Nancy writes: 'Dès que l'apparence d'un dehors du monde est dissipée, le hors-lieu du sens s'ouvre *dans* le monde [...], il appartient à sa structure, il y creuse [...] sa *transimmanence*, ou plus simplement et plus fortement, son existence et son exposition' (SM, 91).[30] Deconstructing the opposition between immanence and transcendence, Nancy suggests that the negativity of existence at once empties existence out and opens it up, causing it to continually transcend or surpass itself, to emerge in its concrete singularity. It is surely this dynamic of emptying out and opening up in which the poet is caught up at the end of 'Hopkins Forest'. As he surrenders to this dynamic, the poet realizes that his being is not diminished but becomes buoyant. The poet feels himself to be part of the mysterious force of becoming by which the world continually ungrounds and exhibits itself. He sees being and nothingness, summer and winter, the earth and the sky, one within the other and one alongside the other. He enters 'pour un instant dans la grande neige' (DF, 135).

In the final stanza of 'Hopkins Forest', Bonnefoy uses images of the very big and the very small, of swirling universes and clusters of particles, to make us feel the visible and invisible forces that transverse us. In the final stanza, the air grows thick. Matter grows more spacious. Space is no longer conceived as an inert and empty medium but is shown to be alive with dancing particles. All that we ignored just a second before, thought to be inert or empty, is suddenly charged and resonant. The world feels at once more intimate and more immense. The poetic syntax too grows more expansive: enjambments and monosyllables proliferate; the visual and sonorous patternings of language intensify. The poem stages a tremor, a rustling, and a clustering motion. We are drawn into its increasingly atmospheric presence and made to feel the way that its material forces rustle and resonate all through us. This is the experience that Bonnefoy describes in his critical essays as 'la présence'. It is not to be confused with the Christian and Romantic conception of communion for it deconstructs the dualisms—interior and exterior, self and world, transcendence and immanence—that underpin its logic. On the contrary, 'la présence' is an experience of radical exposure that makes us feel our own intimate involvement in the spatializing

[29] See Jean-Luc Nancy, 'Calcul du poète', in *Demande: Littérature et philosophie* (Paris: Galilée, 2015), pp. 111–43.

[30] In *Noli me tangere*, the philosopher writes: 'le "divine" n'a plus de place ni dans le monde ni hors le monde car il n'y a pas d'autre monde. Ce qui "n'est pas de ce monde" n'est pas ailleurs: c'est dans le monde l'ouverture' (NM, 78).

dynamics of material presence. It is the realization that the transcendent is not 'elsewhere' but that it is the very dynamic by which material existence opens. The poet feels worldly dynamics of dissolution and exposition acting through his own body, bringing him into being. This is the feeling of 'l'un' or 'le tout' that is so central to his descriptions of 'la présence'. It is the sensation of being part of the world's common dynamic of exposure.

The painted board that rises up in 'Hopkins Forest' and that refuses to be touched thus triggers a new kind of epiphany. It overturns the discourse of lack or loss that is produced by the structures of representation. This is because it presents a new conception of the poetic image, one that cannot be read or understood with reference to some prior or truer reality. Similarly, in his analysis of *Noli me tangere*, Nancy suggests that the epiphany this scene offers resides in the fact that its image can no longer be conceived 'dans la relation de la "figure" au "propre", ni dans la relation de l'"apparence" à la "réalité", ou dans la relation mimétique' (NM, 14–15). He argues that we are set before the image and asked to understand it 'dans la relation de l'image à la vue' (NM, 15). Nancy continues: 'Entre l'image et la vue, ce n'est pas imitation, c'est participation et pénétration. C'est participation de la vue au visible et du visible à son tour à l'invisible qui n'est autre que la vue elle-même' (NM, 15). In the final stanzas of 'Hopkins Forest', the image that Bonnefoy cultivates also dissolves oppositions between the perceiver and the perceived, inner and outer, foreground and background, transcendence and immanence. The image exposes the negative force by which material presence exhibits itself and withdraws, refusing to be touched. Opening onto nothingness and opening out of nothingness, the image becomes a force of exposition in its own right. We as viewing subjects are drawn into its unstable trembling motion. Its liminality is infectious. We feel ourselves being exposed by it. We feel visible and invisible, tangible and intangible forces at play all through us.

A similar account of the image's force of exposition is offered by Bonnefoy at the end of his essay on Mondrian's *The Red Cloud*. Bonnefoy argues at the start of his essay that we're tempted to read the red cloud as a sign. He then decides that its image is too unstable, its tones are too dynamic and inconsistent. He suggests that this image refuses to be deciphered and, in doing so, affords us a different kind of epiphany. Bonnefoy proposes that *The Red Cloud* offers:

> un regard sur cette totalité dont le sens, aussi obscur nous demeure-t-il, nous semble désormais le réel ultime. En somme, c'est là un autre "nuage rouge". Non plus une chose de notre monde qui se fait le signe d'un absolu,

> mais notre univers comme tel qui, de l'intérieur, se révèle à la fois la diversité des êtres et l'unité qui les lie – à la fois le rien et la plénitude, à la fois la ténèbre et une lumière. (NR, 122)

Like the atomistic images at the end of 'Hopkins Forest', the red cloud offers a vision of our material world 'de l'intérieur'. Its atmospheric image immerses our gaze, allowing us to see *from within* the cloud, the squall of snowflakes, or the cluster of particles. It reminds us that we are not outside the play of presence and absence, light and dark that animates it. We too are caught up in its dynamics of opening and withdrawal, creation and destruction. We are part of 'cette totalité dont le sens, aussi obscur nous demeure-t-il, nous semble désormais le réel ultime'.

Adulthood and Infancy: Learning to be Surprised by the World

As Bonnefoy considers the metaphysical ambitions that can inhabit the act of touching in *Début et fin de la neige*, he often plays with the verb 'prendre'. The verb appears as the poet seeks to take possession of and preserve a snowflake. It also appears repeatedly within the verb 'comprendre', as the poet seeks to take possession of material reality in more abstract terms. Bonnefoy explores how viewers who seek to comprehend material existence set themselves apart from it and then circumscribe its form, immobilizing and objectifying it. Etymologically, 'comprendre' means to 'saisir ensemble, embrasser quelque chose, entourer quelque chose'.[31] In a sequence of three poems at the end of *Début et fin de la neige*, 'Le Tout, le rien', Bonnefoy counterpoints the verb 'comprendre' with the verb 'surprendre'. The poet addresses a small child in these poems (in all likelihood his granddaughter) and, as he speaks to her, he juxtaposes the adult's desire to comprehend material reality with the child's simple willingness to be surprised by it, to allow herself to be taken 'à l'improviste, au dépourvu'.[32] Etymologically, the 'enfant' is of course the one who is 'unable to speak'.[33] She has not yet

[31] 'Comprendre' in *Centre national de ressources textuelles et lexicales*, http://www.cnrtl.fr, accessed 19 June 2018.

[32] 'Surprendre' in *Centre national de ressources textuelles et lexicales*, http://www.cnrtl.fr, accessed 19 June 2018.

[33] From Latin 'infans', meaning 'not able to speak', from 'in-', meaning 'not, opposite of', and 'fans', the present participle of 'fari', meaning 'to speak'. 'Infant', in *The Online Etymological Dictionary*, http://www.etymonline.com/infant, accessed 19 June 2018.

learned to use the conceptual structures of language to instrumentalize material existence. Receptive to the ways in which the material world in its infinite finitude keeps opening itself anew, she allows herself to be caught up in it and overtaken by it. Bonnefoy's address to the infant explores how poetry might emulate this way of perceiving and participating in the physical world. It is an *art poétique* that reflects on how poetry can infantilize linguistic consciousness and open us up to the excessive force of material existence's presentation, the dynamic by which it continually surges up and surprises us, overturning our normative systems of perception.

The capacity to allow oneself to be surprised by the sense of material existence is a prominent theme in Nancy's philosophy. In *L'Oubli de la philosophie*, Nancy defines 'l'attitude et l'acte philosophiques' as 'accueillir l'étonnement devant ce qui se présente'. He observes: 'C'est cet accueil qui fait la pensée. La pensée ne donne pas du sens: elle éprouve l'exigence du sens.'[34] In this respect, we can perceive the influence of phenomenology on both Bonnefoy's and Nancy's writings. Phenomenology seeks to 'surprise' the structures of human perception in action, before theoretical or metaphysical consciousness intervenes.[35] Phenomenologists such as Heidegger and Merleau-Ponty investigate how humanity 'always already' understands the world in pre-reflective terms, through its practical engagements with the world. Heidegger's *Dasein*, for example, disregards the Cartesian theoretical distinction between subject and object and suggests that Being, *Dasein*, is 'thrown' into a shared horizon of pre-linguistic sense. Heidegger situates 'meaning in a more contingent and temporally finite sphere', as James writes.[36] But Bonnefoy's and Nancy's use of the motif of naive or childish surprise also suggests that their understanding of the subject's immersion in a world of sense differs from that developed by phenomenology. In *Le Sens du monde*, Nancy critiques the way that phenomenologists perceive human consciousness or bodily orientation as the event that entrances the sense of existence. For Heidegger, he argues, 'l'homme existe et est seul à ex-ister'; 'il transit—traverse et partage—l'avoir-lieu du sens de l'être comme événement d'un être-là' (SM, 93). Nancy suggests that sense should instead be conceived in 'naive' terms. 'Naïf', etymologically, comes from the Latin 'nativus', meaning 'qui naît, qui a une naissance, un commencement'.[37] Nancy proposes that

34 Jean-Luc Nancy, *L'Oubli de la philosophie* (Paris: Galilée, 1986), pp. 102–3.
35 Moran, *Introduction to Phenomenology*, pp. 5–6.
36 James, *The Fragmentary Demand*, p. 95.
37 'Naïf' in *Centre national de ressources textuelles et lexicales*, http://www.cnrtl.fr, accessed 19 June 2018.

sense is the originary force by which all material things come into being, a dynamic of exposure that is not activated by humankind but that inevitably precedes us, and thus always takes us by surprise.[38]

Each of the three poems of 'Le Tout, le rien' contains four quatrains. The opening lines of the first poem describe the last snowfall of the season. Bonnefoy evokes a liminal point in the year in which of apparently opposing forces interact: Winter and Spring, creation and destruction, old wood and new life. The poet watches soft snow fall on blocks of dead wood, stitching up their wounds, before they are taken in and burned (DF, 41). As he does so, he addresses the small child who is by his side. He has witnessed the snow fall many times but the child now sees it for the first time. An internal rhyme highlights this juxtaposition: 'la dernière neige de la saison' is 'la première neige de ta vie' (DF, 41). The poet shows us the transformation that the world undergoes through the child's eyes: '[…] hier, ce n'étaient encore que des taches / De couleur, plaisirs brefs, craintes, chagrins / Inconsistants, faute de la parole' (DF, 41). Yesterday, the world was a patchwork of different colours that the child perceived fitfully, as a series

[38] It is important to specify that Bonnefoy's poetry departs from the conceptions of sense that are developed in Heidegger's early work, notably *Being and Time*. Bonnefoy attributes more agency and creativity to concrete and worldly forces than Heidegger does in *Being and Time*. Bonnefoy's conception of 'la présence' is less anthropocentric than Heidegger's conception of *Dasein*. However, it should also be noted that the '*Kehre*' that Heidegger's work undergoes in 1930 seeks to correct the anthropocentrism of his earlier project and to abolish the lingering influence of metaphysical subjectivity that Heidegger feels hangs over *Dasein*. In the late 1940s, things assume a new importance for Heidegger's writings as he develops a conception of the 'four-fold' (earth, sky, mortals, divinities) and the relationality of material existence assumes greater agency. Andrew J. Mitchell writes: 'In this thinking of thing and world, what phenomenally appears (earth) does so in a medium (sky) that fosters community (mortals) and communication with a beyond (divinities).' Mitchell adds: 'The fourfold is the key to understanding the utter relationality of worldly existence, for things are now understood to be the gathering points of the fourfold.' It is beyond the scope of this study but it would be interesting to explore how Heidegger's conception of the relationality of the fourfold relates to the relationality that manifests itself in Bonnefoy's poetics. Heidegger's conception of the limit as the site where these forces interact seems particularly pertinent. Mitchell writes: 'The fourfold names the reverberating extent and radiant fringe of the thing, the way it issues out beyond itself in an infinite belonging to world' (Andrew J. Mitchell, 'The Fourfold', in *Martin Heidegger. Key Concepts*, ed. Bret W. Davis (Durham: Acumen, 2010), pp. 215–6, p. 208, p. 210). One might still object, however, that a residual anthropocentrism still haunts the 'four-fold'. One might argue that the object remains a rather static entity that is traversed by these four forces. We might also contend that the capacity for disclosure merely shifts from *Dasein* to the four-fold but that the operative or agential element is no less anthropocentric. Michael Zimmerman argues that Heidegger's new ethos is only possible because he hypostasizes Being and personalizes it as a divine agent (Michael F. Zimmerman, 'Toward a Heideggerean ethos for radical environmentalism', *Environmental Ethics*, 5.2 (1983), 99–131).

of shifting emotions, 'faute de la parole'. Today, the blanket of white that has descended dispels these 'chagrins / Inconsistants'. The poet observes:

> Et je vois que la joie prend sur la peur
> Dans tes yeux que dessille la surprise
> Une avance, d'un grand bond clair: ce cri, ce rire
> Que j'aime, et que je trouve méditable.
>
> (DF, 41)

Joy *overtakes* fear and opens the child's eyes wide in surprise. We move into an enjambment as the feeling spreads through the child. Surprise comes as a great discontinuous jump, a sudden incursion into the world. Bonnefoy suggests that this leap is utterly unexpected and at the same time 'clair': transparent, obvious, or right. This 'avance' is finally articulated in: 'ce cri, ce rire'. The paratactic poetic syntax enacts the leap that the child makes. Bonnefoy uses the spaces between words, the jumps we make from one noun to another, to suggest the way that this emotion overtakes the infant. And he suggests that, paradoxically, it is the preverbal nature of this experience that captivates him. What is both lovable and ponderable, what provokes thought, is precisely the way that 'ce cri, ce rire' exceed rational experience.

In the final stanza, the poet affirms the closeness of his relationship to the infant: 'Car nous sommes bien proches' (DF, 41). He alludes to Wordsworth, the poet of childhood delight. He suggests that the child: 'Est le progéniteur de qui l'a pris / Un matin dans ses mains d'adulte et soulevé / Dans le consentement de la lumière' (DF, 41). Bonnefoy half-quotes the famous line of verse 'The child is father of the man'.[39] Wordsworth's image reverses the traditional chronology of human development: it suggests that childhood is a time of unparalleled sensual richness and that adulthood is the process by which we lose this privileged access to the material world through the steady acquisition of language, reason, and experience. Re-envisaging Wordsworth's image in gestural terms, the poet lifts the child up. A potentially appropriative and authoritative gesture becomes a consensual one. Accepting that the child and not the adult is 'le progéniteur', the poet learns the true nature of 'genesis' from the child. He accepts that creation is not a force that he can control or dictate. Rather, like the child, he can only allow it to overtake him, '[d]ans le consentement de la lumière'.

[39] William Wordsworth, 'My heart leaps up when I behold', in *A Wordsworth Selection* (London: Macmillan, 1963), pp. 104–5.

Many of the key motifs of the first poem of 'Le Tout, le rien'—the cry, the outpouring of light, the infant, the act of consent—echo images from 'La Terre'. Bonnefoy suggests that the child experiences the ecstatic nature of material existence: she allows herself to be overtaken by its dynamics, to opened up in new and singular ways. In the second poem of the sequence, the poet expresses his desire to articulate the child's cry: 'Oui, à entendre, oui, à faire mienne / Cette source, le cri de joie' (DF, 42). Describing this cry as a 'source', Bonnefoy suggests that he seeks to take possession of its vital force, this wellspring of life. As one line flows into the next in a series of enjambments, however, this originary force flows upwards and outwards, 'bouillonnante', 'd'entre les pierres de la vie' (DF, 42). It arrives '[t]ôt, et si fort' and then gushes away (DF, 42). The second stanza of the poem uses a series of negatives to describe the poet's inability to grasp this force. A series of infinitival clauses suggest the way that the activity of writing pursues this dynamic without ever encapsulating it: 'Mais écrire n'est pas avoir, ce n'est pas être' (DF, 42). Language can neither contain nor produce this cry. The act of representation changes all that is mobile and vital into a series of static objects: 'Dans des mots qui encore se souviennent // De tant et tant de choses que le temps / A durement labourées de ses griffes' (DF, 42). The verb 'se souviennent' reaches out wistfully in an enjambment across the stanzaic break. Another regretful enjambment suggests that all that is vibrant is obliterated by language's closed structures of representation: 'le tressaillement de la joie n'y est / Qu'une ombre' (DF, 42). Spontaneity and effusiveness are lost. They become nothing but a faint echo or trace within language, 'une ombre, serait-elle la plus claire' (DF, 42).

The final stanzas of the poem unfold in a further series of enjambments, running across the ends of lines and stanzas, as if to suggest the unravelling of the poet's initial affirmative desire. The poet observes: '– Et je ne puis donc faire que te dire / Ce que je ne suis pas, sauf en désir'. Unable to represent being, Bonnefoy suggests that he can only use language negatively, expressing '[c]e que je ne suis pas'. He deconstructs or exhausts language's closed structures of signification, allowing the text to become the negative image of embodied existence, the place in which the body is 'ex-crit', to use Nancy's expression.[40] Using two further appositional clauses, the final stanza suggests that poetry becomes:

[40] Nancy uses the term 'l'excription' to suggest that writing is a gesture that opens out of the interaction of the body, material presence, and signification. It comes into being through the exteriorizing action that brings all these forces into being. In *Corpus*, Nancy writes: 'Écrire : toucher à l'extrémité. Comment donc toucher au corps, au lieu de signifier ou de le faire signifier

Une façon de prendre, qui serait
De cesser d'être soi dans l'acte de prendre
Une façon de dire, qui ferait
Qu'on ne serait plus seul dans le langage.

(DF, 42)

The poem becomes an act of taking that nonetheless disavows its own sovereignty or closure. Refusing to grasp 'something', poetic language pushes onwards from one word to the next. Bonnefoy's repeated infinitives and enjambments keep language in motion. The poem continually overreaches and overspills. It enacts what Nancy describes as '[s]on inscription-dehors, sa mise *hors-texte* comme le plus *propre* mouvement de son texte: le texte même abandonné, laissé sur sa limite' (C, 14). Embracing the dynamic by which existence continually opens outwards, 'en désir', Bonnefoy manages to communicate something of the ecstatic force of the child's cry and laughter. He finds a way of speaking 'qui ferait / Qu'on ne serait plus seul dans le langage' (DF, 42).

In the final poem of 'Le Tout, le rien', the poet turns back to the child by his side and expresses a series of wishes for her future. Translator of Yeats' poetry, Bonnefoy perhaps has his 'Prayer for my Daughter' in mind.[41] Like Yeats' prayer, this final poem expresses a series of aspirations for a child's future but also for the future of poetry and humankind. It begins with an image of 'la grande neige', echoing the conclusion of 'Hopkins Forest'. Addressing the child, the poet observes: 'Te soit la grande neige le tout, le rien, / Enfant des premiers pas titubants dans l'herbe' (DF, 43). The poet hopes that the child will continue to accept the world's atomistic flux as everything and nothing, as all that there is and as the emptiness from which all things arise. He speaks to the infant who still teeters as she walks, who hesitates, much like the falling snowflake or leaf he evokes in other texts. Foregrounding this tottering motion, Bonnefoy suggests that her existence has not been corralled yet into the purposeful movement of adult life. She stumbles forward: 'Les yeux encore pleins de l'origine, / Les mains ne s'agrippant qu'à la lumière' (DF, 43). We feel the uncertain force of becoming in her movements. The

? [...] L'écriture touche aux corps *selon la limite absolue* qui sépare le sens de l'une de la peau et des nerfs de l'autre. Rien ne *passe*, et c'est là que ça touche' (Jean-Luc Nancy, *Corpus* (Paris: Métailié, 1991), p. 12). All subsequent references will appear within the text, using the abbreviation C.

[41] W. B. Yeats, *The Collected Poems* (London: Macmillan, 1993), pp. 211–14.

poet wishes that, with the acquisition of language, the child will not grow insensitive to this productive instability. In a similar manner, he wishes in the next stanza that she might always perceive sense, not as something to be abstracted, but as something emergent: 'Te soient ces branches qui scintillent la parole / Que tu dois écouter mais sans comprendre / Le sens de leur découpe sur le ciel' (DF, 43). Like the 'sens' communicated by the newborn's cry in 'La Terre', this is a sense that makes itself felt without making itself comprehensible. It is articulated, not by language, but by the dynamics of material existence itself. It is what Nancy describes as 'la structure du sens en tant que sens du monde' (SM, 12).[42] And Bonnefoy suggests that if we attempt to signify it, 'tu ne dénommerais qu'au prix de perdre' (DF, 43). The structures of signification inevitably extinguish the very force that they hope to capture. The poet hopes that the child might always receive this sense, allowing it to be articulated by the world itself, by the very dynamics by which existence teeters forwards.

The poem ends by wishing that the child might always recognize the coterminous nature of two values: 'Te suffisent les deux valeurs' (DF, 43). The first of these values is a vision of a shining hill in the distance, glimpsed 'dans l'échancrure des arbres' (DF, 43). It is the dream of a more essential reality that might be possessed fully, the vision of 'l'absolu' or 'l'éternel' evoked in earlier poems in the collection. The second of these values is the endless movement of finite material existence. The poet writes: 'Et que l'eau qui ruisselle dans le pré / Te montre que la joie peut survivre au rêve' (DF, 43). The illusion passes. The stream rushes onwards 'Quand la brise d'on ne sait où venue déjà disperse / Les fleurs de l'amandier, pourtant l'autre neige' (DF, 43). Bonnefoy suggests that humanity will always essentialize or objectify existence, reifying some divine essence or instrumentalizing some concrete form. But, in the same gesture, material existence continues to distribute and disperse itself. It endlessly exceeds the constraints that we impose upon it. The water flows, the wind rises, and the petals fall from the branches of the almond tree. The landscape transforms itself and the viewer with it. And Bonnefoy suggests in this final poem that this force of transformation is nothing other than 'la joie' itself. Joy is the force that *sur*prises and that *sur*vives: 'l'eau qui ruisselle dans le pré / Te montre que la joie peut survivre

[42] Nancy writes in *Le Sens du monde*: '*monde* n'est pas seulement corrélatif de *sens*, il est structuré comme *sens*, et réciproquement, *sens* est structuré comme *monde*' (SM, 18). He continues later: 'il s'agit du sens du monde comme de sa concrétude même en tant que cela à quoi notre existence *touche* et par quoi elle est touchée, en tous les sens possibles' (SM, 24).

au rêve'. It is the dynamic by which material existence continually overtakes us and opens us up, exhausting our fears and fixations, and projecting us out into the physical world.

'Le Tout, le rien' ends with an image that compares falling almond blossom with a shower of snow. This final image echoes all the other instances in the sequence in which Bonnefoy draws oppositions into apposition: all and nothing, adulthood and childhood, warmth and cold, Summer and Winter, life and death. All these appositions reinforce Bonnefoy's conception of the coterminous nature of presence and absence. In doing so, Bonnefoy very deliberately displaces the central Cartesian opposition between interiority and exteriority, subject and object. He focuses our attention instead on the simultaneously creative and destructive nature of finite material existence. He insists that this material dynamic is 'le tout, le rien' and invites us to perceive the way in which we are immersed in processes of emergence and dissolution that continually unground us and open us up. And he suggests that to attune ourselves to this ecstatic motion is to experience the joy of existence. Similarly, in *Une pensée finie*, Nancy writes: '[La joie] fait toucher, *et* elle laisse aller l'essence même du partage qu'est l'être dans sa finitude' (PF, 263). Nancy puns on the verb 'jouir' here in order to stress the corporeal, sensual, and erotic nature of this experience. He suggests that, when we talk about joy, 'C'est la question d'une présence: jouir est une extrémité de présence, *soi* exposé, *de soi* jouissant hors de soi, dans une présence que nul présent n'absorbe, et qui ne se (re)présente pas, mais qui s'offre sans cesse' (PF, 264). Like Bonnefoy, Nancy presents joy as the force that we experience when we feel ourselves being projected outside ourselves. It is the moment in which we feel existence offering itself up endlessly, in a cry of pleasure, a gush of running water, or a shower of almond blossom.

Bonnefoy suggests that it is through the acquisition of language that the human subject learns to control these dynamics, to immobilize and instrumentalize the flux of material existence, and to view the material world as a static sphere in which human action unfurls. And so, like Wordsworth, Bonnefoy considers poetry to be an activity that attempts to prolong or sustain the experience of infancy. He describes poetry, in an interview in 2004, as 'ce beau combat de la poésie contre le langage – contre et avec le langage' (IN, 427). Throughout 'Le Tout, le rien', we perceive this 'combat' in the poet's syntactical and rhythmic structures. One line continually pushes through into another in enjambments. Infinitival and optative structures resist the desire for closure and possession and keep reaching outwards and forwards. The address to the infant too is sent outwards. Bonnefoy uses these structures to communicate a sense that is not abstract but emergent, that is coterminous with the world's own dynamic of exposition. In *Le Sens du monde*, Nancy writes that we can only communicate sense when our thought:

> se perd tendanciellement comme "pensée" dans sa propre exposition au monde, ou qui s'y *excrit*, qui laisse le sens l'emporter, toujours d'un pas de plus, hors de la signification et de l'interprétation. Un pas de plus, toujours, et dans l'écriture de la pensée un tracé de plus *que* l'écriture elle-même.
>
> (SM, 19)

Nancy suggests that it is only when we embrace a loss or absence that is central to the experience of thinking and writing that we can open ourselves up to the dynamism that carries thought and existence outwards. It is because existence continually loses itself—loses any form of self-containment, self-identity, self-control—that it continually exceeds and transforms itself. This excessive or ecstatic dynamic opens existence up and gives it its infantile, fledgling, or nascent force. It is 'le tout, le rien' of material existence. It exposes what Nancy describes as 'un sens inouï, [...] un sens qui précède tous les sens, et qui nous précède, prévenant et surprenant à la fois' (SM, 11).

Exposing the Body of Language

Throughout *Début et fin de la neige*, Bonnefoy critiques the way in which the structures of conceptual thought colonize material reality and seeks instead to use language to approach the material world, not from above or beyond its material processes, but *from the inside*. Poems like 'Hopkins Forest' explore how embracing the negativity of material existence can allow us to feel our own intimate implication in an endlessly dynamic and spacious material world. 'Le Tout, le rien' 'infantilizes' the appropriative structures of conceptual thought in order to communicate the sense of material existence in a participative manner, in gestures that endlessly open or reach outwards. In many other poems in *Début et fin de la neige*, however, one of the key ways in which Bonnefoy trains us as readers to perceive material existence from the inside rather than the outside is by foregrounding poetic language's material substance and its spatial dynamics. The poet draws attention to the text's sonorous, graphic, and material performance, emphasizing the way that words distribute themselves across the page. He foregrounds the text's atmospheric nature, inviting us to perceive the ways in which language behaves a lot like snow and snow like language. And as he does so, he makes us aware of the contact that continually occurs between language and matter in this performance. Continuing to reflect on the scene of *Noli me tangere*, Bonnefoy emphasizes that the contact that occurs between language and the snow in the scene of writing is neither fusional nor appropriative but spacious. He dramatizes the spacious interaction that occurs between signification, sense, and materiality right at the heart of the poem. And, in doing so, he dramatizes the poem's own dynamic of emergence, its worldly force of exposition.

As Bonnefoy foregrounds the material presence of language in the snow poems, he frequently returns to the motif of a light and spacious touch. In one of the short poems at the beginning of *Début et fin de la neige*, the poet approaches the snow in a remarkably cautious fashion, seeking to attenuate the appropriative nature of signification. Strikingly, the snow itself is never named in this poem. It is invoked indirectly as the poem unfolds in a series of loose and tentative comparisons:

> On dirait beaucoup d'e muets dans une phrase.
> On sent qu'on ne leur doit
> Que des ombres de métaphores.
>
> On dirait,
> Dès qu'il neige plus dru,
> De ces mains qui repoussent d'autres mains
>
> Mais jouent avec les doigts qu'elles refusent.
>
> (DF, 22)

Without naming the snow, the poem speculates about what might be said about it. We could compare it to a cluster of mute 'e's. The *e atone*, this partially sounded or unsounded vowel, might suggest something of the snow's diffuse and fugitive presence. Using this formulation in the conditional, 'On dirait', the poet clearly feels the need to attenuate his approach to the snow, to use language in a way that is provisional and speculative. He suggests in the next line that a traditional metaphor would be too appropriative or too fusional. The snow requires 'des ombres de métaphores' (DF, 22). What is a shadow of a metaphor? It is perhaps the shadowy simile that the poet cultivates here, a hypothesis of what might be said. It is perhaps the very subtle comparison between the snow and the mute 'e's, so delicate in nature that it is practically diaphanous. As soon as the poet offers these gentle comparisons, a space intervenes between the two very short stanzas. It perhaps functions as another 'ombre de métaphore', the white space subtly suggestive of the snow's presence.

As we move into the next stanza, the snow falls more heavily. It is compared to hands that push away hands but that nonetheless play with the very fingers they refuse. We see another configuration of the scene of *Noli me tangere* here: an image of refusal and play, withdrawal and interaction. The gesture of rebuffal is evoked as the line runs into an enjambment across a line break and the empty space of the page intercedes once again. The delicate interplay of the fingers unfurls in the *rejet*. The poem ends on this final image that vibrates alone in the white space of the page. Bonnefoy uses the poem's spatial performance to emphasize how the snowflakes pull away from each other and swirl outwards, spurring further interaction. Bonnefoy suggests that it is the very spaciousness of their interaction that drives this performance. He hints that we can learn, as we use language, from this spacious interaction. We can resist the linguistic impulse to appropriate or enclose on material presence. By retreating or pulling away from the snow, refusing to represent it, as he does here with his shadowy and delicate similies, we can perhaps come closer to it. The poem can open up beside it, exploring its own inherently spacious dynamics of exposition.

In the next poem of *Début et fin de la neige*, which appears on the adjacent page, Bonnefoy once again compares the snow to the material substance of language:

> Flocons,
> Bévues sans conséquences de la lumière.
> L'une suit l'autre et d'autres encore, comme si
> Comprendre ne comptait plus, rire davantage.
>
> Et Aristote le disait bien,
> Quelque part dans sa *Poétique* qu'on lit si mal,
> C'est la transparence qui vaut,
> Dans des phrases qui soient comme une rumeur d'abeilles,
> comme une eau claire.
>
> (DF, 23)

The snowflakes are presented as '[b]évues sans conséquences', small errors in a text or speech. It is as if the snowflakes, breaking the light as they fall, are like scratches or scorings in a text. They interrupt the transparent flow of meaning, allowing the material substance of language to become apparent. As the snowflakes fall thick and fast, immersing the poet, he accepts that their material presence is not to be comprehended. It is simply to be experienced, like laughter, like an outburst of joy or pleasure. And so Bonnefoy tells us, 'C'est la transparence qui vaut'. He suggests that we read Aristotle's *Poetics* badly. We surely do so because we interpret 'la transparence' in semantic terms. A transparent language offers a clear window onto a meaning or onto the world. But Bonnefoy suggests that transparency is not a semantic but a sensible property of language. The transparent phrase flows 'comme une rumeur d'abeilles' (DF, 23). Its parts sound together in one continuous phrase and this sensory clarity that renders all things limpid, 'comme une eau claire'. Its presence is diffuse and expansive. Relinquishing any desire for possession or preservation, it vibrates *outwards*. It makes us feel the transparency of existence, which is to say, its fluidity and dynamism, its common spaciousness.

The same conception of the common spaciousness of existence is celebrated in one of the long poems, 'Les Flambeaux'. It forges a similar analogy between the cluster of words on the page and the falling snow. It begins, like so many of Bonnefoy's poems, by reflecting on an appropriative desire. The poet perceives the snow-filled landscape as 'notre chemin [...] pour aller prendre [...] [c]es flambeaux, ce qui est' (DF, 30). When he finds himself unable to grasp this essential force, however, he feels the light that he sought to possess disperse. Addressing the falling snowflakes, the poet urges them to fall downwards and to touch the flames of 'les flambeaux':

> [...] ô neige, touche
> Encore ces flambeaux, renflamme-les
> Dans le froid de cette aube; et qu'à l'exemple
> De tes flocons qui déjà les assaillent,
> De leur insouciance, feu plus clair,
> Et malgré tant de fièvre dans la parole
> Et tant de nostalgie dans le souvenir,
> Nos mots ne cherchent plus les autres mots mais les
> avoisinent,
> Passent auprès d'eux, simplement,
> Et si l'un en a frôlé un, et s'ils s'unissent,
> Ce ne sera qu'encore ta lumière,
> Notre brièveté qui se dissémine,
> L'écriture qui se dissipe, sa tâche faite.
>
> (DF, 31–2)

Bonnefoy encourages the snowflakes to fall towards and to touch the flames. He urges them to embrace their own force of expenditure, suggesting that their fall and their expiration generates a new light. As he does so, the imperative 'touche' falls just before the stanzaic break. Once again, we're subtly encouraged to perceive touch in spacious terms. As the snowflakes fall nonchalantly towards the flames, the poet suggests that they assail it '[d]e leur insouciance'. Seeing them fall so freely, he feels language stirring within him in a similar way. Words too start to fall. They let go of their feverish and nostalgic longing for possession and tumble outwards and downwards. As they do so, one continuous sentence stretches over two stanzas and twenty-two lines. This sentence had started by reaching outwards covetously but then, as the object it sought dissolved, it embraced its own spatial dynamic, a *praxis* that pursues no exterior object. And so, words start to fall freely side by side, revelling in the spaciousness of their physical performance. One fifteen-syllable line stretches outwards in a leisurely manner: 'Nos mots ne cherchent plus les autres mots mais les avoisinent'. The poet suggests that as words embrace their own *praxis* or dance in this way, sometimes one word brushes up against with another—'l'un en a frôlé un'—and this collision produces a flash of light. There's a moment of poetic illumination. We are reminded of the *clinamen* that Lucretius describes in *De Rerum Natura*. Lucretius suggests that particles do not simply fall endlessly through a void because a swerve and a collision occurs. This collision is generative because it triggers the conglomeration of forms and the emergence of life. When the collision between two words produces a flash of light here, the poet continues to address the snow and insists that it is 'ta lumière'. Bonnefoy perceives this linguistic event in finite material terms, as a fleeting physical encounter between two bodies. Its flash of light exposes 'Notre brièveté qui se dissémine, / L'écriture qui se dissipe, sa tâche faite'. Bonnefoy presents the practice of writing—and even the flash of insight it produces—as another fleeting physical performance. Writing performs its function, he suggests, when, like the snow, it dramatizes its own passing, when it makes us feel the force of its own diffusion and dissipation. We perceive words falling outwards, touching one another in passing, and this touch captures and holds nothing. It does, however, *release* a light. We are reminded of the images of light, fire, and unreserved expenditure that dominate 'La Terre'. Bonnefoy invites us to perceive the contact that occurs here in similar terms, not as an appropriative but as an 'expropriative' act (to use Nancy's term). Whether it occurs between two bodies or two words, touch is presented as the very force that keeps existence flashing or sparking outwards. It is the dynamic by which existence disseminates itself. It releases or throws us—like the falling snowflakes or the dancing flames—into being.

The poet has kept the same sentence running for twenty-two lines, using parentheses and subclauses. As the words keep tumbling downwards, he suggests that his task is simply to keep removing the linguistic obstacles that might impede this current. The final two stanzas of the poem extend its flow even further by adding a long parenthesis. These lines no longer evoke the movement of words on the page, however. They instead return to the image of the falling snow and describe the flight of a few isolated snowflakes:

> (Et tel flocon s'attarde, on le suit des yeux,
> On aimerait le regarder toujours,
> Tel autre s'est posé sur la main offerte.
>
> Et tel plus lent et comme égaré s'éloigne
> Et tournoie, puis revient. Et n'est-ce dire
> Qu'un mot, un autre mot encore, à inventer,
> Rédimerait le monde? Mais on ne sait
> Si on entend ce mot ou si on le rêve.)
>
> (DF, 32)

The falling motion that we saw enacted by the text is now enacted by the snowflakes. And as the poet describes their dance, he uses the stresses and the pauses of the line of verse to dramatize each twist and turn. One snowflake lingers and we pause at the caesura: 'Et tel flocon s'attarde'. A snowflake drifts away and the line flows into an enjambment. The line turns into *rejet* and the snowflake turns too, dancing back towards us: 'Et tel plus lent et comme égaré s'éloigne / Et tournoie, puis revient.' Bonnefoy uses the dynamics of the poem's movement across the page to suggest the contingency and uncertainty of the snowflake's movements. In doing so, he reminds us that the poem's dance—like the snowflake's—is not a teleological movement. It is not imagined and understood by the poet in advance. The poem and the snowflake find their way forward erratically and unpredictably. Their movements remind us that space is not a medium though which things move in a predetermined or fatalistic fashion. Space is the very dynamic by which material existence opens outwards, finding its own form in a hesitant and fitful motion. As the poet dramatizes this creative force, he asks: 'Et n'est-ce dire / Qu'un mot, un autre mot encore, à inventer, / Rédimerait le monde?'. He has the sensation that reaching for another word—just one more—might redeem the world. This is not the teleological impulse that the poet explored at the start of 'Les Flambeaux', however. The word that might prove redemptive is always just on the horizon, just out of reach. The poem ends with the words 'Mais on ne sait / Si on entend ce mot ou si on le rêve.' The perfect formulation, the final light, never arrives. The poet suggests that it is the gesture of reaching, rather than the word itself, that is redemptive. For as we keep reaching outwards, trying to grasp this word, existence keeps voiding this gesture. We save nothing. And yet, we are exposed to the dynamics by which existence saves itself—and us too—by continually 'expropriating' itself.

Many twentieth-century French poets, such as Jacques Dupin or Lorand Gaspar, foreground the materiality of language in their poems by stressing the dense way that it deposits itself on the page. They explore how the substance of words fuses with other forms of matter. Bonnefoy takes the opposite approach in the poems of *Début et fin de la neige*. He stresses the spacious nature of language's material presence. He does not seek to approach the snow directly. Pulling back from it, he explores the spatial dynamics of the poem's own physical gesture of exposition: the resonance by which words vibrate through the air or the swirling motion by which they distribute themselves across a page. Insisting that linguistic consciousness is not a vantage point that allows us to view the material world from the outside, the poet refuses to use language to 'comprehend' material existence. His snow poems repeatedly remind us that we are immersed in language's atmosphere, just as we are immersed in the world's atmosphere. We experience both the poem and the world from within. The act of reading or writing poetry, Bonnefoy suggests, is the act of giving oneself over to the poem's material processes, allowing them to overtake us and to carry us outwards, like a burst of laughter, or a cry of delight. We are asked to feel the creative force of material existence at play throughout the body of the poem and throughout our bodies, to understand space not as the empty and inert medium through which bodies fall fatalistically, but as the generative force that opens material bodies up and that projects them outwards.

Touch is conceived as the generative force that drives this performance. It is a vibratory or resonant dynamic that allows different forces to 'spatialize' one another in singular and unpredictable ways. Constantly figuring and reconfiguring the scene of *Noli me tangere*, Bonnefoy suggests that touch necessarily involves a certain gesture of withdrawal. It is this absenting motion that allows material existence to continually void and expose itself, to foster its infinitely spacious and playful forms of interaction. The poet likens touch to a flash of light. In doing so, he asks us to perceive it as an endless release, as the motion by which existence never ceases to liberate itself and to open outwards. Conceived in these terms, touch is no longer a gesture that approaches the bodies of the material world from the outside, as if they were a series of closed things. Bonnefoy insists that we are not, as we so often are in Dupin's and Gaspard's poetry, or in Bonnefoy's early poetry, on the outside, trying to 'get in'. The body—whether it is the human body, the body of the text, or of a material thing—is perceived as a force that is brought into being by the endlessly generative, spatializing capacities of touch. This is why the image of the light touch is so crucial to the poems of *Début et fin de la neige*. It is touch that gives existence its levity, its vibratory or resonant energy, its capacity to endlessly transport and transform itself.

Bonnefoy uses the spatial dynamics of the poem's own performance to ask us to situate ourselves within this motion. He uses the snowflakes' hesitant, darting, sinuous dance to make us feel the creative and unpredictable way a poem comes into being as it is continually spatialized—projected outwards—by the interaction of many different forces. We are asked to surrender to the poem's motion: to allow it to carry us outwards and to make us experience the generatively spatial force of '[n]otre brièveté qui se dissémine'.[43] The poet's use of the term 'dissemination' here invites us to conceive of this motion as a creative force that deconstructs traditional conceptions of an origin. Similarly, in *Le Sens du monde*, Nancy writes: '"Le monde est l'origine" veut dire que l'origine est *là*, où ça ouvre [...] car exister s'espace, se singularise selon une infinité de rythmes de sa propre venue, de sa propre décision d'exister' (SM, 242). Strikingly, Nancy uses this conception of the originary force of the spacing of material existence to deconstruct the distinction that Heidegger makes between the earth as an inert material sphere and world as the 'being-there' that is entranced by *Dasein*. Like Bonnefoy, Nancy conceives of creativity as a worldly and concrete force, rather than as a uniquely human one. He suggests that it emerges in the first instance in the spatializing dance that brings concrete existence into being. Nancy suggests that we encounter this conception of creativity in Democritus' writings, in his meditations of 'la *chute* des atomes dans le vide et le *clinamen*: l'écart et le contact, l'assemblage, la séparation, la tangence, l'entre-deux et l'entrechoc de l'il *y* a diffracté singulier' (SM, 97). He continues: 'La singularité est matérielle, qu'on l'entende plutôt comme événement ou plutôt comme unicité d'existence, ou comme les deux ensemble, et toujours

[43] Bonnefoy might use this word as a subtle tribute to Derrida, but it is perhaps more likely that he uses it to reclaim it from him, to emphasize that the originary or generative spacing that brings being into being is not textual but material. For Bonnefoy, the play of signification is always preceded by the play of sense, by concrete dynamics of spatial orientation, disposition, and dispersal.

comme sens' (SM, 97). The Democritean images that Nancy uses here resemble the images of falling words and snowflakes that we encounter in 'Les Flambeaux'. Like Nancy's text, Bonnefoy's poem also seeks to dramatize material existence's own singular force of emergence, 'l'il *y* a diffracté singulier'. They ask us to situate ourselves within this dynamic, to feel it at work within us, allowing it to open us up, to effract and diffract us, and to carry us away with it. His poems do not try to master or control this dynamic but consent to it. And we in turn, as readers, are asked to consent to the poem, to give ourselves to it. For its spacious dynamics expose a generative, material force that precedes and exceeds us, and that promises to redeem us. This is not an act of redemption in the traditional sense. Nothing will be possessed or preserved. The poem can, however, should we let it, attune us to dynamics by which existence endlessly opens through us and steadily 're-originates' us.

A Spacious Worldly Performance

In poems such as 'Noli me tangere' and 'Hopkins Forest', the poet realizes that the gesture of withdrawal or dissipation that he perceives at the heart of material existence does not lead us 'elsewhere', towards some higher or more essential reality. He senses that the destructive current that he perceives throughout existence is unreservedly negative and realizes in the same moment that it permeates his own being. He feels his own existence being ungrounded and opened up, immersed in an infinitely mobile and mutable material universe. He experiences an ontological crisis, a Mallarmean intuition of 'le néant', as his faith in his own distinction and integrity as a human being, in his capacity to transcend a world of material process, dissolves. The poet realizes that his subjectivity is not grounded 'elsewhere'. His desire to capture some form of essential or absolute meaning seems risible. The poet feels that his physical form is falling through a processual material universe, just like any other material body, like snowflakes or particles. This realization is greeted with profound anxiety and despair at the beginning of 'Hopkins Forest'. And yet, by the end of the poem, it is a source of hope and excitement. For, as the poet watches the falling snow, he realizes that the negativity that dynamizes material existence is not only a destructive force but also a generative one. The motion by which existence continually withdraws is also the motion by which it projects itself outwards, exceeding or transcending its own immanence, endlessly re-originating itself in unpredictable ways. When the poet realizes that this negative force is active within him, he realizes that he participates in its creative force. His own subjectivity is endlessly overtaken by it. No longer approaching material existence from the outside, no longer lamenting his inability to grasp its hidden meaning or essence, he feels the dynamism of material existence at work within him. He senses the interplay of material and immaterial, tangible and intangible, creative and destructive forces all through him. He celebrates the dynamic of exposure that brings being into being *from within*.

Of course, Bonnefoy remains acutely aware that language encourages us to perceive existence from the outside. This is what he seeks to demonstrate when he recounts the story about the falling leaf in 'Poésie et Liberté'. He explains that the person who watches a leaf fall tends to perceive its descent as if it were a linear trajectory, a coherent and complete action. We represent the action to ourselves, viewing it retrospectively, as if it had already unfolded. In doing so, we perceive the world in a determinist manner. And yet, Bonnefoy insists, the leaf hesitates in mid air. And this simple motion reveals material existence's emergent force. It exposes the dynamic by which material existence is continually renewing and transforming itself. It is for this reason that, in 'Poésie et Liberté', Bonnefoy describes poetry as an activity that is synonymous with freedom. He proposes that poetry is '[le] travail d'une libération intérieure' that mobilizes 'l'esprit' 'contre l'inertie du langage au sein de sa propre parole' (E, 317). Poetry opens up the closed structures of language to the creative force of material existence. It is this desire to 'open up' our linguistic consciousness that Bonnefoy explores when he addresses the small child in 'Le Tout, le rien'. The poet suggests that the infant—the one who does not speak, who is not yet practised in normative modes of linguistic perception—allows herself to be continually surprised by the material world. She allows the dynamics of material existence to play through her, to transport and to transform her. And if Bonnefoy proposes that poetry emulates the child's response to the world, it is precisely because poetry too seeks to allow the dynamics of material existence to *play through it*. For Bonnefoy, the practice of writing is a way of actively resisting the closure of signification, of keeping words in motion and making language continually overspill its own limits, so that the poem can communicate something of existence's excessive or ecstatic force. The poet conceives of freedom and creativity in these terms too. Neither are understood as an ability to control material existence, to act on it according to our will from the outside. Freedom and creativity are perceived as concrete and worldly dynamics, as forces that we participate in and inflect rather than master.

They can be articulated *in us and through us*. But to do so, Bonnefoy argues, we must be willing to let ourselves be taken by surprise. This means letting diverse forces—material, sensual, and linguistic dynamics—negotiate within us and articulate themselves anew. It means *actively* allowing ourselves to be reconfigured and redistributed, arriving in the world in ways that we could not know or predict, like a burst of laughter or cry of pleasure, a shower of snow or falling almond blossom.

Whereas poets like Dupin or Tarkos stress the plasticity of the material substance of language, Bonnefoy focuses on its inherently spacious nature. He insists that matter's spaciousness gives it its transformative or creative force: it is only because material existence continually voids itself that it can expose itself anew. And what is perhaps most enabling about this conception of the inherently spacious nature of material bodies, Bonnefoy suggests, is that it transforms our conception of touch. For when—like Lucretius—we perceive the void enmeshed in all things, we no longer perceive touch in an appropriative or closed manner. We no longer understand it as the sovereign act by which one body approaches another from the outside and seeks to take hold of it. Bonnefoy insists that touch is not to be conceived from the outside but from the inside, as the inherently spatializing dynamic of exposure. Touch is thus dispersed in an endless series of vibrations or resonances. We see this form of touch in the falling snowflakes that are like 'ces mains qui repoussent d'autres mains / Mais jouent avec les doigts qu'elles refusent'. The delicate interaction of these fingers shows us the vibrant force that continually thrusts worldly presence outwards and singularizes it. This conception of touch opens up our bodies and makes us aware of their participation in an actively spacious physical world. It opens up the body of the poem too. Bonnefoy presents the poem as a performance in which material, sensual, and linguistic forces interact. The contact that occurs between these forces is light and spacious. It is for this reason that Bonnefoy continually draws our attention to the atmospheric nature of the poem's physical performance: the resonance of words, the clustering of phonemes, a flurry of letters on a page. His snow poems dramatize how matter, sense, and meaning inflect and deflect one another in spacious ways, how they 'expropriate' one another, to use Nancy's term. The poem does not emulate or represent the snow. By dramatizing the spacious dynamics of its own emergence, it moves closer to the snow. It enacts the worldly dynamic of exposition that brings both their material performances into being.

And so, the poem affirms the ontological and materialist nature of its own performance. James writes, in reference to Nancy's writings on art, that the text 'exists in, or as, a relation to the world, a relation to shared finite existence, and more specifically to that movement of sense which is, or opens up, world-hood'.[44] The poem celebrates the dynamics by which words appear, move, interact, and disperse. The text does not reach outwards, towards an outside world. It does not present itself as 'une aventure dans l'élément étranger' nor explore 'un risque venu du dehors', as Nancy writes in *Le Sens du monde* (SM, 55). The text explores its own condition of 'l'être-au-dehors', 'l'être-étranger or étrangé' (SM, 55). Language is 'exposé à, et par, l'*ex* qu'il est, exposé à, et par, cette défaillance d'essence plus ancienne et plus affirmative qu'aucune constitution d'essence, et qui le constitue, c'est-à-dire qui le jette au monde' (SM, 55). This is the motion of Bonnefoy's falling leaf and his falling snowflakes. It is also the motion of Mallarmé's falling feather in *Un Coup de Dès* and of the graphic poem that dramatizes the adventure by which words drift in an oblique, zigzag motion across the two pages of the folio. Bonnefoy suggests that this vagrant, hesitant, oscillating motion is itself redemptive. He proposes that the material *praxis* of the poem takes language—as well as its readers and its writer—somewhere we did not know we were heading. It exposes material existence's force of creation, the opening motion that continually renews existence, the dynamic that never ceases to suprise us, that continually opens us up and carries us outwards.

[44] James, *The Fragmentary Demand*, p. 203.

3
Voice and Subjectivity in *Les Planches courbes*

le son brouille le sens, ouvre à la lumière en avant.
L'Inachevable (IN, 239)

cette musique des mots est un acte de connaissance
dont le lieu en nous est la voix.
'La Parole poétique' (SPV, 203)

'La Voix lointaine'

Bonnefoy's writings offer a powerful critique of visual sense. In the essay 'Les Yeux qui se font regard', he suggests that vision is uniquely complicit with linguistic consciousness and the act of representation (SPV, 213). He argues that, when we allow our visual sense to dominate our perception, we distance ourselves from the material world and objectify the landscape that appears before us. Bonnefoy observes axiomatically, 'Le regard, si j'ose dire, ne voit pas' (SPV, 214). In the collections of poetry that we have examined already in this book, *Dans le leurre du seuil* and *Début et fin de la neige*, Bonnefoy uses the sense of touch to cultivate a different conception of the relationship between one person and another, or between the subject and the material world. He urges us to conceive of touch in inherently spacious terms, as the dynamic by which all worldly forces rebuff and refract one another, and project one another outwards. He emphasizes how this newly spacious conception of touch opens up the human body in particular, allowing us to perceive it as 'un lieu d'existence', to use Nancy's phrase (C, 16), and invites us to conceive of human subjectivity as a dynamic of opening. This chapter will analyse how Bonnefoy develops this notion in his next collection of poetry, *Les Planches courbes*, published in 2001. It will investigate how he foregrounds the aural sense rather than the tactile sense in this collection, using reciprocal acts of listening and voicing to develop a

Yves Bonnefoy and Jean-Luc Nancy: Ontological Performance. Emily McLaughlin, Oxford University Press (2020). © Emily McLaughlin.
DOI: 10.1093/oso/9780198849582.001.0001

properly temporal and spatial understanding of the dynamics of exposure that bring human subjectivity into being.

Shifting the emphasis from the hand to the ear, from the poet's relationship to the material world to the poet's relationship to his own subjectivity, this chapter explores how Bonnefoy uses the act of listening to a distant voice to explore the experience of self-presence in *Les Planches courbes*. Throughout his career, Bonnefoy criticizes how the dominance of linguistic representation and the visual sense encourage us to perceive our own subjectivity as a process of self-reflection and self-representation. He argues that this way of thinking about subjectivity either offers the subject the hope that its image will be returned to it and it will gain full possession of its 'self', or makes us perceive our own subjectivity as a doubled and divided force, something that is never located there where it seems to be, and that evades the endless representations that we offer of it. In *Les Planches courbes*, Bonnefoy uses the aural sense to cultivate a very different understanding of subjectivity. He uses the motif of listening to a distant voice to explore the inherently spacious and expansive nature of subjectivity and encourages us to understand self-presence in resonant rather than in reflective terms. Across the eleven poems of 'La Voix lointaine', the poetic 'je' listens to a resonance that echoes both through its own body and the forms of the physical world. Bonnefoy suggests that this resonance allows the subject to attune itself to dynamics of relation that are more primary than language's structures of reference, differentiation, and division. For him, the rhythms of the versified line of poetry are uniquely capable of exploring—and experimenting with—this inherently generative resonance. The resonance of the poetic line allows us to explore the ways in which human subjectivity emerges from the world's endless dynamics of relation, reverberating outwards, through the surfaces of the human body and the things of the material world.

A preoccupation with voice is, as many critics have observed, evident at each stage of Bonnefoy's career.[1] In *Du mouvement et de l'immobilité de*

[1] In his essay 'Yves Bonnefoy. L'Évocation d'une voix', Pierre Brunel suggests that Bonnefoy's dramatization of voices in *Douve* and *Hier régnant désert* grows out of his early fascination with Rimbaud's notion of an 'opéra fabuleux' (Pierre Brunel, 'Yves Bonnefoy. L'Évocation d'une voix', in *Yves Bonnefoy. Poésie, peinture, musique*, ed. Finck, pp. 23–32, p. 24). In *Les Mots comme le ciel*, Vernier writes that Bonnefoy's poetry is defined by 'cette croyance que le poème peut et doit maintenir envers et contre tout la résonance d'une voix, et que là, dans cette obstination, résident notre vérité et notre espoir' (Richard Vernier, *Yves Bonnefoy, ou les mots comme le ciel* (Paris: Éditions Place, 1985), p. 19).

Douve, poems bear the titles 'Une voix', 'Douve parle', and 'Voix basses et Phénix'; in *Hier régnant désert* too, 'Le Bruit des voix', 'Une voix', and 'La même voix toujours'. As explored in the first chapter of this book, the entire structure of *Dans le leurre du seuil* is voiced, organized around a series of apostrophes, addresses, and incantations. Throughout Bonnefoy's career, in many different collections of poetry, the title 'Une voix' recurs (much like the title 'Une pierre'). These poems appear at intervals, forming one long, temporally-dispersed series. Each one dramatizes a live and yet mysterious speaking voice, a disembodied and fleeting presence. As Dominique Rabaté writes in his essay on Bonnefoy's poetry, 'L'Appel des voix':

> La voix semble toujours se surprendre, s'entendre derrière un rideau (d'arbres, le plus souvent). Et c'est une voix proche et lointaine où se dit aussitôt la qualité même, l'essence pourrait-on dire, de la voix qui est le médium de la présence comme de l'absence, la marque du concret et de l'abstrait, le signe d'un corps qui ne peut pas être là tout à fait.[2]

This voice that recurs in Bonnefoy's poetry is a fugitive presence, one that hovers between presence and absence. In contrast to the fixity of the printed word, it foregrounds the fleetingness of utterance. It suggests the strangely atmospheric and contingent nature of the human body.

Of all Bonnefoy's collections of poetry, *Les Planches courbes* is perhaps the one that is traversed by the greatest number of voices. The opening lines of the first poem are: 'Rauques étaient les voix / Des rainettes le soir' (PC, 11).[3] Later, we read: '. . . La voix que j'écoute se perd, / Le bruit de fond qui est dans la nuit la recouvre' (PC, 75) or 'Ils me parlent. Quelle étrange chose que leurs voix!' (PC, 117). Across the collection, attention is constantly drawn towards the act of listening. One poem (cited in the opening paragraph of this book) opens with the words 'Passant, ce sont des mots. Mais plutôt que lire / Je veux que tu écoutes: cette frêle / Voix comme en ont les lettres que l'herbe mange' (PC, 40). The whole volume also reverberates with descriptions of sounds: 'le murmure' (PC, 40), '[le] roucoulement' (PC, 37), '[le] clapotement' (PC, 46), '[le] bruit de l'eau' (PC, 46), 'le tumulte' (PC, 77), 'un

[2] Dominique Rabaté, 'L'Appel des voix', in *Poétique et ontologie. Colloque international, Yves Bonnefoy*, ed. Serge Canadas, Mary-Ann Caws, and Michel Demangeat (Bordeaux: William Blake & Co, 2008), p. 232.

[3] In her essay 'Poétique de la voix rauque', Michèle Finck suggests that 'la voix rauque' is the 'clé de voûte de l'évolution de la tessiture de la voix poétique'. It is 'la matrice' of a poetry that seeks to open up language to a corporeal, material, and finite existence (Michèle Finck, 'Poétique de la voix rauque', in *Yves Bonnefoy. Poésie, peinture, musique*, ed. Finck, pp. 33–42, p. 33).

chant' (PC, 61), '[la] musique' (PC, 64), '[la] rumeur' (PC, 64). In a speech given in 2000, one year before the publication of *Les Planches courbes*, Bonnefoy discusses the role that sound plays in poetry, observing:

> c'est un fait [...] que cet aspect sonore du mot, cette dimension spécifiquement et uniquement sonore de la parole ont été peu étudiés, dans les travaux de critique littéraire, ou, disons plutôt, ne l'ont guère été d'une certaine façon qui va nous permettre d'accéder à une pensée nouvelle du rapport de l'être parlant au langage. (SPV, 181)

One can hear this corrective impulse, this concern for the 'aspect sonore du mot', all across the pages of *Les Planches courbes*, in the dramatization of voices, in the pleas to listen, and in the use of sound effects. Bonnefoy asks us to attune ourselves to the sonority of the human voice—a sonority that cannot be reduced to any kind of significance—and to open ourselves up to 'une pensée nouvelle du rapport de l'être parlant au langage'.

Etymologically, the word 'subject' (from the Latin 'subiectum') implies the existence of a base or foundation.[4] In the Cartesian tradition of the *Cogito*, the subject is conceived as a stable base—one which cannot be doubted—from which the world can be measured, known, and mastered.[5] Across the poems of 'La Voix lointaine', however, the experience of subjectivity is explored through voice, this most 'baseless' resonance. And so too are experiences of memory, emotion, thought, and desire. Many critics have observed that the voices that appear in Bonnefoy's early poetry are all dying voices, voices that destroy our illusion of possessing a fixed and stable self and reveal the groundlessness of existence. The voices that Bonnefoy presents in *Les Planches courbes*, however, are nascent voices. The same emphasis is still placed on mobility and groundlessness but voice is now associated with infancy, the emergence of human subjectivity, and material finitude's generative dynamics. There is increasing evidence of the influence of psychoanalysis too in *Les Planches courbes*: the long sequence of poems 'La Maison natale' explores early dreams and memories of a childhood home (PC, 81–98). 'La Voix lointaine' describes a distant voice that has

[4] 'The Latin, "subjecta materia", is a loan translation from the Greek "hypokeimene hyle" (Aristotle), literally, "that which lies beneath"' ('subject', in *Online Etymological Dictionary*, http://www.etymonline.com, accessed 10 July 2012).

[5] Critiquing Descartes's conception of the subject, Heidegger writes: 'According to the concept of its essence, *subiectum* is in a distinctive sense that which always lies before and so lies at the basis of something else whose ground it therefore is' (Martin Heidegger, *Nietzsche*, *I* (San Francisco: Harper and Row, 1987), pp. 96–7).

accompanied the poet since earliest infancy. This voice assumes different guises from one poem to the next but it is continually associated with processes of self-individuation and self-exploration, from the scene of childhood babble to the act of poetic voicing. Throughout the sequence, Bonnefoy investigates how a specifically aural sensibility develops *prior* to linguistic consciousness. Overturning the specular tropes that have governed linguistic conceptions of self-reflexivity, he invites us to reflect on the physical dynamics of resonance that allow language to come into being, the forces that gestate or 'birth' linguistic consciousness.

'La Voix lointaine' is also replete with echoes of other voices. The sequence reflects on meditations on voice and subjectivity by other writers, notably Paul Valéry and his long poem 'La Jeune Parque'. The correlative acts of voicing and listening dramatized in 'La Voix lointaine' resemble the vocative structure of Valéry's 'La Jeune Parque'. The final poem of the sequence directly addresses the voice that it has been pursuing and names it as 'la Parque'. Bonnefoy reworks and reinvents Valéry's monodialogue, however, challenging the way that Valéry presents human consciousness as a primarily self-reflexive structure in this poem. Certainly, as Valéry's Parca pursues echoes her of own consciousness, she uses a series of specular images: 'Je me voyais me voir, sinueuse, et dorais / De regards en regards, mes profondes forêts'.[6] In an interview, Bonnefoy observes that Valéry's Parca experiences its existence only through the play of reflections and replications. He criticizes the poem's 'intériorité [...] fantasmatique et sans vie' (IN, 124). Bonnefoy seeks to correct the sollipsistic nature of Valéry's poem about listening in 'La Voix lointaine'. In a similar manner, he also critiques the specular images that are central to Lacan's psychoanalytic writings. He considers Lacan's conception of the 'mirror phase', the moment when the infant perceives its own reflection and discovers its own distinction or individuality. Wary of how specular imagery has been reified in twentieth-century writings on human self-consciousness, Bonnefoy critiques the way it suggests that the limits of human experience are determined by language. He argues that this mode of thinking traps human consciousness in endless processes of self-representation that never open out onto the physical world. The subject turns over endless reflections that never lead it towards any kind of exterior or prior 'reality'. Life itself is presented as nothing other than an endless series of mimetic substitutions. Writing in dialogue with twentieth-century writers like Valéry and Lacan, Bonnefoy is subtly protesting against the

[6] Paul Valéry, *Œuvres*, I, pp. 96–111 (p. 97).

'textual turn' that Valéry's work inaugurates. He is resisting what he describes variously as 'le mirage d'une intelligence, d'une pensée, imaginées souveraines' (IN, 104); '[une] mainmise de l'intellect sur ce qui est bien plus important que lui, et qu'il faut donc protéger' (IN, 104); 'un vaste réseau de représentations anthropocentrées ou anthropomorphes' (IN, 116).[7]

In *À l'écoute*, Nancy also argues that a visual conception of human subjectivity is one that encourages us to perceive ourselves as a reflected object, a solid and appropriable 'self'. Vision is, he writes, 'tendanciellement mimétique': 'selon le regard, le sujet se renvoie à lui-même comme objet'.[8] He proposes that sound, on the other hand, is 'tendanciellement méthexique', that it is 'dans l'ordre de la participation, du partage, ou de la contagion' (AE, 27). The aural sense attunes us to a more primary experience of self-relation, one that has not yet been concretized or objectified by the structures of linguistic perception. Nancy writes: 'Selon l'écoute, c'est en quelque sorte en lui-même que le sujet se renvoie ou s'envoie' (AE, 26). The listening subject is sent outwards and returns to itself in an endless series of reverberations: it experiences itself as 'le rapport en soi', 'la résonance d'un renvoi' (AE, 30). Our subjectivity loops back and forth between the body's 'caverne sonore' to the surfaces and recesses of the material world (AE, 73). The term 'renvoi', as Charlotte Mandell notes in the preface to her translation of *À l'écoute*, means 'return, send back, repeat, a musical refrain, refer, allude back'.[9] The term suggests reflection, repetition, and referral but also invites us to think of these processes in the manner of a musical refrain. Like Bonnefoy, Nancy encourages us to conceive of subjectivity as the very dynamic of reverberation that endlessly relays us back and forth, as we simultaneously echo ourselves and the world, and reverberate between many different experiences of sense.

'À l'écoute': Listening to a Distant Voice

'La Voix lointaine' begins suspensefully. The poet is on tenterhooks, trying to grasp a distant and intermittent voice. As he strains to hear it, he reaches

[7] Writing against *La Jeune Parque*, Bonnefoy is also—we should not forget—writing *for* the other side of Valéry's poetry, the exteriority of 'Le Cimitière marin' that he so cherishes, the Valéry who produces, in 'Fragments de Narcisse', one of Bonnefoy's favourite lines of verse, 'La voix des sources change, et me parle du soir' (IN, 113).

[8] Jean-Luc Nancy, *À l'écoute* (Paris: Galilée, 2002), p. 26, p. 27. All subsequent references will appear within the text, using the abbreviation AE.

[9] Charlotte Mandell, 'Translator's Note', in Jean-Luc Nancy, *On Listening* (New York: Fordham University Press, 2007), p. xi.

back towards the past. He remembers scenes in his childhood in which this voice spoke to him. As in so many of Bonnefoy's sequences of poems ('L'Été de nuit' in *Pierre écrite* or 'Le Haut du monde' in *Ce qui fut sans lumière*), the first poem is quasi-mythical. An idyllic voice calls out to the child and draws him towards a luminous threshold. At the end of the poem, this idyllic voice reveals itself to be a cruel lure. It awakens desires within the child that condemn him to lifelong experiences of loss, exile, and suffering. And so, the sequence opens with a kind of parable that depicts a 'primal scene' in the child's aural consciousness. In the two poems that follow, however, this mythic story is immediately counterpointed with two very different scenes: one depicts the gestation of a child's voice as it babbles, wandering 'entre voix et langage' (PC, 58); the other shows us the emergence of the adult's poetic voice as he experiments with the interplay of sound and sense. The liminal imagery that dominated the first poem is equally prevalent in these two poems, but the threshold that is evoked is no longer depicted in visual terms: it flickers or dances through the human voice itself. The poet dramatizes a scene of listening and voicing out of which knowledge and cognizance gradually appear. There is no irrevocable 'fall' as the child crosses a fatal threshold and finds itself cut off from the origin. The emphasis is placed not on loss but on emergence, not on severance but on the interplay of forces.

'La Voix lointaine' begins *in medias res*, like so many of Bonnefoy's poems. The opening decasyllables show us the poet in pursuit of a mysterious voice: 'Je l'écoutais, puis j'ai craint de ne plus / L'entendre, qui me parle ou qui se parle' (PC, 57). These energetic opening lines contain five verbs and no nouns. They circle around an uncertain presence that remains unidentified. Its presence is designated only by the object pronoun 'la' and even this is elided, concealing its grammatical gender. The poet was listening to it but wasn't sure if he would ever accede to it. He didn't know if the voice was addressing him directly or talking to itself, if he was its chosen recipient or just an intrusive eavesdropper. All these equivocations give rise to structural repetitions: '[j]e l'écoutais', '[l]'entendre', 'qui me parle', 'qui se parle'. A labial alliteration runs from 'puis', to 'parle', to 'plus' and an internal rhyme on 'puis', 'qui', and 'qui' is later picked up in 'nuit'. It is as if the poet is using soundplay to try to find some way back towards this voice.

Apostrophizing this voice directly in the third line, the poet associates it with childhood: 'Voix lointaine, un enfant qui joue sur la route, / Mais la nuit est tombée, quelqu'un appelle' (PC, 57). There is a vague aura of menace as the child plays late into the evening, out on the dark road. This is juxtaposed with the apparently domestic and familiar voice that calls out to the child, drawing him back towards a luminous threshold. The words 'quelqu'un appelle' run into the stanzaic break in an enjambment, resonating outwards. This voice calls out there, where the light shines, where the door squeaks as it opens wide on its hinges: 'Là où la lampe brille, où la porte grince / En s'ouvrant davantage' (PC, 57). All these images open, shine, or resonate outwards, like beacons guiding the child home. And the musicality of the lines too functions as a kind of siren song. The soft rounded vowel [u], that sounded previously in 'écoutais', 'ou', 'joue', 'route', sounds out again in 'où', 'où', and 's'ouvrant'. The laterals of 'quelqu'un appelle' are taken up mellifluously in 'Là où la lampe brille, où la'. They sing bitter-sweetly of a call, an appeal, a light, that is nonetheless always 'là', 'là', 'là'. As the voice calls the child back, a series of vibrant [ʀ]s—echoed in the words 'rayon' and 'ombre'—roll out from the back of the speaker's throat: 'Rentre, chuchote-t-on, rentre, il est tard' (PC, 57).

As the voice calls us back, the poem cultivates an aura of suspense. Prosodically too, the reader hesitates over whether to observe the rhythms of conventional prosody or to read these lines spontaneously and vernacularly. The poem opens with two decasyllables, an alexandrine, and a decasyllable, signalling to the reader from the outset that we have 'rights of expectation'. Given the emphasis that the poem places on voicing, it also seems particularly appropriate to articulate the *e atone*. And yet, as we move into the second stanza, we oscillate between decasyllables and hendecasyllables. The poet keeps the rules of traditional prosody in play whilst also subverting them in a Verlainian manner, alternating between *le pair* and *l'impair*. We discern familiar rhythms constantly but we can never count on their steady return. The use of the *impair* introduces an element of improvisation into the experience of reading. As Clive Scott writes in *The Poetic of French Verse*, rhythm becomes 'a *devinette*' as 'the reader strains to pick out the rhythmical contours, to hear a design, to discover an authority, both formal and authorial. The poem becomes a space occupied by many rhythms half-realised, by structural divisions whose status is never resolved'.[10] Bonnefoy's reader is on the *qui vive*, listening out and picking her way forward tentatively. Like the poet, we too are straining to discern some form of meaningful pattern, to discover the contours of this hesitant voicing.

As the distant voice calls the child back towards a threshold, the lines run into a series of enjambments. The punctuation breaks (a comma and a

[10] Clive Scott, *The Poetics of French Verse. Studies in Reading* (Oxford: Clarendon Press, 1998), p. 24.

semi-colon) fall at the medial caesura. And so, the central caesura assumes a greater prominence. It starts to feel emblematic of the very threshold towards which we are being drawn:

quelqu'un appelle
Là où la lampe brille, | où la porte grince
En s'ouvrant davantage; | et ce rayon
Recolore le sable | où dansait une ombre.

(PC, 57)

The *e atone* sounds out at times, 'Là où la lampe brille, | où la porte grince', but more often it goes unsounded, at the medial caesura and line ends, after 'appelle', 'brille', 'grince', 'davantage', 'sable', and 'ombre'. As the voice, rich with promise, calls out to the child, the *e atone*, this instance of pure voicing, is repeatedly annulled.[11] We feel its cancellation all the more acutely because of the use of final consonant combinations that seem to naturally elicit a phonated [ə]: '-ille', '-ince', '-able', '-ombre', and even '-age'. There's perhaps a subtle warning here that this voice that promises us accession to an origin is more volatile and ungraspable than it first appears. It's also possible that, because of the use of so many of the rich final consonant combinations, the *e atone* still ends up being partially uttered by the reader. In this case, its decasyllables start to feel like hendecasyllables or even alexandrines. The poem's prosodic contours start to feel more unstable. Whatever reading we adopt, it's clear that we have to make decisions about how to negotiate the presence or absence of the *e atone*. Its shadowy phonetic presence haunts the poem, rather like the voice haunts the child.

This uncertainty prepares the reader for the stark reversal that occurs in the final stanza of the poem. By setting the final stanza in parentheses, Bonnefoy signals a change of tone. He shifts back into the present tense and adopts a detached and critical perspective: '(Rentre, a-t-on chuchoté, et je n'ai su / Qui appelait ainsi, du fond des âges [...])' (PC, 57). The poet admits that he did not know who called. The voice that we might have assumed to be a parental figure came 'du fond des âges'. The idyll turns towards nightmare and the poem ends with the words '([...] Quelle marâtre, sans mémoire ni visage, / Quel mal souffert avant même de naître)' (PC, 57). The 'marâtre' is

[11] Of this elided 'e', Clive Scott writes, 'If the articulated e is a real event in regular French verse, its cancelling by elision [...] is no less so. The elided e is not an enunciation which never existed in our consciousness but rather an enunciation which we thrust away, which is swallowed into the following vowel' (Clive Scott, *A Question of Syllables* (Cambridge: Cambridge University Press, 1986), p. 105).

not the true mother but the false replacement, the cruel stepmother of fairy tales.[12] The musicality of the poem now assumes a sinister aspect. The nasal of the negative—'je n'ai su'—permeates the description of this maternal figure: '*m*arâtre', 'sa*n*s *m*é*m*oire ni visage', a '*m*al souffert avant *m*ê*m*e de *n*aître'. She is presented as a relentlessly destructive force, a negativity that precedes even birth. She is the voice that calls us homewards but that leaves us endlessly suspended, restlessly searching for what we can never achieve. Provoking a desire that is always disappointed, she inflicts an endless suffering.

The first poem of 'La Voix lointaine' describes how this voice calls the child homewards, towards a place of plenitude and satisfaction. We are reminded of the traditional association between the human voice and the promise of spontaneous and unmediated state of self-presence, a form of pure interiority. This is the myth that Derrida deconstructs in *La Voix et le phénomène*.[13] The voice promises a return to a natural centre or origin but this desire is never sated. The poet uncovers nothing but duplicity and deception, the doubling of *mère/marâtre*. We are subtly reminded of Lacan's account of the 'mirror phase': the child's loss of its sense of unity with the '(m)other' as it acquires language and enters the symbolic. Lacan suggests that the child who learns to recognize the reflected or represented image never returns to the satisfaction and plenitude of earliest infancy. Elizabeth Grosz writes: 'From this time on, lack, gap, splitting will be its mode of being.'[14] In an interview with Paul de Sinéty in 1994, Bonnefoy describes this fall and suggests that the pain inflicted is all the greater because of 'la censure qui interdit à l'enfant de comprendre la déception qu'il y a dans son attachement à sa mère, censure d'autant plus grand que l'attachement a été plus grand et d'autant plus agitant qu'il sait que sa mère fut la première victime de l'aliénation dont il hérite' (IN, 243). The mother who shares a

[12] It seems fair to suggest that Bonnefoy uses the image of the 'mâratre' here in a lucid and self-critical way, seeking to expose how idealized modes of thought can lead to vitriolic and misogynist ones. In his interview with Serge Bourjea in 2006, he critiques the way that late nineteenth-century French male poets, particularly Valéry and Mallarmé, codify the female voice as 'other'. He suggests that in male-dominated 'sociétés du concept, de la loi', females are 'écartées [...] des systèmes de significations' (IN, 119). He argues that Valéry's and Mallarmé's idealization of the 'otherness' of the female voice is symptomatic of society's repression of non-conceptual modes of experience. He observes: 'le rapport non-conceptualisé à la réalité, l'intuition poétique, est refoulé dans des aspects du comportement social que l'on dira féminins parce qu'on les voit plus facilement chez ces femmes écartées de beaucoup des autres' (IN, 119).

[13] Jacques Derrida, *La Voix et le phénomène* (Paris: Presses Universitaires de France, 1967).

[14] Elizabeth Grosz, *Jacques Lacan. A Feminist Introduction* (London, New York: Routledge, 1990), p. 35.

state of pre-linguistic oneness with the child teaches the child language. And she too suffered this same process of estrangement in the arms of her own mother. These feelings of attachment and estrangement, love and betrayal resonate through 'La Voix lointaine I'. This is perhaps the suffering that is passed down, from generation to generation, 'du fond des âges', in the first poem of the sequence. Voice is the key agent of enrapture and disillusionment here. It promises a return to an origin and bequeaths nothing but exile.

The second poem of the sequence associates this voice firmly with childhood once again. The poet observes: 'Je ne savais rien d'elle, sinon l'enfance' (PC, 58). The poet presents the voice as an acousmatic presence that drifts towards him from some other place. It is a musical presence, a song, that has been with him since childhood. The poet describes it as his 'bien unique', as all that is good or worthy in his existence. In the second stanza, as the poet attempts to describe this voice, he wavers between positive and negative constructions: 'Elle chantait, si c'est chanter, mais non'. The poet hesitates between one possibility and another and then suggests that the voice itself is this vacillating motion: 'C'était plutôt entre voix et langage / Une façon de laisser la parole / Errer, comme à l'avant incertain de soi' (PC, 58). 'Errer' is to go 'd'un côté et de l'autre sans but ni direction précise'.[15] Between voice and language, sound and sense, this voice wanders. It moves 'à l'avant incertain de soi'. Its meandering motion has not yet concretized as any kind of 'soi', any kind of stable object or linguistic representation. Always moving 'entre voix et langage', it remains an indeterminate and prospective force.

In the next stanza, sound prevails: 'Et parfois ce n'étaient pas même des mots, / Rien que le son dont des mots veulent naître.' A series of monosyllables and a steady assonance on [o] dominate. These sounds fall away at the end of the line as the structures of language 'veulent naître'. The poet describes this burgeoning murmur as 'Le son d'autant d'ombre que de lumière, / Ni déjà la musique ni plus le bruit' (PC, 58). This voice wavers between shadow and light, music and noise. If we observe a *césure enjambante* in these final lines, reading them as 5 + 5, 6 + 5, the final *e atone* of both 'ombre' and 'musique' is pushed into the next measure and sounded, evoking the melting motion by which oppositions start to intermingle: 'Le son d'autant d'om|bre que de lumière, / Ni déjà la musi|que ni plus le bruit'. The movement between *le pair* to *l'impair* from one line to the next also enacts the

[15] 'Errer' in *Centre national de ressources textuelles et lexicales*, http://www.cnrtl.fr, accessed 11 July 2017.

vacillating motion. We hear the same gentle oscillation between closure and flux, form and formlessness. The liminality that was so central to the first poem—a voice calling a child towards a threshold—is rearticulated in a very different way here. The motif of the threshold recurs but it is the liminality of the voice that wanders *between* sound and sense that is stressed here. And just as the first poem depicted a seminal childhood scene of awakening or discovery, it's possible to read this poem as an account of childhood babble. This semi-choate voice mixes the patterns of language with raw sounds. We are reminded of an infant who, 'à l'avant de soi', before having mastered the conceptual structures of language, experiments with the resonance of voice, allowing it to wander between sound and sense. If Bonnefoy is dramatizing a scene of childhood awakening and discovery here, he is depicting one that occurs prior to the act of representation, prior to the doubling or splitting of the subject. Strikingly, the adult poet describes this meandering voice as his 'seul bien', as an inherently life-giving or generative force. He evokes what Nancy describes in 'Vox Clamans in deserto' as 'une précession de la parole, une parole infante qui se fait entendre en-deçà de tout parler, jusque dans le parler lui-même' (PP, 21). Nancy suggests that this voice precedes but also engenders language; it coaxes linguistic consciousness and self-reflexivity into being. But it is a gestative force that is always more primary than the structures of signification. Nancy adds: 'car si elle [la voix] est infiniment plus archaïque que lui [le parler], en revanche il n'y a pas de parole qui ne se fasse entendre par une voix' (PP, 21).

The third poem of the sequence describes how, throughout his entire adult life, the poet has sought to preserve this 'naive' voice and to keep it with him. 'La Voix lointaine III' begins with the words 'Et je l'aimais comme j'aime ce son / Au creux duquel rajeunirait le monde' (PC, 59). The standard formulation 'au cœur de' becomes '[a]u creux de'. This voice's capacity for rejuvenation comes not from some centre or base but from the very hollowness of its resonance. The next lines describe its force of renewal by gently rocking between oppositions once again, from one hemistich to another: 'Ce son qui réunit quand les mots divisent, / Ce beau commencement quand tout finit' (PC, 59). Uniting what words divide, opening up what language concludes, voice is presented as a force that always starts again, that always opens outwards. In the second stanza, the poet presents it as a rhythm: 'Syllabe brève puis syllabe longue' (PC, 59). The particular rhythm that he evokes here is the iamb, the canonical rhythm of Anglophone poetry. As he does so, he allows an articulated 'e' to fall at each word-end in this line (but one, 'puis'), prolonging the preceding syllable. The word 'puis' falls just before the medial caesura so it too carries a stress. And so, in this French decasyllable, we hear a rhythm that resembles the alternately stressed and unstressed feet of the iamb: 'Sy-*lla*-be *brè*-ve *puis* sy-*lla*-be *lon*-gue'. In the next lines, Bonnefoy writes: 'Hésitation de l'iambe, qui voudrait / Franchir le pas du souffle qui espère / Et accéder à ce qui signifie' (PC, 59). Presenting the iamb as a hesitating motion, the poet suggests that its long syllable leaps over the short one, expressing our longing for meaning. As we move into the next lines, this aspirational force is again suggested by the rhythm of the next two decasyllables (4 + 6). The second hemistich's longer, outward thrust suggests the force of desire: 'Franchir le pas | du souffle qui espère / Et accéder | à ce qui signifie.'

Bonnefoy suggests that the iamb is particularly effective at making us feel the tremulous dance that occurs between sound and sense in the line of poetic verse. We hear the echo of Valéry's definition of poetry as 'cette hésitation prolongée entre le son et le sens'.[16] Bonnefoy suggests that—to quote Giorgio Agamben's gloss on Valéry's phrase—'the poem tenaciously lingers and sustains itself in the tension and difference between sound and sense'.[17] Certainly, in the essay 'La Parole poétique', published in 2000, Bonnefoy argues that there are '[d]eux faces donc dans le mot: la notion qui porte la signification, le concept, et le son qui s'ouvre sur la présence' (SPV, 183). He affirms that rhythm emerges when the poet experiments with the materiality of language: 'Qu'il y ait rythme, du fait du vers, rythme qui naît de la matérialité du son et nullement de son sens, et le son sera entendu' (SPV, 201). Bonnefoy suggests that rhythm makes us hear the sound of the phrase in a way that rivals and resists its semantic function: '[le son] désaffecte chez le lecteur les points de vue conceptuels, il conteste leur prétention à monopoliser l'approche de ce qui est' (SPV, 201–2). The poet's experimentation with rhythm thus works against the structures of conceptual thought and seeks to use language to find another means of approaching 'ce qui est'.

The final stanza of 'La Voix lointaine III' once again depicts the interplay of sound and sense that the poem cultivates as the interaction of shadow

[16] Valéry writes: 'Entre la Voix et la Pensée, entre la Pensée et la voix, entre la Présence et l'Absence, oscille le pendule poétique' (Valéry, *Œuvres*, I, p. 1333). Valéry, like Bonnefoy, treats sound and sense as two separate variables. He describes poetry as 'le pendule poétique', for it oscillates 'entre deux points symétriques'. It oscillates between 'les caractères sensibles du langage, le son, le rythme, les accents, le timbre, le mouvement' and 'toutes les valeurs significatives, les images, les idées' (Valéry, *Œuvres*, I, p. 1333).

[17] Agamben, *The End of the Poem*, p. 112.

and light. But now Bonnefoy personifies these forces. The aspirational lurch of the iamb is depicted as a desirous light that reaches outwards:

> Telle cette lumière dans l'esprit
> Qui brille quand on quitte, de nuit, sa chambre,
> Une lampe cachée contre son cœur,
> Pour retrouver une autre ombre dansante.
>
> (PC, 59)

Bonnefoy describes the rhythm's reaching motion in romantic terms here, as if the voice embarks on an amorous or erotic adventure. The 'esprit' goes out to dance with a force that remains dark and elusive. This striking final image is not simply a fanciful way of evoking the voice's hesitant dance. Bonnefoy uses this passionate image to insist that rhythm is not merely ornamentation but that it is a psychological and sensual journey in its own right. It is the very process by which linguistic consciousness, 'l'esprit / Qui brille', is exposed to the obscure material and sensual forces. Language dances with all that exceeds and evades it. In *A Voice and Nothing More*, Mladen Dolar argues that the resonance of the human voice allows us to hear two mechanisms 'in one and the same place [...], one which strives toward meaning and understanding, and on the way obfuscates the voice (that which is not the matter of understanding), and on the other hand a mechanism which has nothing to do with meaning but, rather, with enjoyment'.[18] Dolar suggests that these two mechanisms are the rival psychoanalytic dimensions of desire and drive. In Bonnefoy's poem, the 'esprit' is sent out to dance with its shadow. Its quest is presented as a passionate or even compulsive one. The intellect engages in a sensual and even erotic process of discovery. And if the scene in which the intellect confronts its other, or desire confronts drive, is so highly charged, it is perhaps because it recalls the scene in infancy in which our voices wandered between sound and sense, 'à l'avant de soi'.

In the first poem of 'La Voix lointaine', Bonnefoy dramatizes a voice that seems to promise us access to an origin, a place of plentitude. The child who pursues the voice is cast out into a negative world. The light and satisfaction that he seeks are endlessly displaced and decentred. At the outset of the sequence, we're presented with a myth or parable. It is pregnant with Lacanian psychoanalytic ideas about the child's relationship to the mother's

[18] Mladen Dolar, *A Voice and Nothing More* (Cambridge, MA: MIT Press, 2006), pp. 71–2.

voice, the entry into language, and the development of a sense of one's own distinct identity. It is a story of oneness and severance, fusion and loss. This fall narrative that it presents is juxtaposed, however, with a very different experience of the voice in the second and third poems of the sequence. Bonnefoy evokes a childhood, babbling voice that gradually enters into contact with language in 'La Voix lointaine II'. This voice slips in and out of speech; it luxuriates in its own resonance, occasionally coaxing these sounds towards some form of coherent semantic form. And yet, it always remains 'upstream' of language, just short of or in advance of coherent linguistic structures of meaning and identity, 'à l'avant de soi'. And whilst the voice is firmly associated with infancy, Bonnefoy insists it remains with him throughout his entire adult life. The poet can access this 'précession de la parole' and bring it to life by experimenting with the rhythms of language. Overturning the fall narrative of 'La Voix lointaine I', Bonnefoy presents a scene of voicing that keeps linguistic consciousness in steady contact with other physical and sensual forces. He refuses to present the acquisition of language as a scene of representation, duplication, division, and loss. He rejects the discourse of severance that is so central to Lacanian psychoanalysis. Instead, Bonnefoy dramatizes a babbling voice in which there is continual contact and interaction between sound and sense. The emphasis is placed not on loss but on gestation. The voice's spatio-temporal dance, its hesitant motion, is presented as a nurturing force, an inherently desirous or erotic force that keeps all things interacting with others. Bonnefoy thus insists that our entry into the symbolic is not a definitive moment of severance from the physical world. More primary and more crucial than the experience of representation is resonance's gradual and gestational force. It coaxes linguistic consciousness, and indeed all forms of existence, into being. And whilst it precedes and exceeds linguistic consciousness, Bonnefoy insists that we, as linguistic beings, never cease to have access to it. We can always feel it at work, just prior to language, within our own voices.

The Subject of Division and Lack

The early poems of 'La Voix lointaine' suggest that the sonority and rhythm of the human voice is a rejuvenating force. In the central poems of the sequence, this rhythmic imagery is interrupted by a series of striking visual images. The poet-narrator describes a painful memory that repeatedly returns to him. In this instance, a visual image imposes itself; it rises up forcibly and imprints itself upon his consciousness. In the fifth poem of the sequence, the voice to which the poet has been listening comes forwards and sings to him. The poet cites her song in full and it too presents a long series of visual images. The voice interrogates these images, attempting to read them as if they are signs. The song is remarkably simple and repetitive, almost like a nursery rhyme, but it reflects on the way that human consciousness interrogates traces or reflections of its existence. It explores the iterable nature of signs in particular, the way they appear in the absence of the one who made or inscribed them. It suggests that those who seek to understand their existence by simply studying these signs find themselves confronting an absence at the heart of the human condition. When the subject looks for itself, it encounters nothing but a gap and a loss. Language's structures of diffentiation and deferral cause us to experience our own subjectivity according to a logic of absence and lack.

The first quatrain of 'La Voix lointaine IV' opens with the words 'Et la vie a passé, mais te garda / Vive mon illusion' (PC, 60). His hope and desire stubbornly keep this voice alive: 'de ces mains savantes / Qui trient parmi les souvenirs, qui en recousent / Presque invisiblement les déchirures' (PC, 60). The voice is presented as a nourishing presence here, one that cares for the poet in ways that exceed his understanding. It helps the poet to sift through the difficult or damaged parts of the human consciousness. Its rhythm is presented as a stitching or a knitting motion that heals wounds. As we move into the second quatrain, the poet points to one striking exception. The word 'Sauf' stands in stark isolation: 'Sauf: que faire de ce lambeau d'étoffe rouge?' (PC, 60). The image of red fabric impresses itself forcibly. The stanza continues: 'On le trouve dans sa mémoire quand on déplace / Les années, les images; et, brusques, des larmes / Montent' (PC, 60). The first enjambment suggests the sifting motion, the second the more brusque and unexpected motion by which tears rise. The poet is powerless in the face of this feeling and the stanza ends, 'et l'on se tait dans ses mots d'autrefois' (PC, 60). The poet falls silent but hears *her* past words. His defencelessness and speechlessness when faced with 'ses mots' is suggested by the final end-stopped line.

The image of red fabric seems to be a substitutive image for an experience that is too painful to be voiced. Images of red garments and fabrics recur throughout Bonnefoy's poetry. Naughton suggests that they are associated with the mother and links them to the red garments of the maternal figure in Poussin's *Moïse sauvé des eaux*.[19] Whatever interpretation we might give it, it is clear that here the image rises up to express something that the poet cannot articulate in other terms. Both the image and 'ses mots' are representations that the poet cannot move beyond. Beneath them, there seems to be nothing but an absolute alterity, an unconfrontable emotion. The poet uses the rhetorical question, 'que faire de ce lambeau d'étoffe rouge?', to suggest his own impotence when faced with such traces. We are reminded of the reference that the poet makes to a difficult memory of his father, an image of them playing cards together when he was a child, in the sequence 'La Maison natale'. Bonnefoy writes: 'J'aurai barré / Cent fois ces mots partout, en vers, en prose, / Mais je ne puis / Faire qu'ils ne remontent dans ma parole' (PC, 91).

These images and words rise up within the poet countless times. They cannot be ignored but they also cannot be articulated, nor absorbed into the fabric of the work, no matter how many times the poet tries. The poet reflects on what he hoped to achieve through the act of writing in the final stanza of 'La Voix lointaine IV': 'Parler, presque chanter, avoir rêvé / De plus même que la musique' (PC, 60). The enjambment 'avoir rêvé / De plus' suggests the poet's desire to articulate something more than speech or music. He seeks to cultivate a voice that almost sings, but not quite. Yet, in spite of his ambitions, he suddenly becomes like a child once again and lapses into silence and inarticulacy. The poem ends with the words 'puis se taire / Comme l'enfant qu'envahit le chagrin / Et qui se mord la lèvre, et se détourne' (PC, 60). The sonority of language cannot be used to sing and to nurse this emotion. The poet merely bites his lip and turns away. The feeling retreats behind a series of substitutive images that loom large in the poet's consciousness. These forms recur endlessly and, yet, they leave the poet suspended on an impossible threshold. As he confronts his own feelings, he faces an unmasterable alterity.[20]

The next poem of the sequence stages a striking departure. The voice sings to the poet and he reports the words of her song. The singer interrogates a series of traces in the sand, repeatedly asking who it is that made these marks. We encounter the Robinson-Crusoe-style figure that appears in Valéry's

[19] 'In Poussin's painting of 1647, [...] Pharoah's daughter is dressed in the red robes Bonnefoy uses to evoke feminine presence in poems from *Pierre écrite* onward' (Naughton, *The Poetics of Yves Bonnefoy*, p. 157).

[20] We are reminded of Freud's early conception of the 'drives' down into which, Malcom Bowie writes, Freud did not want 'speech, or even a ghostly premonition of speech, to penetrate' (Malcolm Bowie, *Lacan* (London: Fontana Press, 1991), p. 52).

poetry: the one who, stranded alone on a desert island, questions the footprint that it finds in the sand.[21] The images and words that haunted the poet's consciousness in 'La Voix lointaine IV'—'ce lambeau d'étoffe rouge', 'ses mots'—seem to have triggered this meditation on traces and signs. The first quatrain reads:

> Elle chantait, mais comme se parlant:
> Qui a tiré sa barque sur la rive,
> Qui a posé sa rame sur le sable,
> Qui est passé, que nous ne savons pas?
>
> (PC, 61)

The voice that sings appears to be talking to herself. The poet seems to have stumbled upon some kind of introspective murmuring, a sollipsistic conversation that was not directed to him. The song scours the traces of an event on the sand—an arrival, a landfall—that is now past. The voice repeatedly seeks a figure that has moved onwards. As the poem progresses, the traces increase in complexity. The tracks of the boat and oars are followed by a footprint in the sand, then an iridescent shimmer on the surface of the water. The song culminates, at the end of the second quatrain, with the question 'Qui dessina ce visage d'enfant?' (PC, 61). This drawing of another human face is a different kind of sign from the others. It is an intentional marking, perhaps a parent's drawing of its own child's face, or a child's representation of its own reflection. Each of these traces prompts the same question, 'Qui…?', as the voice continually seeks to identify the 'other' who made these marks. This 'other' never manifests itself and the questions keep coming.

The poet's voice intercedes again at the start of the final quatrain: 'C'était un chant de rien que quelques notes, / Qui a voulu le chant dans la parole?' (PC, 61). It is as if the voice's style of questioning has proved infectious. The poet now scrutinizes the song in precisely the same way that the voice scrutinized the traces in the sand. He interrogates this song that drifts towards him but that has no discernible origin. Its 'quelques notes' are now also perceived markers of absence, traces of some other presence. The poet does not ask who sang this song, however, but who *willed* that there be song in the first place? 'Qui a voulu le chant dans la parole?' This question has clear metaphysical overtones: it interrogates the origins of song itself. And

[21] See Valéry, 'Robinson', in *Œuvres*, I, pp. 411–21 (p. 415).

this final question causes us to perceive all the previous ones in a new light. Bonnefoy suggests that the voice's mode of enquiry—one focused on the substitutive nature of the sign—is driven by a metaphysical impulse. The voice that scours these traces always goes in search of an origin, an exterior agent. And yet, where it seeks presence, it encounters only alterity. The origin it seeks reveals itself to be endlessly dispersed and deferred. And so, knowledge and identity are perceived in purely negative terms. The final two lines of the poem offer a stern rebuke to this mode of questioning: '– Nul n'a voulu, nul n'est venu ni parle, / Nul s'est passé, que nous *ne sûmes pas*' [my emphasis] (PC, 61). The poet insists that the only world is the world we know. In other words, the 'other' that we perceive is produced by language itself. It is the effect of language's own doubling and substitutive mechanism. When consciousness sits in isolation, as it does in Valéry's 'La Jeune Parque' and 'Robinson', questioning nothing but its own structures, it is relayed from trace to trace endlessly. The human subject can grasp nothing other than an endless series of traces, behind which no authentic or originary presence is discovered. The subject seeks itself everywhere in language and it encounters nothing but the 'other'. It is troubled by the way that its own existence is continually doubled, by the alterity that haunts its scene of self-perception. It does not find the full self-knowledge or self-identity that it seeks—the original agent behind the trace—but only difference, deferral, alterity, and lack.

Bonnefoy presents this series of questions about the traces in the sand as a circular song, as if to suggest that this is an endless refrain, one that humanity repeats on loop. The song explores how the very structure of the linguistic sign leads us to expect *more* from material existence. We endlessly scour the physical world for signs, trying to access some hidden origin or agent. And as these signs never grant us access to an origin or agent, everything seems to be characterized by lack. Behind all things, there yawns an absence, a distance. Our world seems to be characterized by its essential otherness. The song is very simple in structure but it is endlessly allusive. We can hear echoes of Valéry's self-reflexive monodialogues but also of Derrida's conception of the 'trace' or of Lacan's notion that the human unconscious is 'structuré comme un langage'. For Lacan, unconscious experience slips away from us down a chain of signifiers in an endless chain of displacements and substitutions.[22] The song contains endless possible

[22] Jacques Lacan, *Les Quatre concepts fondamentaux de la psychanalyse* (Paris: Seuil, 1973), p. 23.

allusions to various different strands of post-structuralist thought, but they all play very lightly through the text. The reader is placed in a very similar situation to the voice who scours the marks on the sand: we perceive a series of allusive traces that have no clear centre or origin. And it is precisely this conception of the 'text' that Bonnefoy is critiquing here. He strenuously resists the way that twentieth-century thinkers have reified language's substitutive play to the point of perceiving it as a fundamental or originary operation. We perceive the world only according to the doublings and displacements of our linguistic systems. And in doing so, we reduce all that exceeds and evades these systems to the status of other.

The next poem protests that the negative force that is at the 'origin' of existence is nothing other than material finitude itself. It proposes that its structure of exposition is not a series of reflections that steadily 'other' our existence. On the contrary, finitude opens us up physically and exposes us to the world, allowing us to *know* the world in these terms. 'La Voix lointaine VI' describes a scene of offering, an expectant gesture that awaits an answer or a resolution, like the questions posed in the previous poem. No answer comes. The poem opens with the words 'Et nul n'a bu au verre que je pose / Ni pris du fruit qui était devant moi' (PC, 62). Bonnefoy invites us to perceive the way that the gesture itself—its expectations—engenders a sense of lack. The poem continues: 'Un peu de vent fait remuer la poussière / D'herbes sèches, de graines, sur le chemin' (PC, 62). Bonnefoy uses a natural and seasonal imagery to suggest the dynamism of physical existence, its force of destruction and renewal. Then, in the next stanza, a radiant imagery is used to explore how these dynamics overtake the linguistic subject: 'L'été: un éblouissement comme est la neige, / Celle qui vient légère et ne dure pas' (PC, 62). The subject is caught up in changing seasons and weathers, in material 'economies' that far exceed its linguistic consciousness. The second quatrain ends with the words 'Et rien de nous n'en trouble la lumière / D'eau qui s'est condensée puis s'évapore' (PC, 62). Bonnefoy suggests that we have no control or mastery over the changing weather or the movement of the light. We are contained within or carried by these processes, like the leaves and seeds carried by the wind. Our exposure to their negativity does not come as a source of anxiety in this poem. The poet no longer feels distanced from the physical world as he did in the previous poem but is overcome by a profound sense of peace: 'D'où la sérénité, même l'allégresse / De ces instants qui savent que n'est rien' (PC, 62). The poet realizes that nothing *is*. Nothing stands in full self-presence and nothing is given to us completely for our comprehension. Strikingly, the subject of the verb 'savoir' is not a human being here but is 'ces instants'. These fleeting moments *know* that nothing is. Knowledge is not presented as something that the linguistic subject seeks and possesses here. Knowing is an activity that is continually voided or negated, that refuses to yield any object or essence. And this refusal liberates the subject, triggering an immense sensation of serenity and happiness. The sense of loss and alterity that pervaded the previous poem falls away. The subject realizes that each of its acts is ungrounded and exposed, opened up to the world's endless processes of dispersal and renewal. Every human gesture is perceived as just another ephemeral physical act. The poem thus ends with the words 'Flocon la main qui avait pris le verre, / Autres flocons l'été, le ciel, les souvenirs' (PC, 62). Human existence is not perceived to unfold at a distance from material reality but to be an intimate part of it. The emphasis is no longer placed on the substitive presence of the image—or on reflection, doubling, and splitting—but on the gesture by which existence opens through us. This dynamic overtakes the poet, immersing him in a spacious and dynamic physical world. It makes him feel the common structure of the world's exposition. All physical things are exposed in the same way: 'Flocon la main qui avait pris le verre, / Autres flocons l'été, le ciel, les souvenirs'.

The central poems of 'La Voix lointaine' foreground images of visual and linguistic signs. They show us a subject that seeks to understand itself and the world self-reflexively, by interrogating a series of representations. These structures never lead the subject back to an appropriable and knowable 'self' but leave it scouring an endless chain of substitutions. In 'La Voix lointaine IV', the subject turns over the image of the scrap of red fabric and nurses 'ses mots', unable to access the emotion that inspires these images. In 'La Voix lointaine V', the voice interrogates each trace in the sand, seeking the human presence at its origin. Each question simply provokes another question. The structures of human knowledge promise a referent that they never deliver, until the linguistic subject starts to feel that this lack must be an essential feature of material existence itself. We perceive all that exceeds the structures of language as 'other'. We become convinced that the world is defined by this essential absence and that loss and alienation are hard-wired into our very being. At the end of 'La Voix lointaine V', Bonnefoy protests that our existence is the existence we know. Our reality only seems to retreat from us endlessly and to assert its infinite difference if we conceive of knowing in narrowly linguistic terms and ourselves only as subjects of self-reflexive consciousness. Bonnefoy insists in the sixth poem of 'La Voix lointaine' that the human subject is not first and foremost a self-reflexive subject but a subject of finite and embodied action: we are caught up in a physical world that continually opens us up and exposes us to its physical structures of exchange and renewal. Presenting 'ces instants' as the subject of 'savoir', Bonnefoy suggests that knowing is not an appropriative gesture, not a gesture that succeeds or fails, grasps or loses. It is simply a gesture of opening. This gesture does not reinforce our sense of being outside material existence, confronting its essential alterity. On the contrary, it reveals all that we have in common with it. We are always already caught up in its dynamics of exposure. Existence is always 'othering' and transforming itself, but we are part of this endlessly shared process.

The Dancing Voice: 'un sujet en battement'

After this reflective series of central poems, a performative interlude ensues. As in so many of Bonnefoy's poems, once the poet embraces the negativity of material existence and the way that it plays through his own body, he discovers that he is free to embrace a new performative space. The poet's attention turns once again to the voice to which he has been listening. Moving into the present tense, the poet apostrophizes '[la] voix dansante'. Emphasis is placed increasingly on the voice's movement and images of song and dance intermingle. The poet urges the voice not to stop. He apostrophizes '[la] voix proche', coaxing it outwards where it can dance with 'l'ombre de [son] corps'. When the voice finally sings in 'La Voix lointaine IX' and the poet cites her song in full, the song narrates the steps of her dance. Stressing not only the sonority but the movement of the human voice in these poems, Bonnefoy draws our attention to the physical dynamics of resonance. He invites us to perceive human subjectivity as a resonant force. Bonnefoy encourages us to perceive it in dynamic terms as a reverberative movement outwards that resonates between the human body and other material bodies. The poet presents this outward movement as a dance between interiority and exteriority, the conscious and the unconscious, activity and passivity, light and darkness.

In 'La Voix lointaine VII', the poet urges the voice to stay in motion. As he does so, the lines of verse run into a series of enjambments. The poet urges the voice to keep ungrounding and dispersing the dynamics of signification, and to keep making its own resonance felt. The poem begins with the words 'Ne cesse pas, voix dansante, parole / De toujours murmurée, âme des mots' (PC, 63). Bonnefoy presents this voice as the very soul of language. He affirms that its capacity to murmur and dance, its sonority and dynamism—rather than its capacity to signify—is the 'âme des mots'. The poet suggests that this vibrant movement 'colore et dissipe les choses / Les soirs d'été où il n'est plus de nuit' (PC, 63). The voice is presented as a contagious presence that resonates through the physical world and allows us to see it anew. It exposes the material world's processual nature of existence, allowing things to emerge for a moment in their lustre and vitality, and then to dissolve into the shadows again. An inherently liminal presence, it hovers, in a kind of half-light, between day and night, recalling Verlaine's 'chanson grise'.[23] We move from the decasyllables of the first stanza into two more metrically tentative and searching lines at the start of the second stanza. In a hendecasyllable and a trimetric alexandrine, the poet apostrophizes the voice again, suggesting that it reunites being and appearance: 'Voix qui porte de l'être dans l'apparence, / Qui les mêle comme flocons de même neige' (PC, 63). In each of these images, Bonnefoy plays with the conceptual oppositions that underpin the Western philosophical tradition: body and soul, colour and form, being and appearance. The voice's dance shows us that these oppositions are inextricably intertwined. The vibrations of the voice continually gain and lose form. The soul of existence, its essence, emerges in the very physical dynamics that brings it into being. Spirituality and physicality vibrate side by side, 'comme flocons de même neige'. This vibration is enacted by the articulation of the *e atone* across these lines: 'Voix qui port*e* de l'êtr*e* dans l'apparence, / Qui les mêl*e* comm*e* flocons de mêm*e* neige' (PC, 63). A *césure enjambante* pushes the final syllable of 'l'être' into the next measure, 'Voix qui porte de l'ê|tre dans l'apparence', as if to stress that 'l'être' is not a pre-existing essence but the very dynamic by which the appearances of things are dynamized, changed, and dispersed. In the final two lines of the stanza, we then slip back into two clearly defined decasyllables: 'Voix qui presque s'est tue, lorsque le rêve / Demanda trop et crut presque obtenir' (PC, 63). Linguistic consciousness dreams of appropriating this force—of grasping 'l'âme', its essence or origin—but, when it attempts to do so, it only halts the very motion of which it is in pursuit. The stanza closes on the end-stopped line, with the word 'obtenir', as if to suggest how this gesture of appropriation brings the voice's dance to a halt.

The thought that the poet is articulating does not end at the full stop, however, but continues in the next stanza. The poet inserts the conjunctive

[23] Paul Verlaine, 'Art poétique', in *Œuvres poétiques complètes*, 2 vols, ed. Y.-G. Le Dantec (Paris: Gallimard, Bibliothèque de la Pléiade, 1989), I, p. 326.

'Et' and then continues to ascribe epithets to this voice: 'Et qui jouera à clore nos paupières / En se pressant riante contre nous' (PC, 63). He suggests that we obliterate being when we try to grasp it conceptually and, yet, before we know what is happening, the voice is rising up again. It presses itself against us. Seduced by its physicality, we close our eyes laughingly. Detached visual contemplation gives way to more immersive, tactile, and aural forms of exposure in this final stanza. The final lines combine vibrant and plosive alliterations which culminate in the 'pr' of 'pressant': 'Et qui joue*r*a à clo*r*e nos *p*au*p*iè*r*es / En se *pr*essant'. We too feel our own voices resounding through our bodies, echoing inside and out. The *e atone* of 'clore' and 'riante' are sounded and disperse outwards as the laughter does. The poem ends with a strong nasal assonance which culminates in the apparition of a nasal consonant in 'nous': '*En* se press*an*t ri*an*te c*on*tre *n*ous'. The use of the first-person subject pronoun in the plural suggests the inherently plural or shared—or even promiscuous—nature of resonance.

In the final lines of the poem it is as if we emerge blinkingly from this state of rapture, opening our eyes: 'Puis nous verrons ces signes sur le sable / Qu'égratigna en dansant son pied nu' (PC, 63). As the voice has danced with us, we have moved along the sand, our feet inscribing a set of traces. Here is the play of being and appearance that the poet evoked earlier. This image echoes the traces in the sand evoked in 'La Voix lointaine V'. These traces are no longer static forms now, however, but steadily evolving ones. The body that inscribes them in the sand immediately dances over them again, erasing and renewing them. The [ʀ] of 'verrons' resurges in 'égratigna'; the sibilant alliteration of 'ces signes sur le sable' resurges in 'en dansant son pied nu'. It is as if the play of sound itself is inscribing and uninscribing these traces, making and unmaking them. Bonnefoy dramatizes the physical movements that bring acts of inscription and representation into being. He enacts the more primary movement—the resonance, the oscillation, the dance—that inscribes the verbal or written trace. This resonance is at once sonorous and tactile. It resonates out from the body but also returns to reverberate *against* it, to act upon it and dance with it: 'En se pressant riante contre nous'. It is this resonance that seduces the poet as he writes, and the reader too, as she articulates the sounds of the poem, feeling them resonate back and forth through her. As we are drawn into this dance, a writerly or readerly performance emerges, and another set of verbal or written traces appear. But they are always rewritten and reinvented as the resonance starts up again. Bonnefoy's poem foregrounds this restlessness above all. He insists that voice is constantly relayed between the corporeal, the material, and the meaningful, and between aural, tactile, and visual modes of sensing. Its resonance moves between different bodies and surfaces and assumes different forms. The dancing voice exposes what Nancy describes as 'la résonance de l'être ou l'être comme résonance' (AE, 44).

'La Voix lointaine VIII' renews the poet's plea to this voice not to stop. After the intimate, tactile, and sonorous performance of the previous poem, its movements are now figured visually and spatially as a dance out upon an open stretch of sand. The first quatrain coaxes the voice outwards into the light: 'Ne cesse pas, voix proche, il fait jour encore, / Si belle est même la lumière, comme jamais' (PC, 64). As the voice is drawn outwards, the lines of verse move continually out across the page, in a series of enjambments that run over line ends and stanzaic breaks:

> Reviens dehors, petite vie dansante. Si le désir
> De danser, même seule, t'enveloppe,
>
> Vois, tu as sur le sable assez de lumière
> Pour jouer avec l'ombre de ton corps.
>
> (PC, 64)

It is by dancing outwards, the poet suggests, that the voice finds enough light to dance with its own shadow. Bonnefoy subverts the classical image of self-reflexivity, the mirror image. The voice does not dance with its own reflection but with its own shadow. Its image is not returned to it or distanced from it; this is not a dance of the selfsame and the other, desire and loss, unity and separation. Rather, the voice dances with 'l'ombre de [s]on corps'. It dances with the dark and resistant force that is its own body. It is exposed to other side of corporeal perception, the opaque physical presence that facilitates sensing but that is not penetrated by it. At the end of the second stanza, the poet urges the voice to reach out and 'sans plus craindre, offrir tes mains / Au rire qui s'enténèbre dans les arbres' (PC, 64). The voice is encouraged to keep moving self-expansively outwards, to allow itself to disperse out into the physical world. It becomes a laughter that simultaneously disseminates and darkens. It resounds through the trees even as it loses itself in their dark folds.

Bonnefoy once again uses the image of laughter to suggest the ecstatic nature of human subjectivity, the way that it projects continually outside itself. Overturning the ocularcentric conception of self-relation that has been cultivated within the Western tradition, he presents subjectivity not as a scene of self-reflection but of reverberation. Bonnefoy asks us to conceive of subjectivity not as the cool and detached act of contemplating an image of oneself, but as the ecstatic gesture of being projected outwards. He suggests that subjectivity is projected outwards as it dances with 'l'ombre de son corps'. It reverberates against the body's physical surfaces and then reverberates out amongst the things of the physical world. It comes into being precisely through this spatializing or self-expansive motion. By urging this voice to keep moving outwards, the poet is urging the subject to recognize its inherently spatial and worldly nature. He is reminding us that our conscious lives only come into being because they continually touch upon unconscious physical forms. These are the surfaces that resist resonance and, in doing so, return it to us. Their refusal—their darkness—keeps sense in resonance. It allows it to return to us deflected, diffracted, and diverted. Similarly, in *À l'écoute*, Nancy urges us to understand subjectivity as a resonance:

> à l'état naissant, à l'état de renvoi pour lequel n'est donné la fin de ce renvoi (le concept, l'idée, l'information), et donc à l'état de renvoi sans fin, comme un écho qui se relance lui-même et qui n'est rien que cette relance. (AE, 53)

To conceive of subjectivity in this way, Nancy writes, is to shift from 'le registre de la présence à soi' towards the understanding that 'le "soi" n'est précisément rien de disponible (de substantiel et de subsistant) à quoi on puisse être "présent", mais justement la résonance d'un renvoi' (AE, 30). And so Nancy suggests listening does not appear to us as:

> [...] une figure de l'accès au soi, mais comme la réalité de cet accès, une réalité par conséquent indissociablement "mienne" et "autre", "singulière" et "plurielle", tout autant que "matérielle" et "spirituelle" et que "signifiante" et "asignifiante". (AE, 30–1)

Resonance allows us to conceive of subjectivity as an ecstatic projection outwards, as a force that is endlessly returned and dispersed, scattered and singularized. By thinking of subjectivity in this way, Nancy, like Bonnefoy, very deliberately foregrounds the traffic that occurs between cerebral and material, signifying and unsignifying, conscious and unconcious forces. He suggests that we emerge from the constant reverberations that occur between these forces.

In the ninth poem, the poet no longer describes the voice's resonant dance. The voice herself steps forward and performs a song. Her song is rather like a child's playground rhyme for it narrates the steps of the dance that she performs. The song appears *entre guillemets* and spans the poem's full three quatrains. And almost every phrase in its simple, almost rudimentary structure begins with the word 'Je'. This subject pronoun appears ten times in all. This song and dance is thus a sustained reflection on the nature of subjectivity. And it unfolds in a series of assertions and counter-assertions, turns and counter-turns. It begins: 'Elle chantait: "Je suis, je ne suis pas, / Je tiens la main d'une autre que je suis [...]"' (PC, 65). It is as if Rimbaud's famous axiom—'Je est un autre'—has been worked into the steps of a dance. Bonnefoy puns on the first-person present tense of the verbs 'suivre' and 'être'. The voice is and is not; she holds the hand of an 'other' that she herself *is*. And equally, she follows and does not follow; she is lead by an 'other' that she follows. This play on words allows the poet to present being as a dance. For as the voice trembles between presence and absence, she simultaneously dances with herself and another, leading and being led, following and being followed. Bonnefoy shows us the voice reverberating between presence and absence, interiority and exteriority, activity and passivity, sameness and otherness. In an earlier poem in *Les Planches courbes*, Bonnefoy writes: 'Presque de même poids / Être, ne pas être' (PC, 37). The dynamic by which the voice slips in and out of existence here is presented as the very same dynamic by which it echoes back and forth.

As in the previous poem, this voice dances with its shadows: 'Je danse parmi mes ombres, l'une se tourne / Vers moi, elle est riante, elle est sans visage' (PC, 65). The voice dances with a dark and laughing presence, one that—like the 'marâtre' of the first poem—is 'sans visage'. It has no discernible features. As the voice dances with this shadow, the 'e' atone of the word 'autre' is pushed into the next measure by a *coupe enjambante*: 'Je tiens | la main || d'une au | tre que je suis'. And whilst, with the articulation of so many mute 'e's, these shadows seem to loom large in the third line, 'Je dans*e* parmi mes ombr*e*s, l'un*e* se tourne / Vers moi', as soon as the voice turns to face the figure in the fourth line, the 'e's are all elided: 'elle est riante, elle est sans visage'. The shadow no sooner presents itself than it withdraws. As it does so, we move from the *pair* into the *impair* (two decasyllables and an alexandrine are followed by a hendecasyllable). And as the shadow turns, so too does the line of verse: 'l'une se tourne / Vers moi, elle est riante, elle est sans visage'. The word 'tourne' falls just before the *versus* and the word 'Vers' falls after. Etymologically, 'le vers' is the line which turns: the Latin 'versus' signifies 'le retournement de la charrue au bout du champ' (to cite Nancy).[24]

[24] Nancy comments, 'Je ne me lasse pas d'exploiter cette mine qu'est l'*étymon* et la pensée du *vers*. Elle m'enchante parce qu'elle donne tout à penser: la suspension du cours, l'inversion, le retour (vers quoi?), le passage à la limite (le bout du champ), le rythme des aller-retour, le

The turning motion of the line of verse enacts the voice's twisting dance, the shadows' continual ebb and flow.[25]

The second stanza stages a more reflective interlude, as the voice feels the passing of time and observes: 'Je sais pourtant qu'avant l'aube le fer / Déchirera l'étoffe de la danse'. We slip back into the well-defined rhythm of the decasyllable. The dance's turning motion is likened to the weave of a fabric. The dance will not give rise to any kind of lasting substance, however. As soon as the weaving motion that brings it into being fades, its 'étoffe' will be destroyed. Reading the metre of this second line as 4 + 6, a tremendous emphasis is placed upon the verb 'Déchirera'. It is perhaps also tempting to read it as 6 + 4, however, to produce a *césure enjambante*, dissolving the integrity of the word 'l'étoffe' and suggesting that it is no more substantial than the 'ombres'. The voice resumes her dance and now she is the one who turns towards the shadow: 'Et je me tourne alors vers cette plus gauche, / Cette plus hésitante et comme étonnée / Qui se tient en retrait, dans la musique' (PC, 65). She turns towards this gauche and tremulous presence that always holds itself back. Etymologically, 'gauchir' comes from the Proto-Germanic word for 'to turn aside, swerve'.[26] The dancing figure thus turns towards this presence which is itself nothing other than a turning motion, another series of *renvois*. She turns towards resonance itself, this force 'Qui se tient en retrait, dans la musique'. The poem ends with the words 'Vois, ce n'est que

labour...' (Jean-Luc Nancy and Emmanuel Laugier, 'Penser la poésie, avec Jean-Luc Nancy', *L'Animal. Littératures, arts & philosophies* (2003), 14–15; available at http://remue.net/cont/Laugier_Nancy.html, accessed 10 April 2019, (para. 17 of 36)). Agamben also describes the *versus* as the 'essential trait of verse' (Agamben, *The End of the Poem*, p. 111).

[25] The rhythm of these lines already places a great deal of emphasis on the *versus*. Across the sequence, the repeated use of elisions or *césures enjambantes* could even be seen to weaken the medial caesura. The reader always has the option of delivering these decasyllables and hendecasyllables as *vers simples*. In this case, the whole line orients itself towards the final turning point, the *versus*. It is striking that in Nancy's only essay on Bonnefoy's poetry, Nancy foregrounds Bonnefoy's use of the *coupe*. Nancy suggests that the *coupe* is the place where a tension between a metaphysical desire to enclose sense and an awareness of its continual effraction or fissuring are articulated. He thus plays on the connotations of 'coupe' as 'container' and as 'cut' (Nancy, 'Nécessité du sens', in *Yves Bonnefoy. Poésie, peinture, musique*, ed. Finck, pp. 49–50). Bonnefoy foregrounds the *coupe* more heavily in 'La Voix lointaine' than in most of his poems but it is very clear that it is a site of turning for the poet rather than a site of rupture. The poet clearly finds the connotations of 'le vers' and 'le versus' more fertile here than those of 'la coupe'. His use of the *versus* is far more supple and energetic than Nancy's description of 'la coupe' in 'Nécessité du sens'. His playful and winding lines of verse present the *versus*—as Nancy's texts also do—as the motion that articulates 'le rythme des aller-retour' of sense.

[26] 'Gauche' derives from 'gauchir', meaning 'to turn aside, swerve', from the Proto-Germanic 'wankjan', and from the PIE 'weng', meaning 'to bend, curve'. 'Gauche' in the *Online Etymological Dictionary*, http://www.etymonline.com, accessed 7 March 2017.

pour toi que je ris et danse' (PC, 65). The voice dances for its own resonance, for the dynamic by which it is endlessly relayed. This is the force that continually ungrounds and interrupts the voice and thus keeps deflecting or projecting it outwards. Repeating the subject pronoun 'je' steadily throughout the poem, Bonnefoy suggests that its reverberation is the very motion by which human subjectivity emerges. Self-presence becomes a scene of resonance in which sense is endlessly projected outwards and bounced back. The subject is thus always dilating and dissipating, casting itself outwards and awaiting itself, trying to catch up with itself. It is, as Nancy writes, 'un rebond qui ne s'achève en aucun retour en soi sans aussitôt relancer en écho un appel à ce même soi' (AE, 44); 'une figure qui s'est déjà perdue et qui s'attend encore, et qui s'appelle' (AE, 75).

This vibratory form of self-investigation necessitates continual contact or collision with other forces. It is for this reason that the voice's turn and counter-turn is presented as a dance with a shadow. In the swerve of resonance, there is interruption, rupture, resistance, and deflection. There is contact with all that remains resistant and impenetrable, what Nancy describes as 'un toucher clair au seuil obscur du sens' in *Le Sens du monde* (SM, 132). The motion by which we sound ourselves out is thus necessarily hesitant and vacillating. It is 'comme étonnée', taken by surprise, cast back in new and unexpected ways. In the final line of the poem, 'Vois, ce n'est que pour toi que je ris et danse', the imperative '[v]ois' can be also be heard homophonically as 'voix'. Bonnefoy acknowledges that two different modes of sense are in resonance here: visual and aural. The reader is at once deciphering signs and listening to their sounds. The poem moves outwards by keeping these different modes of sense in resonance. They touch and deflect one another, 'expropriate' one another, so that sense's restless dance never ceases. Bonnefoy suggests that human subjectivity is born of this motion and we can only experience the sense of our own existence if we are prepared to let sense be continually disrupted and deflected, continually reborn, in this way. In an interview in which he discusses poetry, Nancy suggests that 'le rythme des aller-retour' of the poetic line of verse is particularly adept at articulating this conception of sense.[27] The dynamics by which the line of verse turns allow the poem to explore what Nancy describes elsewhere (in his text on dance, *Allitérations*) as: '[u]n sens tourné,

[27] Jean-Luc Nancy and Emmanuel Laugier, 'Penser la poésie, avec Jean-Luc Nancy', *L'Animal. Littératures, arts & philosophies* (2003), 14–15; available at http://remue.net/cont/Laugier_Nancy. html, accessed 15 July 2011, (para. 17 of 36).

plié et déplié vers les ouvertures des sens. Un sens dépliant les sens, dépliant ou déliant le sens, absolument'.[28]

The inherently dualist confrontation between the subject and its reflection that is foregrounded in Valéry's poems and Lacan's writings gives way to a much more sinuous and heterogeneous series of reverberations, deflections, swerves, and echoes here. The voice is an endlessly dynamic network of frictions and collisions. It explores the negativity of its own motion, making us feel the space that penetrates it and that allows it to continually open outwards. As the poem beats its rhythm, reaches outwards and then turns back, it luxuriates—to use Agamben's word—in the fertile tensions between signification and sense, speaking and listening, passivity and activity, reading and performing. Nancy writes in *À l'écoute*:

> [la] présence est [...] toujours dans le renvoi et la rencontre. Elle *se* renvoie à *soi*, elle *se* rencontre ou, mieux, elle se fait contre soi, à son encontre et tout contre. Elle est co-présence [...] Mais pour autant qu'elle ne consiste pas dans un être-présent-là, dans un être stable et posé, elle n'est cependant pas ailleurs ni absente: elle serait plutôt dans ce rebond du "là" ou dans sa mise en branle, qui fait de lui, du lieu sonore [...] un lieu-à-soi, un lieu *comme* rapport à soi, comme avoir-lieu d'un soi, un lieu vibrant comme le diapason d'un sujet ou, mieux, comme un diapason-sujet. (AE, 37)

The subject comes into being in the resonance that occurs between different modes of sensing, be they corporeal, spatial, or intellectual: '[il] se fait contre soi, à son encontre et tout contre'. Subjectivity is thus born of the motion back and forth that spatializes and singularizes the different forces at play. We emerge from this encounter, friction, and resonance. The highly performative poems that Bonnefoy dramatizes in 'La Voix lointaine' murmur, sing, and dance. Their performance is at turns visual, sonorous, and tactile. We at first hear an acousmatic voice, then it presses itself seductively against our bodies, and then it performs a dance of light and shadow on the sand. The poems reflect self-reflexively at different moments on the act of speaking, writing, or reading. And from one poem to the next, throughout the sequence as a whole, these acts are all shown to reverberate against each another and

[28] Nancy's text on dance was co-written with Mathilde Monnier and so, rather appropriately, it is impossible to say whether Nancy or Monnier is the source of this quotation. In the exchange between the two writers and their two different disciplines, sense is 'tourné, plié et déplié'. It is also important to note that their co-authored text was written to be performed and accompanied by a dance (Nancy and Monnier, *Allitérations*, p. 150).

to stimulate each another. The poems thus attune us to what Adrienne Janus in her article on Nancy's *À l'écoute* describes as 'a resonance that begins before and continues after, penetrates and envelopes, the voice, speech, and writing'.[29] This is the originary resonance that gives rise to writing and speaking, to subjectivity and indeed all existence. It is what keeps the material world in a perpetual state of agitation and transformation. Its dynamic of 'expropriation' continually projects sense outwards in new and singular ways. Its force overtakes and surprises us, seduces us and casts us overwards, and draws us, once again, into its endless dance.[30]

'En résonance', 'l'extimité'

After these three poems which coax the voice outwards and urge it to sing and to dance, the final two poems of 'La Voix lointaine' reflect on the passing of this motion. 'La Voix lointaine X' presents the voice as a fleeting shadow and this shadow is then compared to a mist that envelopes and dissolves the world's stable forms. In the final poem of the sequence, 'La Voix lointaine XI', the poet reaches out to the mysterious figure, the anonymous female, who has accompanied him ever since childhood. The poet moves close to her, seemingly now having some kind of hold on her. The sequence ends with a series of rhetorical questions that probe the identity of this female in the manner of Valéry's 'La Jeune Parque' and which, in the very same gesture, manage to insinuate that these questions are redundant. We have the answers to these questions, Bonnefoy suggests, if only we will listen to the sound of our own voices. As the poet writes in another sequence of poems in *Les Planches courbes* 'Que ce monde demeure!', 'nos voix, / Qui se prennent au rien / L'une de l'autre soient / Notre suffisance' (PC, 31).

[29] Adrienne Janus, 'Listening: Jean-Luc Nancy and the Anti-Ocular Turn in Continental Philosophy and Critical Theory', *Comparative Literature*, 63.2 (2011), 182–202 (p. 192).

[30] In his writings on dance, Nancy suggests that dance's distinguishing feature is that it calls us to participate in it: 'la danse est *méthexique* avant d'être mimétique'. He proposes that dance attunes us to the interdependence of representation and participation, *mimesis* and *methexis*: 'transmettre un geste n'est pas le donner à reproduire [...], c'est faire passer son énergie propre. On pourrait dire que c'est un mélange d'imitation et de participation'. However, he accords a certain primacy or inaugural force to the gesture of participation: 'Élan et saut, ou bien bond, voilà le dansant de tout travail, de toute pensée, j'aimerais même dire la *praxis* de toute *poiésis*—et aussi, pour renouer avec ce motif, la *methexis* de toute *mimesis*: on n'entreprendrait pas de représenter quoi que ce soit si l'on n'était saisi par le mouvement, par le jet d'un commencement, d'un départ...' (Nancy and Monnier, *Allitérations*, p. 54, pp. 52–3, p. 78).

The penultimate poem of the sequence suggests that this mythical Other that we personify—the 'marâtre' that appeared in the opening poem—is merely a shadow: 'Et ombre elle était bien, une fantasque / Découpe du langage sur le ciel' (PC, 66). Playing on the two meanings of 'fantasque', 'fantastical' and 'unpredictable', Bonnefoy suggests that this mythical Other is nothing other than material contingency itself. She cuts language up and scatters it in shreds across the sky. She is the force of interruption—the 'coupe'—that continually breaks sense and that allows it to disseminate in new ways. This negativity scatters, composes, and decomposes the structures of language.[31] But Bonnefoy also suggests that it restores language to the physical world: 'Ainsi nuées et arbres quand ils mêlent / Leurs fumées dans l'eau calme, et c'est le soir' (PC, 66). Words melt—along with all the other presences—back into a dynamic material world. They disperse and settle, like the mist that rises from the trees and hovers over the calm water of the lake. The poet feels the primacy of material finitude. He feels its force that precedes and exceeds language's structures of doubling, splitting, and othering. We slip once again into an atmospheric vision of material existence. Things lose their distinct form. Our vision slackens and we perceive the spacious processes of exchange from which stable forms emerge. No longer outside of a material world that seems insurmountably 'other', the poet feels the serenity that comes from recognizing ourselves to be part of a resonant and atomistic world.

In the second stanza, this negativity is presented as the very good of existence: 'Ombre mais le seul bien qui soit au monde / Puisqu'elle puise à toute chose simple' (PC, 66). Bonnefoy suggests that its continual processes of dissolution and emergence 'puise à toute chose simple'. The simplicity that the poet feels here is not the simplicity of a single origin or element. The poet describes it using a series of images in apposition: 'L'eau qui déborde, avec l'odeur des feuilles, / Du broc posé sur les dalles sonores' (PC, 66). Water lips over the rim of the jug, as the smell of leaves diffuses through the air, and as the crockery sounds out against the flagstones. The conjunction 'avec' suggests the coincidence of these diverse sensory impressions. And each of these presences sounds or spills outwards. They all resonate alongside one another, in and through one another. Even the stones beneath our feet become 'dalles sonores'. The simplicity that Bonnefoy

[31] As discussed earlier, Nancy's essay on Bonnefoy's poetry explores how the interruption and breaking of sense is staged by the poet's use of the *coupe* (Nancy, 'Nécessité du sens', in *Yves Bonnefoy. Poésie, peinture, musique*, ed. Finck, p. 48).

describes here is the simplicity of the spacing of material existence, its common or shared dynamic of exposure.[32] As the poet describes all these expansive presences, the reader feels them—and herself too—resonating outwards. Existence is presented as a force that is always *débordant*, that is productively or creatively spacious. All things are projected outwards, amongst other ecstatic bodies, other resonances.

The final poem of the sequence returns to the notion of song, this excess or surplus in the voice, that cannot simply be reduced to language or signification.[33] It begins once again with the words 'Elle chantait': 'Elle chantait, et j'ai eu dans ses mots / De quoi presque finir ma longue guerre' (PC, 67). The poet has been struggling to capture the voice, to accede to this dark and shadowy 'other'. This song now seems to promise to bring the poet's struggle to an end. It signals a move towards resolution but, even as it does so, the poet hints that this closure will be partial and provisional: 'De quoi *presque* finir ma longue guerre' [my emphasis].[34] He moves towards this most elusive figure and touches her hands: 'je touchais / Ses mains'. This act of touch occurs across the *coupe*, as so often in Bonnefoy's poems. At the very moment that the poet performs this gesture, he sees this figure's fingers undo a thread: 'je regardais ses doigts défaire // Ce fil qui a ses nœuds dans l'invisible'. This 'fil' is perhaps the thread that is spun, measured, and cut by the three Parcae, the thread of destiny. It is perhaps also the thread of conceptual thought, the normative linguistic structures that encourage us to perceive our lives according to pre-given patterns. We might thus suggest that this thread represents the inherently determinist tendencies of our own linguistic consciousness, our love of fixity and security. In his essay 'Il reste à faire le négatif', Bonnefoy refers to 'un de ces nœuds de parole à quoi on se voue quand on veut avoir et non être' (E, 247). Undoing this thread, the Parca seems to demonstrate to us that there is no pre-given measurement for existence. She suggests that nothing can be possessed. As the poet evokes the undoing of this knot, the line runs into an enjambment, over the

[32] We are reminded of the way that Nancy in *Le Sens du monde* argues that Plato's category of *agathon*, the good, has to be thought, not as 'la jonction [...] du donné et de désiré', but as 'l'espacement originaire en tant que matérialité, et cet espacement lui-même comme existential du rapport à l'agathon' (SM, 85, 95). Nancy writes that 'Le Sens, c'est *l'agathon offert*, selon l'excès de son excellence' (SM, 88).

[33] Dolar writes that 'singing takes the distraction of the voice seriously, and turns the tables on the signifier; it reverses the hierarchy—let the voice take the upper hand, let the voice be the bearer of what cannot be expressed by words' (Dolar, *A Voice and Nothing More*, p. 30).

[34] The first chapter of this book examined Bonnefoy's treatment of the theme and the rhythm of 'l'inachevable' in 'La Terre', in *Dans le leurre du seuil*. In 'Les Nuées', another section of *Dans le leurre du seuil*, Bonnefoy writes: 'Ici, la tâche que je ne sais finir. Ici, les mots / Que je ne dirai pas' (DL, 93).

stanzaic break, and the verb 'défaire' falls before the *coupe*. The thread falls just as the *coupe* falls, just as the line which signifies breaks. The *coupe* becomes what Nancy describes in his essay on Bonnefoy's poetry as a '[p]assage à la ligne qui est comme à l'écoute, ou à l'affût, d'une autre nécessité: celle de défaire le sens'.[35] The closed and binding systems of conceptual thought are interrupted or fractured. There's a brief sensation of release and opening, as if we momentarily cast off the weight of linguistic consciousness.

The poem builds towards a resolution, only to reveal the fundamental irresolution of all things. The poet approaches the figure that he has pursued over the eleven poems of the sequence. And he asks: 'Était-elle dehors à jouer, une simple / Servante enfant qui a charge du monde?' Is the Parca nothing more than a little servant girl at play? Is the terribly powerful and calculating figure of mythology—the one who measures and cuts the thread of each life—simply a powerless and innocent being? The final poem returns to the image with which the sequence opened, 'un enfant qui joue sur la route'. The servant child is quite the opposite of a god; she is not in authority but in servitude, not immortal but vulnerable. Playing outside, she is like the 'petite vie dansante' which plays 'dehors', 'sur le sable'. Is it not so, Bonnefoy speculates, that there is neither mastery nor design to the universe but only naivety and play? And is it possible that this is 'le seul bien' of worldly existence? The poem ends with one further question. It runs from the last line of the second stanza through to the end of the poem:

> Était-elle la Parque, qui aurait moins
>
> À mettre à mort qu'à mener sous des arbres
> Où, souriante à qui serait près d'elle:
> "Écoute, dirait-elle, les mots se taisent,
> Leur son n'est plus qu'un bruit, et le bruit cesse"?
>
> (PC, 67)

Bonnefoy overturns the traditional conception of the mythological figure of the Parca. Rather than putting us to death, this figure smiles at us and leads us beneath the trees. Enjambments across the line ends and the stanzaic break evoke this movement. She leads us from the light into the shadows, in amongst the foliage beneath the trees. The calculated end of mythology—spun, measured, and cut by the three Fates—becomes a gentle passing. The

[35] Nancy, 'Nécessité du sens', in *Yves Bonnefoy. Poésie, peinture, musique*, ed. Finck, p. 48.

Parca herself speaks to us. She urges us to listen not to what she says but to her voice. This voice reminds us that all words are passing noise, that we are nothing but a resonance that swells briefly, reverberates amongst all the other presences of the world, and melts away. We are like the laughter, evoked earlier, that darkens as it disperses amongst the trees. Language, heard in this way, functions as a *memento mori*: 'Leur son n'est plus qu'un bruit, et le bruit cesse'.[36] The poem falls silent with these words, dramatizing its own passing, the expiration of voice.

In 'La Voix lointaine', Bonnefoy counters the ocularcentric discourses on the subject of self-presence that have dominated much of twentieth-century French poetry and thought. He proposes that subjectivity should not be conceived in visual terms as an act of self-reflection, the return of one's own image, but as a scene of resonance. To conceive of self-presence in sonorous terms, he suggests, is to explore its dynamic and tactile nature, its emergent force. It is to attune ourselves to a negativity that permeates all material existence and thus reimmerses the human body and human subjectivity into a spaciously resonant physical world. Bonnefoy makes it clear that he conceives of this conception of the resonance of human subjectivity in opposition to the portrait of self-reflexivity that emerges from Valéry's 'La Jeune Parque'. Valéry's Parca is the figure who awakens on an island and questions the structures of her own linguistic consciousness, the reflections and representations of her being. She famously interrogates the visual scene of self-observation: 'Je me voyais me voir, sinueuse, et dorais / De regards en regards, mes profondes forêts.'[37] Her desire for stable self-knowledge is steadily thwarted as she discerns the series of gaps and schisms that separate her from her own self-image. As she interrogates her own thoughts, she turns over image after image, lost in '[s]es profondes forêts'. She gradually comes to terms with a 'subjectivity of lack'. She accepts that self-presence necessarily involves an act of representation that divides the subject and distances it from itself, leaving it wanting. And so, the subject cannot figure and or know itself fully. It can only figure itself over and over again, exploring the structure of lack or alienation that brings it into being and spurs its creativity.

[36] In a similar fashion, in one of the most beautiful poems in *Les Planches courbes*, quoted in the introduction to this book, 'Passant, ce sont des mots', Bonnefoy also makes language itself function as a *memento mori*. He urges that we do not read the letters inscribed on a tombstone but listen to them instead. He urges us to listen to the buzzing sound of the bee that slips past these words and then he urges, 'Puis sache un bruit plus faible encore, et que ce soit / Le murmure sans fin de toutes nos ombres' (PC, 40).

[37] Paul Valéry, *Œuvres*, I, p. 97.

In Bonnefoy's sequence, it is not language that speaks and reflects upon its own structures. It is voice itself that speaks. It murmurs, sings, and dances. It exposes the dynamics of its own resonance and, in doing so, it exposes what might be called a primary or originary resonance: the dynamic of reverberation that brings all things—including human subjectivity—into being. And so, subjectivity is not depicted as the movement of referral by which linguistic consciousness pursues itself down through an endless chain of linguistic traces. On the contrary, subjectivity emerges in the dynamic by which the human voice resonates against a human body and resonates out amongst other material bodies. The subject sounds itself out. It feels the resonance of its voice disperse outwards and return in steadily amplified waves. The physical surfaces against which it acts—the body, the air, the sand, the trees—break or interrupt its flow but also keep it in resonance. And this steady interruption and 'renvoi' allows sense to continually modulate itself, to reverberate between the sonorous, the tactile, and the visual; the corporeal, the spatial, and the intellectual. Sensual perception thus becomes intimate and tactile but also endlessly spaced. Our different sensory impressions continually unsettle and deflect one another, keeping one another in motion. They allow us to experience the body as a place of resonance, a site where the different modalities of sense dance side by side, resounding between interior and exterior spaces. Nancy suggests that this gesture of opening occurs '[d]ans un corps qui s'ouvre et qui se ferme à la fois, qui se dispose et s'expose avec d'autres, résonne le bruit de son partage (d'avec soi, d'avec les autres)' (AE, 79). He suggests that by resonating against the body and other bodies, sense at once shares itself out and singularizes itself. Its act of communication is also an act parturition. As Nancy writes, 'le partage [...] fait sujet: le partage sujet de tous les "sujets"' (AE, 79).

And so, in the penultimate poem of 'La Voix lointaine', the subject finds itself in a profoundly atmospheric or resonant world. We might suggest that this vision of the world inverts and reinvents the Lacanian notion of 'extimité' in a compelling way. Lacan used the notion of 'extimacy' to resist naive conceptions of an ego that is contained within the human body, insisting that the subject is not, as Malcolm Bowie writes, 'a substance endowed with qualities, or a fixed shape possessing dimensions, or a container awaiting the multifarious contents that experience provides'.[38] Lacan instead argues that subjectivity should be conceived as an intimately exterior movement through 'a series of events within language, a procession of turns, tropes,

[38] Bowie, *Lacan*, p. 76.

and inflections.'[39] Lacan's subject is a force that is always on the move, overwritten by the significations and desires of others, and trying to accede to some more authentic articulation of itself. *Contra* Lacan, and *contra* Valéry, Bonnefoy's subject is 'extimate' in a very different way. Without succumbing to a naive logic of the body as substance or container, Bonnefoy presents human subjectivity as a spaciously physical presence. He suggests that it exists ecstatically, resonating outwards, existing in relation with its own body and other bodies. Like the water that flows out from the jug, the smell of leaves that disseminates, and the sound that echoes across the flagstones, the subject is another force that endlessly overflows and that extends itself outwards. This experience of existence in its dynamism and its excess, its 'extimacy', is what Bonnefoy describes as 'la présence'. It is the experience of being, as Nancy writes, 'à l'écoute simultanée d'un "soi" et d'un "monde" qui sont l'un à l'autre en résonance' (AE, 82).

A Corporeal Performance

In the poems of 'La Voix lointaine', Bonnefoy protests that we are all too quick to perceive human subjectivity as self-reflection and to inscribe it within the structures of linguistic and visual representation. He suggests that this assumption leads us to conceive of human subjectivity as a divided or cleft force, one that finds itself cut off from—alienated from—itself and the physical world. All that might have been intimate to us is perceived as different and distant, 'lointain'. If Bonnefoy reworks and reinvents Valéry's monodialogues in 'La Voix lointaine', it's because he perceives them as the seminal modern texts that enshrine notions of severance and alterity within human consciousness. His female speakers interrogate the representative structures of their own self-consciousness and encounter nothing but schism and lack. The many psychoanalytic references that are dotted throughout 'La Voix lointaine' also suggest that Bonnefoy is also reflecting on Lacan's understanding of the human subject's severance from the Real that is inaugurated in 'the mirror phase'. Bonnefoy's sequence of poems subtly critiques the textual turn that overtook psychoanalytic and deconstructive discourses in the twentieth century. He is deeply wary of the way that it leads writers and thinkers to privilege identity over ontology, and linguistic

[39] Ibid.

consciousness over material presence. He distrusts the way that subjectivity, experience, and ethics are inscribed within structures of signification and thus understood from the outset according to a logic of the self-same and the 'other'. For Bonnefoy, this mode of thinking delimits human existence in narrowly linguistic terms and alienates the human subject from its wide range of non-linguistic capacities. These experiences are all 'othered'. Bonnefoy writes in '*Le Dégré zéro de l'écriture* et la question de la poésie' that this form of linguistic hegemony means that 'ce qui aurait pu nous être du proche étant fait ainsi de l'étranger, nous serons obligés de vivre dans un triste univers tout en énigmes, notre propre existence dans celui-ci étant la principale d'entre elles' (SPV, 195). Alienation becomes the operative or driving force within human subjectivity.

Protesting that the self-reflexive act of representation is not the primary structure of human consciousness, Bonnefoy insists that what is basic is the 'turn' of sense, its 'renvoi' (to use Nancy's term). Bonnefoy proposes that, whilst linguistic consciousness and the visual sense tend to try to immobilize and recuperate this turning motion, the sonority of the voice continually makes us feel the emancipating force of its dynamics of reverberation. It is for this reason that the poet asserts in 'La Parole poétique' that the sonority can awaken a new understanding 'de ce qui se joue en nous mais aussi ce que vivent les autres' (SPV, 195). The sonority of the human voice reminds us that all sense touches the human body. It resonates against the body and resonates outwards, in a dynamic of self-dilation. It touches the things of the physical world and resonates back to the body, echoing back and forth, continually exceeding and transforming itself. The subject that Bonnefoy dramatizes is just as mobile as the subject of Mallarmé's or Valéry's poetics, the subject of Lacanian psychoanalysis or Derridian deconstruction. For Bonnefoy, subjectivity is nothing other than a resonance, a rhythm, or a dance. But its mobility is not conceived as the rupture of the self-same and the loss of a state of unity and self-presence promised to us by language. There is no such fall. For Bonnefoy simply insists that resonance *precedes* reflection. It is this basic structure of reverberation that gives rise to all our different modes of sensing. Sense is at once corporeal, spatial, and meaningful; tactile, sonorous, and visual. Our different acts of sensing resonate against one another, shaping and contesting one another, differentiating themselves from one another, renewing and singularizing each impression. Using the motif of the dance, Bonnefoy suggests that this basic physical *praxis* of sense not only precedes linguistic consciousness but steadily grounds and ungrounds its structures, bringing them into and out of being. As the emphasis that is placed on tracks, marks, and inscriptions throughout 'La Voix lointaine' suggests, the differential linguistic structures that poets such as Valéry and thinkers such as Lacan and Derrida prize are still in play. Bonnefoy insists, however, that these dynamics are not primary but secondary. They are generated by the resonance of a concrete or material sense: traces are inscribed by the dancing body, only to be steadily uninscribed. Language constantly tries to control and recuperate the very motion that gives rise to it. But Bonnefoy suggests that the *praxis* of sense—its turn and counter-turn—constantly overturns language's closed structures.

Throughout 'La Voix lointaine', Bonnefoy stresses that voice, resonance, or sense only exist because they touch the body. The voice dances with 'l'ombre de son corps'. The body resists voice—and sense—and, in doing so, returns it to us. Its corporeal structure remains opaque, dark, and impenetrable. And yet, without its resistance we would sense nothing. Just as the notion of self-awareness is conceived in newly physical terms as a 'renvoi', so Bonnefoy hints that the unconscious can be thought *autrement*, as a profoundly corporeal and material force. He suggests that the lines of enquiry undertaken by psychoanalysis can be attuned to the realities of voice, embodiment, and physical relation. His conception of the unconscious thus resembles Freud's early conception of the drives, but Bonnefoy dismantles the language of inwardness and interiority in which Freud shrouded it. He suggests that sense resonates outwards, opening the body up, but that it can only do so by continually touching and being deflected by material surfaces that it cannot penetrate. The resonance of the human voice emerges from the body's deep recesses. It touches its dark surfaces even as it reverberates outwards and touches the bodies of the material world. Nancy writes: '[l]'oreille ouvre sur la caverne sonore que nous devenons alors' (AE, 73). Sense thus exposes its dark physical alterity. Bonnefoy urges us to dance with these shadows in the poems of 'La Voix lointaine'. He suggests that they re-endow the body with an essential mystery. This is not a mystery that directs our gaze endlessly inwards, however, for these shadows echo outwards, from body to body, thing to thing, imbuing the whole physical world with mystery. They spread contagiously, through all physical things, like 'le rire qui s'enténèbre dans les arbres'.

Bonnefoy thus uses voice in 'La Voix lointaine' to encourage us to perceive the body as a concrete force that opens outwards and enters into the worldly play of resonance. But his account of voicing also seeks to change how we perceive the body of the poem. The poem becomes a sonorous performance that dances 'with its own body'. It moves across the empty space of the page, exposing its play of black ink and white paper, shadow and light. There are endless self-reflexive references throughout 'La Voix lointaine'. They all draw attention to the scene of creation, to the way that the poem emerges as a set of vibrations, a physical *élan*, or a gesture of inscription. But there is an equally powerful awareness of the correlative scene of reading by which the poem emerges as the reader scans its metrics and actualizes its rhythm. The poet's use of versification encourages the heightened forms of voicing particular to verse, the enunciation of the *e atone* in particular. Bonnefoy is acutely aware that rhythm acts upon the reader's body, choreographing its movements, and setting it in resonance with the written forms before it. The use of the *impair* signals that these acts of voicing will not conform to any pre-given design. The reader must at once read and improvise, listen and voice, follow and lead. In *À l'écoute*, Nancy defines poetic diction as:

> cette résonance où [le texte] *s'écoute*, en s'écoutant *se trouve* et en se trouvant *s'écarte* encore de soi pour résonner plus loin, s'écoutant plus avant qu'il ne s'entend, devenant ainsi proprement son "sujet" qui n'est ni le même ni non plus l'autre que le sujet individuel qui écrit le texte.
>
> (AE, 69)

The poetic voice listens to itself, reaching outwards and losing itself, delivering itself and waiting for itself. It comes into being hesitantly, between the page, the body, and the air, acts of reading and voicing. It bounces back and forth off all these surfaces. It is at once out ahead and catching up with itself. This is the effect that Bonnefoy's lines of verse create as they shift between the *pair* and the *impair*. They place the reader in a role that is active and passive, responsive and creative. Bonnefoy encourages us to see how the act of voicing the poem itself is an experiment in self-discovery and self-relation. He presents resonance, not simply as a metaphor for the dynamics of subjectivity, but as the very dynamics that bring it into being.

Conclusion

Heure présente, ne renonce pas

(*L'Heure présente*, p. 96)

'L'Heure présente'

I would like to conclude this study by considering a highly summative poem that Bonnefoy wrote late in his life. It is 'L'Heure présente', published in 2011, in the collection that bears the same title, *L'Heure présente*.[1] The poem diagnoses the situation in which humanity finds itself at the start of the twenty-first century. It depicts a state of ontological crisis that has progressively overtaken Western culture since the seventeenth century. Bonnefoy explores how the metaphysical conception of sense, understood as a property of existence that can be identified and possessed, exhausts itself. In the wake of this crisis, he suggests that poetry faces the challenge of affirming and enacting a newly transitive conception of sense. He proposes that sense should now be considered synonymous with finite, worldly action.

In both the poet's diagnosis of our cultural ills and his affirmation of a newly performative conception of poetic action, 'L'Heure présente' bears a very strong resemblance to 'La Terre'. We might suggest that these two crucial works 'bookend' the latter half of Bonnefoy's career. The poems are dominated by the same key images and themes: light, touch, finitude, exposure. Like 'La Terre', 'L'Heure présente' opens by dramatizing the poet's reaction to a disappearing flash of light. In the 2011 poem, however, it is a flash of lightning that briefly illuminates the night sky and then dissipates. The poet recognizes that it was once Zeus' lightning bolt, a sign or even proof, of the existence of a higher power. Now, this light falls across the sky, 'brisée, / Dépossédée de soi, à ces confins, / Là-bas, de notre nuit d'ici, / L'heure présente' (HP, 81). As this luminous form expends itself, the poet shows us God retreating from the world, matter growing dark and thickening.

[1] Yves Bonnefoy, *L'Heure présente* (Paris: Mercure de France, 2011). All subsequent references will appear within the text, using the abbreviation HP.

Yves Bonnefoy and Jean-Luc Nancy: Ontological Performance. Emily McLaughlin, Oxford University Press (2020). © Emily McLaughlin.
DOI: 10.1093/oso/9780198849582.001.0001

Most strikingly of all, Bonnefoy stages a procession of female figures. He uses the Shakespearean device of the procession to dramatize the unfolding of history over a series of generations. Yet, Shakespeare's kings here give way to a line of benighted and suffering women. We see Niobe leaning over Adonis; then Judith covered in blood; Desdemona betrayed; Ophelia overtaken by madness and swept away by the river; J.G.F. consumed by illness and death (HP, 83–4). They are figures from Carravaggio's and Gentileschi's paintings, Shakespeare's theatre, and Baudelaire's poetry. Bonnefoy dramatizes a progressive loss of faith in the absolute value of a human life. He shows how the loss of faith in a metaphysical absolute triggers a crisis of confidence in the value and sanctity of human existence, of which women are the first victims. As each new female figure appears, the individual human life appears increasingly meaningless and inconsequential, until finally, an anonymous woman falls face forward into a mass grave, perhaps one of the victims of the mass slaughter of the twentieth-century concentration camps.

In *Le Lieu d'herbes*, Bonnefoy suggests that humanity is naturally prone to desire the absolute because the structure of linguistic consciousness doubles and deforms our perception.[2] When it becomes clear, however, that language will not grant us any form of special access to some form of higher meaning, humankind experiences a profound sense of loss. In this moment, Bonnefoy suggests, material existence seems to be stripped of all form of meaning or value. We see it, as Bonnefoy writes in his essay on Garache, 'cruellement par le dehors, [...] dans la brutale raréfaction de nos raisons d'exister' (NR, 312). This is the perception of worldly existence that Bonnefoy dramatizes at the start of 'L'Heure présente'. Looking out on dark and leaden world, the poet asks himself if it is only '[d]e la tourbe / Pour rien qu'un dernier feu' (HP, 85). The poet, in this melancholy state, watches the disappearing light of the setting sun. He sees its beams of light grow finer and finer. As the light recedes, the poet perceives that '[l]a visibilité se fait or pur' (HP, 91). Gold is of course the traditional image of the redemption of a sacred essence. And yet, here, as the dream of this essence is voided, the poet suggests that a new conception of the sacred—a different kind of gold—is emerging. Where once there was a higher meaning or essence, an organizing or creative principle, the poet now perceives only an absenting motion. As the light steadily withdraws, he realizes that the world is open to

[2] Bonnefoy, *Le Lieu d'herbes*, p. 15.

the 'beyond' in a different way than before. The world is *opened up* by it. The poet perceives what Nancy describes as creation *ex nihilo*. As Morin describes it: '[t]he world opens from within to an unconditional alterity that is an "outside" of the world without being another world. This "outside" does not exist (it is nothing that "is") but it [...] can "mobilise" existence'.[3] The poet realizes that it is precisely *because* any kind of organizing or original principle is absent that the world can continually dissolve into this nothingness and, projecting itself ecstatically outwards, assume endlessly different forms.

The poet suggests that this negative force calls out to him in 'L'Heure présente'. Its creative force solicits his attention, appealing to him to help in bringing it into being: 'Aimez-moi, donnez-moi forme' (HP, 93). The poet feels its dynamics at work within his own body but also all through the physical world. He affirms: '[l]e ciel du soir / Est, peut-être, une rose. Rose à venir / Par vos travaux d'horticulteurs dans les nuées, / Rose d'arbres, de fleuves, de chemins [...]' (HP, 93). This formulation continues in a very long series of repetitions and appositions. The poet comes to perceive all forms in inherently dynamic and futural terms, as a '[r]ose à venir'. As he becomes aware of the motion by which being continually voids itself and opens outwards anew, he realizes that form is not something to be abstracted or redeemed from the dynamics of worldly existence. Form continually blossoms forth in the shifting forms of material existence. It is inherently futural—'[une r]ose à venir'—because it emerges out of contingent actions. Bonnefoy thus suggests that the artist is no longer to be imagined as a godlike figure who retreats from the world and sanctifies a higher or more essential form of being. He is an 'horticulteur' at work amongst the forms of the physical world. Surrendering himself to the world's physical dynamics of exposure, he allows the world's agency to articulate itself *through him*. He facilitates the flourishing of worldly forms—'Rose d'arbres, de fleuves, de chemins'—by fostering their interaction, their shared dynamic of becoming.

Bonnefoy addresses this dynamic of exposure in the final sequence of 'L'Heure présente'. The final lines of the poem are an apostrophe to 'l'heure présente' itself:

> Heure présente, ne renonce pas,
> Reprends tes mots des mains errantes de la foudre,
> Écoute-les faire du rien parole,

[3] Morin, *Jean-Luc Nancy*, p. 61.

> Risque-toi
> Dans même la confiance que rien ne prouve,
> Lègue-nous de ne pas mourir désespérés.
>
> (HP, 96)

The 'present hour' is the current moment in history. But, 'présente' can be read as a verb as well as an adjective here. The 'heure présente' is thus also 'the hour that presents'. It is the present moment in which existence bears itself forth. On one level, these final lines address the current generation and urge them to have faith in their own voices. The poet asks us to hear the way that 'la parole' can emerge from the world, its 'mots des mains errantes de la foudre' unfurling in new and unpredictable ways. He reassures us that the world's own dynamic of opening will teach us to bear and to live through its processes of destruction. Speaking to a generation of people who are alive now and who will outlive him, Bonnefoy urges them to place their faith in this force of renewal. And yet, in the very same gesture, the poet also adddresses *the present moment*, the moment that unfurls and presents itself. The final sequence of 'L'Heure présente' is also a prayer to the very dynamic by which existence emerges from the nothingness and renews itself. The poet urges this dynamic to keep articulating itself. He suggests that poetry *is nothing but* an articulation of faith in this dynamic of exposure. It is the act by which we allow the world to act in and through us. And so, Bonnefoy urges: 'Risque-toi / Dans même la confiance que rien ne prouve'. He appeals to the world to keep opening in and through him, and to keep carrying him outwards, into an unknown and unmade future.

Like so many of the poems analysed in this book, 'L'Heure présente' dramatizes a crisis in the structures of conceptual thought. Bonnefoy explores how the promise of a higher meaning or essence that precedes material existence's shifting appearances reveals itself to be an illusion. He depicts this crisis in personal terms, dramatizing the intense feelings of dispossession and isolation that he feels as the promise of the absolute dissolves. He dramatizes this crisis in historical terms too, tracing its evolution from Gentileschi's and Carravagio's painting, to Shakespeare's theatre, to Baudelaire's or Mallarmé's poetry. And as he does so, he encourages us to live through this crisis, to 'tenir le pas gagné', as he writes in 'L'Acte et le lieu de la poésie'. He insists that the voiding of our metaphysical ideals by the negativity of finite material existence is not to be lamented. For it is by obliterating this ideal form, Bonnefoy suggests, that this negativity restores value and sanctity to the material *praxis* of existence itself. Existence is opened up to a beyond that is 'nothing that is' but that nonetheless endlessly mobilizes and renews existences. Sense is perceived not as that which we *have* but as that which *is*. It becomes a concrete, dynamic, and relational force. And the poetic performance allows us to feel, unfurling within the body of the poem and within our own bodies, all that is most ungraspable and yet most intimate: existence's own dynamic of exposition.

Presence

In 2011, five years before the poet's death, 'L'Heure présente' offers a summation of the poetic method that Bonnefoy has been elaborating since the publication of *Dans le leurre du seuil* in 1975. Like so many of the poems examined in this book, 'L'Heure présente' explores how humanity's metaphysical consciousness is inspired by structures of representation. Bonnefoy considers how language's mimetic structures cause humanity to perceive the shifting forms of material existence as a mere a copy of a more essential reality. He analyses how, once the promise of the metaphysical exhausts itself, these same structures of representation leave us feeling that the world is nothing but an endless series of empty and meaningless forms. In a very similar way, poems in *Dans le leurre du seuil*, *Début et fin de la neige*, or *Les Planches courbes* sift through the fallen images of the tradition. Bonnefoy explores how the image's promise of a higher sense is exhausted. And he laments that writers nonetheless continue to use its reflexive and dualist structure to understand the meaning of human existence and the structure of reality. In 'La Voix lointaine', he protests that the image's cleft structure causes us to perceive our own existence in fractured terms, as an endless series of displacements and differences, in which meaning and value can only be understood according to a logic of lack. He warns us in 'Hopkins Forest' that this mode of thinking threatens to convince us of 'le non-être' of our embodied and material existence. From one poem to the next, Bonnefoy entreats us to move beyond the mimetic model, to cast off its fallen structures, and to step outside the context of our own dispossession. In the essay 'La Présence et l'image' (1981), Bonnefoy observes that the modern poet or theorist at work in 'la chambre d'études' asserts 'qu'il n'y a bien, dans les ruines du *cogito*, que les milles niveaux de nuées rapides de ce langage que nous ne sommes, pour notre jour fugitif, qu'un froissement léger des structures, qu'un pli que nous ne pourrons prétendre entièrement reconnaître'

(E, 185). Bonnefoy laments that these writers perceive the structures of linguistic consciousness to be identical to the structures of human perception. They read all existence linguistically, tracing a folding motion that endlessly doubles all existence, exploring how meaning seems to be promised everywhere and, yet, endlessly evades us. All that seems so tantalizingly suggestive reveals itself to be *other*. Alienation seems to be the operative force in our own subjectivity. We become convinced that lack and absence are hard-wired into all worldly existence.

Similarly, in 'Poésie et vérité' (1986), Bonnefoy complains that contemporary writers recognize the relativity of language's meanings but that this does not lead them to explore the finite, physical dynamics that produce this play. They affirm the primacy of the play of signification and 'absolutise donc le langage à proportion même qu'elle relativise les acceptions' (E, 263). And so, Bonnefoy observes, they present poetry as 'la rupture d'un code' (E, 263), as a transgressive form of play within the structures of language. These writers suggest that poetry is an intensification or subversion of the ordinary linguistic structures that we use in everyday life. Bonnefoy vehemently rejects this idea and insists that poetry is not 'la rupture d'un code' but 'la mise à distance de l'idée même de code' (E, 263). He protests that that there is a 'différence de nature' between these two activities. The poetic act is:

> ce qui transgresse non un certain état de conceptualisation du monde mais tout système de cette sorte. C'est ce qui, défaisant mais par prescience d'une autre écoute, nous rend la dimension perdue, qui est de présence à présence, et avec elle toute une part de notre être-au-monde, qui avait été réprimée: et nous permet d'y penser, aussi bien, nous permet de comprendre mieux notre condition. (E, 264)

What frustrates Bonnefoy about the notion that poetry is a way of playing with linguistic codes is that it espouses the notion that linguistic consciousness is a transcendental horizon. It suggests that human consciousness can only play with the linguistic parameters by which it accesses the real. No other forms of experience are available to us. He, on the other hand, insists that poetry is a mode of action that refuses to be circumscribed by the diktats of linguistic consciousness and that opens up the self-reflexive structures of linguistic perception to the resonant play of embodied and material existence. He argues in 'La Parole poétique' that poetic prosody has always sought to draw our attention back to the generative resonance between linguistic, sensual, and material forces. It has always cultivated another way of knowing. Language will not express corporeal or material existence *but*, Bonnefoy insists, its signifying structures *are* continually exposed to sensual and material forces. It is by embracing the negativity of finite existence, he contends, that poetry can attune us to the endlessly spacious contact that occurs between signifying, material, and corporeal forces in any linguistic gesture. The poem is thus capable of *relativizing* the structures of linguistic consciousness. It uses all the performative means at its disposal—vocative, sonorous, rhythmic, and graphic—to make us feel a more primary resonance, the fertile exchange or oscillation that occurs between different modalities of sense, and that brings language, poetry, and indeed all forms of existence into being.

And so, Bonnefoy keeps reminding us that the negativity that voids our desire to appropriate material existence's essential meaning does not block our desire for intimacy with the physical world. On the contrary, finitude spatializes our intellectual, corporeal, and material existence. In poems like 'Ô flamme' or 'Hopkins Forest', Bonnefoy dramatizes a moment in which he, like Mallarmé during the *crise de Tournon*, realizes that nothing transcends the motion by which things come into and pass out of existence. Bonnefoy inflects Heidegger's conception of 'being-toward-death' with the highly corporeal understanding of mortality that emerges from Baudelaire's poetics. He presents finitude not as a confrontation with the outer limit of one's life, but as the sensual and embodied reality of perpetually living *through* death in each and every instant (IM, 172). He reminds us that all bodies are infinitely exposed to their ends or limits and that this dynamic of exposure is precisely what brings them into being. Accepting that there is no experience of subjectivity, no linguistic structure of meaning or identity, that precedes the body's structure of opening, the poet affirms that the body itself is the site of existence's exposure. He presents it as 'un théâtre [...] de l'évidence', to return to the phrase from his essay on Baudelaire. And so, finitude's dynamic of exposure inspires a new practice of affirmation. This is the practice that Bonnefoy embraced in the final sequence of *Dans le leurre de seuil*, in which the poet repeats the formulation 'Oui par' over and over again. Bonnefoy insists that we can feel the worldly dynamics of exposure that bring both the human body and the body of language into being. We can affirm the inherently exposed or consensual nature of our existence, 'notre être-au-monde'.

The radical sense of intimacy that the poet feels with the physical world when he realizes that he is part of this common or shared dynamic of exposition is what he terms 'la présence'. It is for this reason that Bonnefoy describes 'la présence' as a sensation of 'le simple', 'l'un', 'la transparence', or 'l'indéfait'. By placing such emphasis on oneness and simplicity, Bonnefoy aligns himself with ancient philosophers such as Plotinus or Lucretius, or Anglo-American process philosophers such as Whitehead. It is crucial to stress, however, that Bonnefoy's conception of 'la présence' does not descend into the materially monist view of existence that we find the in the work of philosophers like Whitehead. Bonnefoy never ceases to foreground the fact that finitude's structure of opening endlessly spatializes and singularizes all existence. Its hesitant or resonant dynamic keeps matter, corporeal sense, and signification projecting and deflecting each other outwards. Bonnefoy presents this resonance as a kind of ontological disposition. Its hesitant motion allows worldly existence to emerge in its heterogeneity, what Nancy describes as its singular plurality.[4] And so, whilst Bonnefoy asserts the primacy of this concrete dynamic of exposition, he never loses sight of the diversity to which it gives rise.

Bonnefoy's critique of conceptual thought and his insistence on the importance of conceiving of subjectivity in relational and situated terms have much in common with Heidegger's attempts 'to uncover a more fundamental, pre-reflective, non-appropriative relation to being', to cite Clark.[5] Bonnefoy's understanding of the poem as a gesture of worldly exposure also resembles Heidegger's affirmation that the work discloses or sets forth the 'world'.[6] And yet, it is also crucial to stress that Bonnefoy's understanding of exposure is less anthropocentric than Heidegger's conception of disclosure. Whereas *Dasein* entrances the sense of existence and activates the world, Bonnefoy insists on the agency of the concrete, worldly, relational dynamics that expose sense. By placing so much emphasis on existence's own force of exposition, Bonnefoy avoids making the ontological distinction that Heidegger makes between Being and beings. Morin observes that Heidegger presents Being as 'nothing but its difference from beings', 'nothing but the "that there is" of anything that is'.[7] For Bonnefoy, the very notion of Being is generated by linguistic representations that encourage us to double and to essentialize existence. He refuses to oppose Being and beings, appearing and appearances, and instead stresses the radical simplicity of existence's dynamic of exposition. He insists that existence does not

[4] In 'La Voix lointaine', for example, Bonnefoy is acutely aware that it is the resonance of the human voice that coaxes linguistic consciousness into being. The dynamics of exposure that he foregrounds within his poems foster not only creation but differentiation.

[5] Clark, *Martin Heidegger*, p. 12.

[6] Ibid., p. 46.

[7] Morin, *Jean-Luc Nancy*, p. 61.

withdraw to hold or maintain itself as a pure form of negativity that we could characterize as Being. On the contrary, material existence dissolves only to distribute itself without reserve, with an infinite generosity and profusion. And so, Bonnefoy deconstructs the specular and dualist logic of Heidegger's 'ontological reduction'. Resisting his inherently visual conceptions of appearing and disclosure, the poet prefers to conceive of the world's dynamic of exposure in tactile terms. He suggests that such a tactile approach allows us to think in immersive terms, exploring how existence's dynamic of opening overtakes us and opens us up, exposing 'un sens qui précède tous les sens, et qui nous précède' (to use Nancy's phrase) (SM, 11). Although language endlessly tries to appropriate this dynamic of opening, to forge oppositions between appearing and appearances, Being and being, Bonnefoy insists that this dynamic remains completely simple, completely unmasterable: existence opens outwards, entering into relation, bringing being into being.

Similarly, in *Le Sens du monde*, Nancy critiques the visual motifs that dominate Heidegger's work and affirms that touch allows us to conceive of sense as a dynamic of opening (SM, 32–5). Nancy uses the motif of touch to stress that the world's transitive force is not unveiled or disclosed by a human subject (or by *Dasein*) but that it is continually exposed by a dynamic of exposure that is concrete, general, and worldly. Nancy argues that touch makes us aware of 'ce qui précède et surprend le phénomène dans le phénomène lui-même, [...] sa venue ou sa survenue' (SM, 32). What he is suggesting here is that touch attunes us the rhythm of separation and contact that brings all stable and substantial forms into being. This conception of rhythmic touching reveals the spaciousness of all bodies and their immersion in world of process. It shows us how all phenomena are caught up in and overtaken by the world's dynamic of opening. As Nancy writes, 'on [...] s'y laisse prendre [...], emporter, mettre à bout' (SM, 34). And so, sense is conceived as a concrete force that is communicated by touch only to the extent that it is never grasped or circumscribed but is continually 'expropriated' or released by the constant interruptions, breaks, reverberations, and openings inherent in touching. Sense never inheres in any body, substance, or object but circulates in the endless dynamics of exposition that bring bodies into being. Sense can keep circulating precisely because touch is continually ungrounded and renewed.

For both Bonnefoy and Nancy, the act of writing cultivates this 'expropriative' form of touch. Without lapsing into a metaphysical logic of revelation, without claiming to make manifest being's hidden essence or interiority, Bonnefoy and Nancy use the performative resources of language to expose existence's radically exteriorized structure. They make us aware of the different forces that continually touch one another in the scene of writing. In *Le Poids d'une pensée*, as Nancy explores the material forces that articulate themselves in the scene of speaking or writing, he observes:

> Le sens a besoin d'une épaisseur, d'une densité, d'une masse, et donc d'une opacité, d'une obscurité par lesquelles il donne prise, il se laisser toucher *comme sens* précisément là où il s'absente comme discours. Or ce là est un point matériel, un point pesant: la chair d'une lèvre, la pointe d'une plume ou d'un style, toute écriture en tant qu'elle trace le bord et le débord du langage. C'est le point où toute écriture *s'excrit*, se dépose hors du sens qu'elle inscrit, dans les choses dont ce sens est censé former l'inscription. (PP, 8)

Nancy suggests that the text unfolds in the dynamics by which signification touches and is deflected by 'un point matériel'. Speaking thus emerges as a kind of vibratory contact between meaning and the larynx, mouth, and lips; writing unfolds between signification and the material supports of paper, pen, and hand. For Nancy, style is nothing other than the exploration of how one force continually spatializes and inflects another. It explores the very process by which writing is 'excribed'. It is by foregrounding the technics of poetic prosody that Bonnefoy urges us to conceive of writing in similar terms. He stresses that poetry emerges from the resonance between the rival forces of sound and signification, meaning and materiality. He suggests that to listen to a poem is to hear one force continually 'disappropriating' or releasing the other (SPV, 183).

In *Corpus*, Nancy suggests that this conception of contact means that touch resembles an address. For we conceive of touch as the dynamic that causes all forces to open or project outwards. He proposes that writing enacts this dynamic: 'celui qui écrit ne touche pas sur le mode de la saisie, de la prise en main […] mais il touche sur le mode de s'adresser, de s'envoyer à la touche d'un dehors, d'un dérobé, d'un écarté, d'un espacé' (C, 19). He adds: 'Sa touche même, et qui est bien sa touche, lui est dans le principe retirée, espacée, écartée' (C, 19). The text attunes us to the contact between forces that spatializes their dynamics. It makes us feel the way that this spatializing force is active within our own bodies, within all the interactive (or intra-active) bodies that populate our spacious material world. The text's spacious gestures expose the performativity of all existence, 'un théâtre du monde', to use Nancy's phrase (SM, 43). In a similar manner, Bonnefoy suggests that poetic rhythm is—and has perhaps always been—a performative way if reflecting on the generative nature of resonance. The technics of poetic prosody allow the poet to explore the dance between forces that keeps all things—the body, the intellect, material phenomena—opening outwards. For Bonnefoy, poetry's ontological performance is inherently *methexic* because it draws us into this resonance. It makes us realize that there is no space for us to view this resonance from the outside but that it is active within us. We have the eerie sensation that we do not articulate it but that it articulates us. The poem thus pulls us into the rhythms of worldly existence and calls us to experience them *from the inside*. We feel the systolic and diastolic motion by which existence steadily opens outwards and withdraws, expands and contracts. We feel sense resonate, departing from us and returning to us, echoing within us and outside us, endlessly diffracting our experience of existence.

The ecstatic or 'expropriative' conception of touch that Bonnefoy and Nancy cultivate transforms traditional conceptions of subjectivity and the human body. Accepting that there is no subject, no 'âme' or 'esprit' that precedes corporeal existence, they present the body as a concrete site of exposure, 'un lieu d'existence' (C, 16). It is the space in which physical, sensual, and cognitive forces endlessly interact. When we address, listen to, or touch ourselves, we are addressing nothing other than the body's own ceaseless feedback loops, what Nancy describes as 'la résonance d'un renvoi' (AE, 30). We are this reverberation, this resonance that occurs back and forth across the body's structures, and between one body and another. And as sense returns to us, continually deflected or inflected, we feel all through it the vibratory touch of the 'other' (PP, 31). In 'Vox clamans in deserto', Nancy suggests that it is this touch of the 'other' is what solicits a reaction in us. It sets us in resonance and thus inspires joy, laughter, or tears (PP, 31). The conception of resonance that is developed here dissolves any clear distinction between inner and outer, the conscious and the unconscious, the transcendent and the immanent. In the final stanzas of 'Hopkins Forest', Bonnefoy asks us to feel subjectivity's or corporeity's atmospheric force. He suggests that our existence is just as tremulous and ungrounded as any other dynamic. Our physicality is as just as spacious, mysterious, and unfathomable as the material universe. We are continually emerging from and dissolving into its infinite depths. He proposes that we feel these depths in the act of touch, that this is what gives touch its uncanny force: we are touched by the body's—and the world's—opacity, distance, depths, death, void, obscurity, and shadows. At the end of 'Hopkins Forest', we feel ourselves to be the quivering threshold across which tangible and intangible forces play. In 'La

Voix lointaine', we feel the way that the resonance of the human voice bounces back off the body's dark and unpenetrated surfaces, dancing with 'l'ombre de [s]on corps' (PC, 64). In *Corpus*, Nancy argues that the body exposes 'le contact étranger, l'étranger restant étranger dans le contact' (C, 19). He adds: 'c'est tout l'affaire du tact, de la touche des corps' (C, 19). Perceiving the body as a 'lieu d'existence', we become aware of the way that our own existence trembles between presence and absence. We feel ourselves emerging out of our own 'naive' bodily action. And as we do so, we perceive—as Bonnefoy writes in his essay on Mondrian—'notre univers comme tel qui, de l'intérieur, se révèle à la fois la diversité des êtres et l'unité qui les lie—à la fois le rien et la plénitude, à la fois la ténèbre et une lumière' (NR, 135).

This form of immersive thinking charges the human body and the material world with a new energy. The transcendent is no longer conceived as somewhere beyond existence but as the infinite depths out of which worldly existence continually emerges and into which it withdraws. The unconscious too is no longer a buried and inaccessible place. It is understood in radically corporeal and material terms as the very obscurity and impenetrability of physicality itself, as the resistant matter against which consciousness reverberates, returning deflected, diffracted, and diverted. By rethinking the transcendental and the unconscious in this way, both Bonnefoy and Nancy allow us to perceive how darkness, emptiness, and void energize existence and give it an ecstatic creativity, a capricious ingenuity. They overturn the familiar forms of perception engendered by the pattern-forming structures of conceptual thought and show us that our material existence is more vital and more mysterious than we often think. All that seems most familiar and solid—our own bodies, possessions, and landscapes—reveal their essential uncanniness and unpredictability.[8] We feel cosmic and subatomic dynamics at work within our own bodies. We feel 'la présence': the feeling of joy and excitement, fear and wonder that comes when we realize the radically exteriorized nature of our own existence.

Some thinkers, such as Simon Critchley and Robert Bernasconi, have raised the concern that the re-emergence of this kind of corporeal and material ontology threatens to undermine the primacy that has been accorded to ethics in French thought since the Second World War. They suggest that such a gesture can legitimize forms of exploitation and

[8] For an investigation of the ecocritical implications of this radical state of intimacy with processual material existence, see Emily McLaughlin, '"Et que faut-il penser / De ces pommes jaunes?" An Ecocritical Reading of Yves Bonnefoy's Punctual Colour Work', *French Studies*, 71.3 (2017), pp. 348–61.

violence. Critchley criticizes the way that an ontology of being-in-relation emphasizes 'the reciprocity of the "with"' and effaces the alterity and asymmetry of Levinas's face-to-face encounter.[9] Bernasconi argues that it minimizes the importance of alterity and ends up practising precisely the kind of philosophy of immanence that it initially sought to deconstruct.[10] In his essay 'A Different Alterity', Watkin argues that such critiques misunderstand an ontology of relation because they fail to appreciate that it does not begin with a specular and self-reflexive linguistic structure that suppresses alterity, appropriating it as 'selfsame'. There is thus, Watkin writes, 'no need for a Levinasian Other to underwrite the ethical relation'.[11] An ontology of being-in-relation presupposes that human existence begins, not with an act of appropriation, but with a gesture of opening. It affirms that the self only exists by being opened up and thrust into relation and that the physical praxis of existence is always already an *ethos*. Watkin writes, 'the basis of the mutuality is not a shared value or essence, or even a reciprocal pact "to look out for each other", but simply this: that its participants have nothing in common; they *are* in common'.[12] We do not exist in relation but as relation. The contact that occurs between us is fundamentally 'expropriative': it projects us outwards in endlessly singular ways and subjects us all to processes of transformation. Similarly, in the essay 'Il reste à faire le négatif', Bonnefoy suggests that ethics never begins with the thought of difference but with the feeling of compassion. He suggests that ethics emerges from an awareness of our common state of finitude and exposure, our shared vulnerability.[13]

Ontological Performance

The at once materialist and ethical stance that Bonnefoy adopts allows us to perceive connections between his work and that of other materially- and

[9] Simon Critchley, *Ethics, Politics, Subjectivity: Essays on Derrida, Levinas and Contemporary French Thought* (London: Verso, 1999), pp. 251–2.

[10] Robert Bernasconi, 'On Deconstructing Nostalgia for Community within the West: The Debate between Nancy and Blanchot', *Research in Phenomenology* 23 (1993), 3–21 (p. 12). For a brief summary of Critchley's and Bernasconi's respective positions, see Christopher Watkin, 'A Different Alterity: Jean-Luc Nancy's "Singular Plural"', *Paragraph*, 30.2 (2007), 50–64 (p. 60).

[11] Watkin, 'A Different Alterity', p. 61. [12] Ibid.

[13] Bonnefoy writes: 'la compassion [...] sait aimer la finitude là où on voudrait le plus oublier les ravages, dans l'existence d'autrui' (E, 251). He proposes that the only way that we can truly experience and face up to the negativity of existence that is provoked by finitude is through the feeling of compassion: 'le seul vrai "négatif", le seul non illusoire déni de ce déni de présence qu'est le langage, c'est cette compassion active qui fait que les mots, pris au plus près du besoin, se ramassent sur l'immédiat, dans tant d'urgence, se taisent' (E, 251).

ethically-minded writers. Some of the strongest affinities that emerge are between his writings and those of Francophone poets, particularly those stemming from the Antillean tradition, Aimé Césaire and Édouard Glissant. Bonnefoy places a similar emphasis on vocal performance, rhythm, song, and dance. He experiments with plastic and haptic qualities of language as they do. Césaire and Glissant use these devices to privilege embodied modes of perception and to reflect on the subject's relationship to its own body, the bodies of others, and the physical world. They also critique the structures of conceptual thought but their analysis is given tremendous political urgency by their desire to resist the colonizing force of the narrowly rationalist structures of French Metropolitan thought and to critique the way that it has been used to dominate, define, and demean the lives and the culture of the Martinican people. There is an affinity too between Bonnefoy's conception of being-in-relation and Glissant's *Poétique de la relation*.[14] Glissant deconstructs the Cartesian model of subjectivity and explores the ways in which human subjectivity emerges from the interaction of myriad cultural, social, political, economic, atmospheric, and material processes. Undoubtedly, however, Bonnefoy is more wary of the signifying structures of language than Glissant and feels unable to experiment as freely as he does with practices of representation, in order to propose newly hybrid and heterogeneous kinds of social and political structure. This comparison undoubtedly challenges us to question Bonnefoy's and Nancy's relation to power. They do not face the same pressing need that Glissant does to contend with and to mitigate the effect of oppressive systems of objectification and instrumentalization. Their work cultivates a salutary and hopeful new ethics but, we might wonder, what resources does it give us to cope with the patterns ingrained in us by systemic modes of oppression? Is there no means of actively engaging with these systems in order to reorient them? Are we content with the lack of social, cultural, and political specificity in Bonnefoy's work, the use of a universalizing language that prevents him from addressing particular social and environmental predicaments in real places? Bonnefoy would surely contend that conceptual thought is at the root of all objectification and instrumentalization and that the task of poetry is to find the embodied and affective means of resisting it, in ways that are accessible to the greatest possible number. He suggests that all other efforts—to work within the system to change the system—will be in vain. To return to the quotation

[14] Édouard Glissant, *Poétique de la relation* (Paris: Gallimard, 1990).

from 'Poésie et vérité', he defines poetry not as 'la rupture d'un code', but as the rupture of 'tout système de cette sorte' (E, 264). He insists that what is required is not another pragmatic attempt to reorient a failed system but an epistemological change, a different way of understanding how we all relate to ourselves, to others, and the physical world.

The most important affinity that exists between Bonnefoy's performative poetics and Césaire's and Glissant's post-colonial writings is undoubtedly the fact that they all address the question of being-in-relation in simultaneously ethical and materialist terms. Bonnefoy's expropriative conception of touch allows him to develop an ethics that is at once social and environmental. He insists that to conceive of human subjectivity and human society self-reflexively is only to conceive of it in conceptual terms. It is to perceive other people and things as objects, as if they were determinate entities rather than beings. If we surrender to this mode of thinking, Bonnefoy writes in the essay 'La Parole poétique' (2000):

> nous allons être coupés de ce qui se joue en nous mais aussi de ce que vivent les autres, nous resterons capables d'analyser les phénomènes de la matière mais serons dissuadés de notre désir d'aimer, [...] ce qui aurait pu nous être du proche s'étant fait ainsi de l'étranger, nous serons obligés de vivre dans un triste univers tout en énigmes. (SPV, 195)

Anthropocentric and self-reflexive modes of conceptual thought edit out the reality of the world's dynamic material processes. In doing so, they cut us off from their processes of exchange and transformation, from the possibility of sharing and renewal. Similarly, Césaire uses the volcano as a symbol of the destructive and creative force of natural existence—Glissant, the sea—and suggests that poetry attempts to attune the metaphysical structures of the French language to the fertile physical processes of exchange and transformation of his 'pays natal'.[15] Césaire uses the adjective 'natal' as Nancy uses the adjective 'naïf', to suggest that the material landscape of his country has the capacity for rebirth.[16] It is an eruptive landscape, one that has the capacity to open, to overturn the visions, narratives, and laws imposed upon it, and to renew itself. Like Bonnefoy and Nancy, Césaire contends that notions like creativity, ethics, or environmentalism cannot be compartmentalized. Creativity is ecosystemic, and ethics is too. They are

[15] See Jean Khalfa, 'Césaire Volcanique', *L'Esprit Créateur*, 45.2 (2005), 52–61.
[16] Aimé Césaire, *Cahier d'un retour au pays natal* (Paris: Présence Africaine, 1956).

embodied and concrete processes. When such forces are not understood in these terms, Bonnefoy never ceases to warn us, when finite physical existence is not perceived as an inherently regenerative and emancipating force, it is at grave risk of being instrumentalized and exploited by conceptual thought.

What makes Bonnefoy's poetics and Nancy's thought innovative is that they both affirm the primacy of sense over linguistic consciousness. They both refuse to reify or to 'absolutize' (to use Bonnefoy's verb) the boundary between human consciousness and physical reality. In doing so, they insist that the human body, the bodies that surround it, and the animate and inanimate presences of the physical world are not foreign or alien to us. They dispense with the need for the Romantic motif of communion and also for the tropes of incision or penetration that recur in Dupin's and du Bouchet's work, insisting that there is no need to engineer such a reunification. They propose that linguistic consciousness emerges out of the resonant dynamics of physical sense, and that language is spatialized and energized by sense's structures of reverberation. One force is never synonymous with or amalgamated with another, but each touches the other lightly, expropriating it, allowing it to bounce or ricochet outwards in unforeseen ways. Bonnefoy suggests that the poem sets sense in resonance. It allows us to feel the ways that sense reverberates back and forth between different modalities: semantic, corporeal, and material; temporal and spatial; tactile, sonorous, visual, and olfactory. Nancy writes in *Les Muses*: 'que fait donc l'art, si ce n'est en somme toucher à, et toucher par l'hétérogénéité principielle du "sentir"?'[17] The ontological nature of the poetic performance resides in the way that it exposes this fundamental resonance between different forms of sense, this 'hétérogénéité principielle'. Nancy suggests that its tremulous gesture exposes the trans-immanence of existence. The work of art allows us to feel the dynamic by which existence withdraws into nothingness and is exposed anew. In doing so, it exposes the inherently creative and spatializing contact that occurs between distinct forces, the dynamic that continually expropriates existence and allows it to keep exceeding or surpassing itself, to keep projecting outwards. Nancy sums up his point axiomatically: 'L'art n'a pas affaire au "monde" entendu comme extériorité simple, comme milieu ou comme nature. Il a affaire à l'être-au-monde dans son surgissement même'.[18]

[17] Jean-Luc Nancy, *Les Muses* (Paris: Galilée, 1994), p. 36.

[18] Ibid.

Bibliography

Texts by Yves Bonnefoy

(i) Poetry

Bonnefoy, Yves, *Du mouvement et de l'immobilité de Douve* (Paris: Mercure de France, 1953)
Bonnefoy, Yves, *Hier régnant désert* (Paris: Mercure de France, 1958)
Bonnefoy, Yves, *Pierre écrite* (Paris: Mercure de France, 1965)
Bonnefoy, Yves, *Dans le leurre du seuil* (Paris: Mercure, 1975)
Bonnefoy, Yves, *Ce qui fut sans lumière* (Paris: Mercure de France, 1987)
Bonnefoy, Yves, *Début et fin de la neige* (Paris: Mercure de France, 1991)
Bonnefoy, Yves, *Les Planches courbes* (Paris: Mercure de France, 2001)
Bonnefoy, Yves, *La Longue Chaîne de l'ancre* (Paris: Mercure de France, 2008)
Bonnefoy, Yves, *L'Heure présente* (Paris: Mercure de France, 2011)

(ii) Prose

Bonnefoy, Yves, *L'Improbable* (Paris: Mercure de France, 1959)
Bonnefoy, Yves, *Rimbaud par lui-même* (Paris: Seuil, 1962)
Bonnefoy, Yves, *Rome, 1630. L'Horizon du premier baroque* (Paris: Flammarion, 1970)
Bonnefoy, Yves, *L'Arrière-pays* (Geneva: A. Skira, 1972)
Bonnefoy, Yves, *Le Nuage rouge* (Paris: Mercure de France, 1977)
Bonnefoy, Yves, *Dictionnaire des mythologies et des religions des sociétés traditionnelles et du monde antique* (Paris: Flammarion, 1981)
Bonnefoy, Yves, *La Vérité de parole* (Paris: Mercure de France, 1988)
Bonnefoy, Yves, *Entretiens sur la poésie* (Paris: Mercure de France, 1990)
Bonnefoy, Yves, *Théâtre et poésie. Shakespeare et Yeats* (Paris: Mercure de France, 1998)
Bonnefoy, Yves, *Lieux et destins de l'image* (Paris: Le Seuil, 1998)
Bonnefoy, Yves, '*Igitur* et le photographe', in *Mallarmé 1842–1898, Un Destin d'écriture*, ed. Yves Peyré (Paris: Gallimard, Réunion des musées nationaux, 1998), pp. 59–85
Bonnefoy, Yves, *L'Imaginaire métaphysique* (Paris: Le Seuil, 2006)
Bonnefoy, Yves, *Notre besoin de Rimbaud* (Paris: Le Seuil, 2009)
Bonnefoy, Yves, *L'Inachevable. Entretiens sur la poésie, 1990–2010* (Paris: Albin Michel, 2010)
Bonnefoy, Yves, *Le Siècle où la parole a été victime* (Paris: Mercure de France, 2010)
Bonnefoy, Yves, *Le Lieu d'herbes* (Paris: Galilée, 2010)
Bonnefoy, Yves, *Sous le signe de Baudelaire* (Paris: Gallimard, 2011)

Texts by Jean-Luc Nancy

Nancy, Jean-Luc, and Philippe Lacoue-Labarthe, *Le Titre de la lettre. Une lecture de Lacan* (Paris: Galilée, 1973)
Nancy, Jean-Luc, *Ego Sum* (Paris: Flammarion, 1979)
Nancy, Jean-Luc, *Le Partage des voix* (Paris: Galilée, 1982)
Nancy, Jean-Luc, *La Communauté désœuvrée* (Paris: Christian Bourgois, 1986)
Nancy, Jean-Luc, *L'Oubli de la philosophie* (Paris: Galilée, 1986)
Nancy, Jean-Luc, *Une pensée finie* (Paris: Galilée, 1990)
Nancy, Jean-Luc, *Corpus* (Paris: Métailié, 1992)
Nancy, Jean-Luc, *Le Poids d'une pensée* (Grenoble, Québec: Presses universitaires de Grenoble, Le Griffon d'argile, 1991)
Nancy, Jean-Luc, *Le Sens du monde* (Paris: Galilée, 1993)
Nancy, Jean-Luc, *Les Muses* (Paris: Galilée, 1994)
Nancy, Jean-Luc, 'Nécessité du sens', in *Yves Bonnefoy. Poésie, peinture, musique*, ed. Michèle Finck (Strasbourg: Presses Universitaires de Strasbourg, 1995), pp. 43–50
Nancy, Jean-Luc, *Être singulier pluriel* (Paris: Galilée, 1996)
Nancy, Jean-Luc, 'Deguy l'an neuf!' in *Cahier Michel Deguy, Le Poète que je cherche à être*, ed. Yves Charnet (Paris: Éditions de la table ronde, 1996), pp. 164–81
Nancy, Jean-Luc, *Hegel. L'Inquiétude du négatif* (Paris: Hachette, 1997)
Nancy, Jean-Luc, *Le Regard du portrait* (Paris: Galilée, 2000)
Nancy, Jean-Luc, *L'Évidence du film* (Brussels: Yves Gevaert Éditeur, 2001)
Nancy, Jean-Luc, *À l'écoute* (Paris: Galilée, 2002)
Nancy, Jean-Luc, *Au fond des images* (Paris: Galilée, 2003)
Nancy, Jean-Luc, *Noli me tangere. Essai sur la levée du corps* (Paris: Bayard, 2003)
Nancy, Jean-Luc, and Emmanuel Laugier, 'Penser la poésie, avec Jean-Luc Nancy', *L'Animal. Littératures, arts & philosophies* (2003), 14–15
Nancy, Jean-Luc, 'Souveraine en peinture', in *Cléopâtre dans le miroir de l'art occidental*, ed. Claude Ritschard and Allison Morehead (Milan: 5 Continents Éditions, 2004), pp. 63–9
Nancy, Jean-Luc, and Mathilde Monnier, *Allitérations. Conversations sur la danse* (Paris: Galilée, 2005)
Nancy, Jean-Luc, *La Déclosion (Déconstruction du Christianisme 1)* (Paris: Galilée, 2005)
Nancy, Jean-Luc, *Le Plaisir au dessein* (Paris: Galilée, 2009)
Nancy, Jean-Luc, *L'Adoration* (Paris: Galilée, 2010)
Nancy, Jean-Luc, 'Calcul du poète', in *Demande: Littérature et philosophie* (Paris: Galilée, 2015), pp. 111–42

Secondary Texts

Acke, Daniel, *Yves Bonnefoy, Essayiste. Modernité et présence* (Amsterdam: Rodopi, 1999)
Agamben, Giorgio, *The End of the Poem* (Stanford, CA: Stanford University Press, 1999)
Alexandrova, Alena, Ignaas Devisch, Laurens Ten Kate, and Aukje Van Rooden, eds, *Re-treating Religion. Deconstructing Christianity with Jean-Luc Nancy* (New York: Fordham University Press, 2012)

Austin, J.L., *How to Do Things with Words* (Cambridge, MA: Harvard University Press, 1962)
Bachelard, Gaston, *La Poétique de l'espace* (Paris: Presses Universitaires de France, 1957)
Bancquart, Marie-Claire, *Dans le feuilletage de la terre* (Paris: Belfond, 1994)
Bastet, Ned, *Valéry à l'extrême. Les Au-delà de la raison* (Paris: L'Harmattan, 1999)
Bataille, Georges, *La Part maudite, précedé de La Notion de dépense* (Paris: Éditions de Minuit, 1967)
Bataille, Georges, *La Place de la Concorde*, ed. Denis Hollier (Paris: Gallimard, 1974)
Bataille, Georges, *L'Expérience intérieure* (Paris: Gallimard, 1978)
Baudelaire, Charles, *Œuvres complètes*, 2 vols, ed. Claude Pichois (Paris: Gallimard, Bibliothèque de la Pléiade, 1975–6)
Bennington, Geoffrey, 'In Rhythm: A Response to Jean-Luc Nancy', *SubStance*, 40.3 (2011), 18–19
Bernasconi, Robert, 'On Deconstructing Nostalgia for Community within the West: The Debate between Nancy and Blanchot', *Research in Phenomenology*, 23 (1993), 3–21
Blanchot, Maurice, *Le Livre à venir* (Paris: Gallimard, 1959)
Bombarde, Odile, and Jean Avice, eds, *Yves Bonnefoy* (Paris: L'Herne, 2010)
Bowie, Malcolm, *Lacan* (London: Fontana Press, 1991)
Brunel, Pierre, 'Yves Bonnefoy: L'Évocation d'une voix', in *Yves Bonnefoy: Poésie, peinture, musique*, ed. Michèle Finck (Strasbourg: Presses Universitaires de Strasbourg, 1995), pp. 23–32
Buchs, Arnaud, *Une pensée en mouvement. Trois essais sur Yves Bonnefoy* (Paris: Galilée, 2008)
Caws, Mary Ann, *The Inner Theatre of Recent French Poetry* (Princeton: Princeton University Press, 1972)
Césaire, Aimé, *Cahier d'un retour au pays natal* (Paris: Présence Africaine, 1956)
Clark, Timothy, *Derrida, Heidegger, Blanchot, Sources of Derrida's Notion and Practice of Literature* (Cambridge: Cambridge University Press, 1992)
Clark, Timothy, *Martin Heidegger* (Abingdon: Routledge, 2002)
Clark, Timothy, *The Poetics of Singularity, The Counter-Culturalist Turn in Heidegger, Derrida, Blanchot and the Later Gadamer* (Edinburgh: Edinburgh University Press, 2005)
Claudel, Paul, *Œuvre poétique* (Paris: Gallimard, Bibliothèque de la Pléiade, 1967)
Collot, Michel, *La Matière-émotion* (Paris: Presses Universitaires de France, 1997)
Collot, Michel, *Paysage et poésie: Du romantisme à nos jours* (Paris: José Corti, 2005)
Combe, Dominique, *Poésie et récit* (Paris: José Corti, 1989)
Combe, Dominique, 'Du "recueil" au "Poème-livre", au "Livre-poème"', *Méthode ! revue de littératures française et comparée*, 2 (2002), 15–22
Combe, Dominique, *Dominique Combe commente Les Planches Courbes d'Yves Bonnefoy* (Paris: Gallimard, 2005)
X Critchley, Simon, *Ethics, Politics, Subjectivity: Essays on Derrida, Levinas and Contemporary French Thought* (London: Verso, 1999)
Crow, Christine, *Paul Valéry and The Poetics of Voice* (Cambridge: Cambridge University Press, 1982)

Culler, Jonathan, *The Literary in Theory* (Stanford, CA: Stanford University Press, 2007)
Davies, Gardner, *Mallarmé et le drame solaire* (Paris: José Corti, 1959)
Davis, Bret W., ed., *Martin Heidegger. Key Concepts* (Durham: Acumen, 2010)
Derrida, Jacques, *La Voix et le phénomène* (Paris: Presses Universitaires de France, 1967)
Derrida, Jacques, *Marges de la philosophie* (Paris: Les Éditions de Minuit, 1972)
Derrida, Jacques, *La Dissemination* (Paris: Seuil, 1972)
Derrida, Jacques, *Ulysse Gramophone* (Paris: Galilée, 1987)
Derrida, Jacques, *Limited Inc.* (Paris: Galilée, 1990)
Derrida, Jacques, *Le Toucher, Jean-Luc Nancy* (Paris: Galilée, 2000)
Dolar, Mladen, *A Voice and Nothing More* (Cambridge, MA: MIT Press, 2006)
Dupin, Jacques, *Gravir* (Paris: Gallimard, 1963)
Fabbri, Véronique, *Paul Valéry. Le Poème et la danse* (Paris: Hermann, 2009)
ffrench, Patrick, *After Bataille. Sacrifice, Exposure, Community* (Leeds: Legenda, 2007)
Finck, Michèle, *Yves Bonnefoy. Le Simple et le sens* (Paris: José Corti, 1989)
Finck, Michèle, 'Poétique de la voix rauque', in *Yves Bonnefoy. Poésie, peinture, musique*, ed. Michèle Finck (Strasbourg: Presses Universitaires de Strasbourg, 1995), pp. 33–42
Finck, Michèle, Daniel Lançon, and Maryse Staiber, eds, *Yves Bonnefoy et l'Europe du XXe siècle* (Strasbourg: Presses Universitaires de Strasbourg, 2003)
Gagnebin, Murielle, ed., *Yves Bonnefoy. Lumière et nuit des images* (Seyssel: Champ Vallon, 2005)
Game, Jérôme, *Poetic Becomings* (Oxford, New York: Peter Lang, 2011)
Gasarian, Gérard, *Yves Bonnefoy. La Poésie, la présence* (Seyssel: Champ Vallon, 1986)
Genova, Pamela, 'White on Black on White: Yves Bonnefoy's *Début et fin de la neige*', *Romance Studies*, 23.2 (2005), 143–58
Giguère, Ronald Gérard, *Le Concept de la réalité dans la poésie d'Yves Bonnefoy* (Paris: A.-G. Nizet, 1985)
Gillespie, Stewart, and Philip Hardie, eds, *The Cambridge Companion to Lucretius* (Cambridge: Cambridge University Press, 2007)
Glissant, Édouard, *Poétique de la relation* (Paris: Gallimard, 1990)
Goldsmith, Elizabeth E., *Sacred Symbols in Art* (Whitefish, MT: Kessinger Publishing, 2003)
Grosz, Elizabeth, *Jacques Lacan. A Feminist Introduction* (London, New York: Routledge, 1990)
Harrow, Susan, *The Material, the Real, and the Fractured Self: Subjectivity and Representation from Rimbaud to Réda* (Toronto, Buffalo, London: University of Toronto Press, 2004)
Heidegger, Martin, *Being and Time*, trans. John MacQuarrie (Oxford: Blackwell, 1962)
Heidegger, Martin, *Nietzsche, I* (San Francisco: Harper and Row, 1987)
Heidegger, Martin, *Poetry, Language, Thought* (New York: Harper & Row, 2001)
Hewson, Mark, and Marcus Coelen, eds, *Georges Bataille. Key Concepts* (Abingdon, New York: Routledge, 2016)
Hill, Leslie, *The Cambridge Introduction to Jacques Derrida* (Cambridge: Cambridge University Press, 2007)

Hill, Leslie, *Bataille, Klossowski, Blanchot: Writing the Limit* (Oxford: Oxford University Press, 2007)

Himy, Olivier, *Yves Bonnefoy. Poèmes commentés* (Paris: Honoré Champion, 2006)

Hölderlin, Friedrich, *Hyperion and Selected Poems* (New York: Continuum, 1990)

Homer, *The Odyssey*, trans. E.V. Rieu (Harmondsworth: Penguin, 1945)

Howells, Christina, *Derrida. From Deconstruction to Ethics* (Cambridge: Polity Press, 1999)

Inizan, Yvon, *La Demande et le don. L'Attestation poétique chez Yves Bonnefoy et Paul Ricœur* (Rennes: Presses Universitaires de Rennes, 2013)

Jaccottet, Philippe, *Une transaction secrète* (Paris: Gallimard, 1987)

Jaccottet, Philippe, *Œuvres*, ed. José-Flore Tappy (Paris: Gallimard, 2014)

Jackson, John E., *Yves Bonnefoy* (Paris: Seghers, 1976)

Jackson, John E., *La Question du moi. Un aspect de la modernité poétique européenne. T.S. Eliot, Paul Celan, Yves Bonnefoy* (Neuchâtel: A la Baconnière, 1978)

Jackson, John E., *À la Souche obscure des rêves. La dialectique de l'écriture chez Yves Bonnefoy* (Paris: Mercure de France, 1993)

James, Ian, *The Fragmentary Demand, An Introduction to the philosophy of Jean-Luc Nancy* (Stanford, CA: Stanford University Press, 2006)

James, Ian, *The New French Philosophy* (Cambridge: Polity Press, 2012)

Janus, Adrienne, 'Listening: Jean-Luc Nancy and the Anti-Ocular Turn in Continental Philosophy and Critical Theory', *Comparative Literature*, 63.2 (2011), 182–202

Khalfa, Jean, 'Césaire Volcanique', *L'Esprit Créateur*, 45.2 (2005), 52–61

Labarthe, Patrick, Odile Bombarde, Jean-Paul Avice, *Yves Bonnefoy. Écrits récents, 2000–2009* (Geneva: Slatkine Érudition, 2011)

Lacan, Jacques, *Les Quatre concepts fondamentaux de la psychanalyse* (Paris: Seuil, 1973)

Lançon, Daniel, ed., *Yves Bonnefoy et le XIXe siècle. Vocation et filiation* (Tours: Publications de l'Université François Rabelais, 2001)

Lançon, Daniel, and Patrick Née, eds, *Yves Bonnefoy: poésie, recherche et savoirs* (Paris: Hermann, 2007)

Loxley, James, *Performativity* (London: Routledge, 2007)

Lucretius, *De Rerum Natura*, trans. Alicia Elsbeth Stallings (London: Penguin, 2007)

McLaughlin, Emily, 'Noli me tangere: Bonnefoy, Nancy, Derrida', *French Forum*, 37.1 (2012), 183–94

McLaughlin, Emily, 'Affirmation Without End: Some Syntactical Similarities between Yves Bonnefoy's poetry and Jean-Luc Nancy's Philosophy', *L'Esprit créateur*, 55 (2015), 110–22

McLaughlin, Emily, '"Et que faut-il penser / De ces pommes jaunes?" An Ecocritical Reading of Yves Bonnefoy's Punctual Colour Work', *French Studies*, 71.3 (2017), 348–61

McLaughlin, Emily, 'Gravity and Grace: Bonnefoy's and Bergson's "Monde-images"', in *Gravity and Grace: Essays for Roger Pearson*, ed. Charlie Louth and Patrick McGuinness (Cambridge: Legenda, 2019), pp. 161–77

Malabou, Catherine, *L'Avenir de Hegel: Plasticité, Temporalité, Dialectique* (Paris: Vrin, 1996)

Malabou, Catherine, *La Plasticité au soir de l'écriture* (Paris: Éditions Léo Scheer, 2004)

Mallarmé, Stéphane, *Œuvres complètes*, 2 vols, ed. Bertrand Marchal (Paris: Gallimard, Bibliothèque de la Pléiade, 1998–2003)

Mandell, Charlotte, 'Translator's Note', in Jean-Luc Nancy, *On Listening* (New York: Fordham University Press, 2007), pp. xi–xii

Marchal, Bertrand, *La Religion de Mallarmé* (Paris: José Corti, 1988)

Moore, Alexander, *Cultural Anthropology, The Field Study of Human Beings* (San Diego: Collegiate Press, 1998)

Moran, Dermot, *Introduction to Phenomenology* (London, New York: Routledge, 2000)

Morin, Marie-Ève, *Jean-Luc Nancy* (Cambridge: Polity Press, 2012)

Mumford, Meg, *Bertolt Brecht* (Abingdon: Routledge, 2009)

Naughton, John T., *The Poetics of Yves Bonnefoy* (Chicago: University of Chicago Press, 1984)

Née, Patrick, *La Poétique du lieu dans l'œuvre d'Yves Bonnefoy, ou Moïse sauvé* (Paris: Presses Universitaires de France, 1999)

Née, Patrick, *La Rhétorique profonde d'Yves Bonnefoy* (Paris: Hermann, 2004)

Née, Patrick, *Yves Bonnefoy: Penseur de l'image. Ou les Travaux de Zeuxis* (Paris: Gallimard, 2006)

Parker, Andrew, and Eve Kosofsky Sedgwick, eds, *Performativity and Performance* (New York, London: Routledge, 1995)

Pearre, Anja, *La Présence de l'image. Yves Bonnefoy face à neuf artistes plastiques* (Amsterdam: Rodopi, 1995)

Pearson, Roger, *Unfolding Mallarmé. The Development of a Poetic Art* (Oxford: Oxford University Press, 1996)

Pearson, Roger, *Mallarmé and Circumstance. The Translation of Silence* (Oxford: Oxford University Press, 2004)

Pearson, Roger, *Stéphane Mallarmé* (London: Reaktion, 2011)

Petterson, James, *Postwar Figures of L'Éphemère* (London: Associated University Presses, 2000)

Pinson, Jean-Claude, *Habiter en poète: Essai sur la poésie contemporaine* (Seyssel: Champ Vallon, 1995)

Preminger, Alex, ed., *The Princeton Encyclopedia of Poetry and Poetics* (2nd edn, Princeton: Princeton University Press, 1974)

Rabaté, Dominique, *Poétiques de la voix* (Paris: José Corti, 1999)

Rabaté, Dominique, 'L'Appel des voix', in *Poétique et ontologie. Colloque international, Yves Bonnefoy*, ed. Serge Canadas, Mary-Ann Caws and Michel Demangeat (Bordeaux: William Blake & Co, 2008), pp. 231–45

Rimbaud, Arthur, *Œuvres complètes*, ed. André Guyaux (Paris: Gallimard, Bibliothèque de la Pléiade, 2009)

Schnusenberg, Christine, *The Mythological Traditions of Liturgical Drama: The Eucharist as Theatre* (Mahwah, NJ: Paulist Press, 2010)

Scott, Clive, *A Question of Syllables* (Cambridge: Cambridge University Press, 1986)

Scott, Clive, *The Poetics of French Verse. Studies in Reading* (Oxford: Clarendon Press, 1998)

Shaw, Mary Lewis, *Performance in the Texts of Mallarmé* (University Park, PA: Pennsylvania State University Press, 1993)

Sheringham, Michael, *Everyday Life. Theories and Practices from Surrealism and to the Present* (Oxford: Oxford University Press, 2006)

Stamelman, Richard, *Lost Beyond Telling. Representations of Death and Absence in Modern French Poetry* (Ithaca, NY: Cornell University Press, 1990)

Starobinski, Jean, 'La Poésie, entre deux mondes', in Yves Bonnefoy, *Poèmes. Du mouvement et de l'immobilité de Douve, Hier régnant désert, Pierre écrite, Dans le leurre du seuil* (Paris: Gallimard, 1982), pp. 7–30

Tarkos, Christophe, *Écrits poétiques* (Paris: P.O.L., 2008)

Thélot, Jérôme, *Poétique d'Yves Bonnefoy* (Geneva: Droz, 1983)

Thomas, Jean-Jacques, and Steven Winspur, *Poeticized Language. The Foundations of Contemporary French Poetry* (University Park, PA: Pennsylvania State University Press, 1999)

Valéry, Paul, *Œuvres*, 2 vols, ed. Jean Hytier (Paris: Gallimard, Bibliothèque de la Pléiade, 1969)

Verlaine, Paul, *Œuvres poétiques complètes*, 2 vols, ed. Y.-G. Le Dantec (Paris: Gallimard, Bibliothèque de la Pléiade, 1989)

Vernier, Richard, *Yves Bonnefoy, ou les mots comme le ciel* (Paris: Éditions Place, 1985)

Watkin, Christopher, 'A Different Alterity: Jean-Luc Nancy's "Singular Plural"', *Paragraph*, 30.2 (2007), 50–64

Wordsworth, William, *A Wordsworth Selection* (London: Macmillan, 1963)

Yeats, W. B., *The Collected Poems* (London: Macmillan, 1993)

Zimmerman, Michael F., 'Toward a Heideggerean ethos for radical environmentalism', *Environmental Ethics*, 5.2 (1983), 99–131

Index

Milton Keynes UK
Ingram Content Group UK Ltd.
UKHW022203070923
428252UK00005B/40

9 780198 849582